DOING DEALS

DOING DEALS

Investment Banks at Work

Robert G. Eccles and Dwight B. Crane

Harvard Business School

HARVARD BUSINESS SCHOOL PRESS
■ Boston, Massachusetts ■

Harvard Business School Press

92 91 90 89   5 4 3

Library of Congress Cataloging-in-Publication Data

Eccles, Robert G.
    Doing deals : investment banks at work / Robert G. Eccles and
Dwight B. Crane.
        p.   cm.
    Bibliography: p. 257
    Includes index.
    ISBN 0-87584-199-6
    1. Investment banking.   I. Crane, Dwight B., 1937–
II. Title.
HG1616.I5E33   1988
332.66--dc19   88-14884
                                                     CIP

The paper used in this publication meets the requirements
of the American National Standard for Permanence of Paper

_____ **TO ANNE AND LORETTO**

CONTENTS

DOING DEALS

INTRODUCTION

This book is about management in the investment banking industry. Upon hearing this description of our research project, some people have expressed surprise and amusement, reflecting the belief that management in the industry is a secondary, or even staff, activity. "Doing deals" is seen to be the primary function. Nevertheless, when we began our study in 1985, management was a topic of increasing concern.

The investment banking industry was in a period of exceptional prosperity when we began the project. Between 1981 and 1986 the volume of domestic public bond issues rose at an annual rate of 36 percent, to reach $196.3 billion; the volume of domestic equity issues almost tripled, from $15.2 to $43.5 billion, in one of the strongest bull markets on record; secondary trading on the New York Stock Exchange tripled, from a daily average of 46.9 million shares to 141.0 million; the dollar volume of mergers and acquisitions (M&A) activity also tripled; and the volume of international bonds multiplied fivefold, from $53.0 to $226.4 billion. Many of the leading firms took advantage of this prosperity to grow, to diversify into other product lines, and to establish offices in London, Tokyo, and other financial centers. The result was strains on the management of these firms.

The strain produced calls for more "professional management" from both within and outside the investment banking industry. Decreasing margins because of increased competition from U.S. commercial banks and foreign banks were another source of pressure for more attention to management. Trading losses in 1987, some of which were quite spectacular, and the events following Black Monday (October 19, 1987), when the Dow Jones Industrial Average dropped a stunning 508 points, appear to make the need for better management even more urgent as the industry sees its period of prosperity severely threatened.

Management in Investment Banks

We agree that the need for good management is more important than ever—a not-unexpected conclusion from two people who teach it. What is perhaps less expected is our conclusion that, despite rhetoric about doing deals being more important than managing, investment banks have developed a set of management practices that are appropriate to the industry. The current challenge is to take the management practices they have developed and apply them to firms that have become larger and more complex. Furthermore, we believe that although we observed these practices during a time of super-abundance, they are equally applicable to times of adversity. Increased size, complexity, and adversity simply make it more difficult to apply the management practices that have been developed; and they are by themselves insufficient reason to change these practices in any fundamental way.

We developed this theory to explain observed practices. Management in the industry must be understood in terms of the function of investment banking, the economic characteristics of the business, and the production process for doing deals. Central to these three determinants of management practices is the concept of a network: management in investment banking means managing networks. The function of investment banking is to mediate the substantial asset flows between issuers (sellers of assets) and investors (buyers of assets). To do so, investment banks create a complex network of external ties between themselves and their two types of customers. Included in the network are ties between investment banks themselves, which result from collaborating on deals, especially security offerings.

A distinctive economic characteristic of the ties between investment banks and their customers is the decoupling or loose linkage between value provided to the customer and fees earned by the firm. (Throughout this book the term *firm* will always be used to refer to an investment bank. Both issuing and investing customers—also called clients—will be referred to as companies.) Investment banks provide a fairly constant stream of information, advice, and even special studies for which little or no compensation is received. They get paid when a deal is done. Furthermore, profitability varies substantially by product line, and low-margin products are often used as a way of maintaining contact with the customer to get information that will make it possible for the firm to sell high-margin products as well.

The firm's external ties create the need for a complex network of internal ties between the people who must work together to serve customers. Coordination between people serving the same issuer, between people serving the same investor, and between people linking issuers and investors requires a variety of integrating devices. The loose linkage between value provided and revenue received further increases the complexity of the internal network because it makes the products of the firm interdependent. In addition, continuously changing market conditions create changes in the external ties that make it necessary to continually revise the corresponding internal network of ties.

Adding to the complexity of the internal network is the production process in which unique deals are performed as a service in real-time interaction with clients. Because each deal is different in terms of the customer problems it seeks to solve and the market conditions existing at the time it is done, the firm must have the capability of bringing to bear whatever resources are needed, regardless of where they are located in the firm, and often at a moment's notice. The impossibility of predicting what deals will be done and what resources each will require means that the internal network must be complex and flexible.

The management practices of investment banks have been developed to manage flexible and continuously changing networks of external and internal ties. The practices include the process for formulating strategy, the design of organizational structure, management control systems, the process for determining bonuses, and relationship management. Because of the complexity of the business and the speed with which it changes, strategy is formulated largely below the most senior level through a grass-roots or bottom-driven process. The organizational structure used to implement the strategy is also largely defined by people below top management. To a great extent, therefore, investment banks are *self-designing organizations*.

The self-designing organization gives people throughout the firm a high degree of autonomy. There is always the risk that people will fail to focus their efforts on the right concerns or fail to coordinate their work with others. Thus complementing the self-designing organization of investment banks are tight management control systems that top management largely designs and imposes. A key aspect of these systems is that they monitor the quality and quantity of external ties with customers and the performance of ties within the firm. These and other systems are used to establish individual and unit accountability and to measure performance. They are a way to focus the activities within the self-designing organization.

Like all systems, the ones used in investment banks are imperfect and subject to manipulation by those affected by them. Manipulation is most likely if people perceive that rewards such as bonuses are largely determined by system measures. This can lead to local optimization that is suboptimal for the firm as a whole, and to efforts to manipulate the numbers that the systems produce. Thus a process that emphasizes a subjective assessment of a person's contribution to the firm as a whole, one that is pointedly *not* based purely on system measures, is used to compensate for the possible dysfunctional consequences of the systems. (Because this evaluation process is very subjective, it is vulnerable to charges of being unfair.)

In addition to all of the data furnished by systems, the information-processing capabilities of the complex and flat network structure make substantial information directly available to senior management, thereby ameliorating the problem of a subjective bonus determination process. Thus structure, systems, and the bonus determination process form a triad of organizational characteristics in which each one compensates for the weaknesses inherent in the others.

However well managed, there are limits to the extent to which the strategy formulation process, organizational structure, control systems, and bonus determination process can provide the necessary focus and coordination in an investment bank. Since the investment banking business ultimately involves balancing the needs of the customer (which entails balancing the needs of issuers and investors) with the needs of the firm, relationship managers are responsible for a specific group of customers. The relationship managers take a firmwide perspective on how resources are used to serve customers, in effect acting as agents of the investment bank's CEO. They are responsible for overcoming any organizational characteristics that inhibit the coordination among product specialists with techniques and trade-offs that best balance the firm's and the customer's interests.

Our argument can be summarized as follows: the management practices (strategy formulation, structure, systems, the bonus determination process, and relationship management) used in investment banks are a consequence of the function, economic characteristics, and production process of the business. Increased size, complexity, and adversity make it more difficult to apply these practices, and require their adaptation, such as more sophisticated systems. Fundamental changes in management practices should only occur, however, if there are fundamental changes in the function, economic characteristics, and production process of investment banking.

Outline of the Book

We begin by describing a series of deals that First Boston Corporation did for Union Carbide (chapter 1). People familiar with the industry should find this an interesting case to compare to their own experience. For people unfamiliar with the industry the case will give them an idea of what investment banking is all about. (For these readers we also provide a Glossary of investment banking terms at the end of the book.) We then present our theory about management in this industry (chapter 2) and use the case to illustrate various aspects of our theory. One of the important trends relevant to our theory is the shift from single to multiple investment bank relationships by issuing customers. The consequences of the shift are examined (chapter 3), as well as how customers deal with the consequences (chapter 4) through the management of their ties with investment banks.

The strategy of an investment bank is reflected in the market segments it serves and the products delivered to these segments, as well as in the ties it has with other investment banks. These networks both influence and are a part of the industry structure (chapter 5). Strategies of firms are developed through a grass-roots strategy formulation process that is implemented through a self-designing organization that is a flat, flexible, and complex network (chapter 6). The configuration of the network is also influenced by performance measures generated by management control systems that complement the self-designing organization (chapter 7). These systems are also used in the bonus determination process, which is designed to ameliorate some of the negative consequences inherent in systems by including a large subjective component in the evaluation of people's contribution to the objectives of the firm as a whole (chapter 8). Supplementing these practices is the role of the relationship manager, who is responsible for coordinating all of the product specialists assigned to a specific customer (chapter 9). Our theory has implications for the management challenges that will be faced by investment banks, by commercial banks entering the investment banking business, and by organizations that have acquired, or will acquire, investment banks (chapter 10).

Methodology and Acknowledgments

This research project began with case studies of Bankers Trust and Paine-Webber conducted in late 1984 and 1985 for the second-year Harvard M.B.A. course "Management of Financial Service Organizations." In both firms an important management issue concerned the role of relationship managers and how they worked with product specialists. We found this a sufficiently intriguing problem that in the spring of 1985 we decided to conduct a formal research project on this subject. As we dug into it, the topic expanded to incorporate a broad look at the management of investment banks.

The foundation of this project was over three hundred interviews conducted in seventeen U.S. investment banks (Bear, Stearns; The Blackstone Group; Dean Witter Financial Services; Dillon, Read; Donaldson, Lufkin & Jenrette; Drexel Burnham Lambert; First Boston Corporation; Goldman, Sachs; Kidder, Peabody; Lazard Frères; L.F. Rothschild Holdings (formerly L.F. Rothschild, Unterberg, Towbin); Merrill Lynch; PaineWebber; Prudential-Bache Securities; Salomon Brothers; Shearson Lehman Brothers; and Smith Barney, Harris Upham). These interviews, most of which were conducted between February and December 1986 with some follow-up interviews throughout 1987, included people in all functions and on all levels, from new associates to top management. We also spent time on trading floors and reviewed internal company documents such as performance evaluation forms. (One of the consequences of studying a rapidly changing industry is that the titles and affiliations of people change frequently, as do the names and affiliations of the firms themselves. In this book we have adopted the convention of referring to both people and firms as they were at the time our data were collected, unless otherwise noted.)

Even though the barriers between investment banking and commercial banking were being rapidly broken down during the course of our project, we decided to focus on investment banks in order to avoid the confounding, although interesting, problem of investment banking activities conducted in the context of a commercial bank. Based upon informal interviews and our previous knowledge of commercial banks, however, we do raise in the last chapter some issues concerning commercial banks and their growing role in the investment banking business.

Another limitation of our study is that we focused primarily on management of investment banking firms located in the United States. We did explore the international aspects of these firms to some extent, however, and we also talked to people in European firms in the investment banking business. In January 1987, we conducted interviews with some forty people in ten European financial institutions (Barclays de Zoete Wedd; Credit Suisse First Boston; Deutsche Bank; the Kleinwort Benson Group; Lazard Brothers; the S. G. Warburg Group; Midland Bank; Morgan Grenfell; Natwest Investment Bank; and Union Bank of Switzerland), and the subsidiaries of three U.S. investment banks and one commercial bank in London (Goldman, Sachs; Merrill Lynch; Salomon Brothers; and Citicorp).

Because the topic of customer relationships was so important in all of the financial firms we studied, we decided to get the customer perspective as well. We focused on issuing customers, since it was with them that the important shift has occurred from single to multiple relationships with investment banks; investors have worked with more than one investment bank for many years. With the assistance of Dr. Wayne E. Baker, who at the time was a postdoctoral research fellow at Harvard and now is on the faculty at the University of Chicago School of Business, interviews were conducted in twenty-one issuing customer organizations (including Burroughs [later renamed Unisys], Citicorp, Digital Equipment Corporation, Exxon, General Motors, and Hospital Corporation of America) between December 1985 and December 1986. These and the other customers interviewed represented a broad range in terms of the extent to which they used investment banking services and how they managed their relationships with investment banks. In all cases these interviews involved members of the financial staff, such as assistant treasurers, treasurers, and chief financial officers and, in some cases, the chief executive officer as well.

We deeply appreciate the cooperation of these institutions and the many people who took time out of busy schedules to talk with us. Their willingness to participate in our research project made it possible for us to broaden it from its original focus to a more general study of management in the investment banking industry. While interviewing relationship managers and product specialists, it soon became clear to us that their activities could not be studied in isolation from those of the people who deal with investors, leading us to study investment banking firms as a whole. Our study, however, still emphasizes the perspective of the side of the firm dealing with the issuer. A larger proportion of our interviews were conducted in the investment banking function (narrowly defined), compared to the sales and trading function, and we did not interview investors in any formal way.

In analyzing the large amount of field data, we identified similarities and differences in management practices within and between firms, and between firms and their customers. We then attempted to articulate a theory to explain why firms use the management practices that we observed. Although participants in the industry can articulate this theory to varying degrees, in general they are (and should be) more concerned with taking actions than with developing a theory for their actions. What we have attempted to do here is to make the theory explicit and to use it to illuminate management challenges in the investment banking industry.

To explore further and quantify some of the practices we observed in field interviews, we supplemented the field data with a large database of deals that we constructed out of data from Securities Data Company (SDC). William French, president of SDC, and Jeffrey Lih, vice president, were very helpful in making the data available. Their data on all publicly reported deals enabled us to analyze the structure of the investment banking industry and the structure of the interface between investment banks and issuing customers. (We discuss the database and analytical techniques in detail in the Appendix.)

Supplemental quantitative data were also made available by Greenwich Associates. Charles Ellis, president, and Jay Bennett, vice president, were very generous in arranging to get the data to us and for producing a number of special analyses that we requested. These data were especially useful for analyzing the customer and investment bank interface.

Other data on this interface were made available to us by John Chalsty, CEO of Donaldson, Lufkin & Jenrette, who gave us permission to report results from a survey his firm sponsored as a field study at the Harvard Business School. This study was performed by Michelle Collins and Michael Goss and was directed by Prof. Samuel L. Hayes of the Harvard Business School.

A project of this magnitude accomplished in such a short period of time by academic standards (although it may seem like millennia to investment bankers) could not have been done without a great deal of help. Wayne Baker worked with us for two years. He played a key role in the customer interviews, most of which he conducted himself, in structuring the SDC database, and in analyzing the data. Glyn Ferguson (now Aeppel), a Harvard M.B.A. graduate, worked with us for a year as a research associate during the data collection phase, both in field interviews and in library research. She was succeeded by Phyllis Dininio, who continued to help with data collection and began to help with data analysis. Paige Woltzen joined the project in 1987 to help with further data analysis and the many tasks involved in finishing a book. A sociology doctoral student, Karl Eschbach, provided particularly insightful and careful assistance with some of the empirical analysis.

We are also grateful to support staff at the Harvard Business School. Philip DeCesar, Mark Indelicato, and Carol Smith in the Division of Computer Services provided more help than they could imagine at the start of the project, as did Marnie Hoyle from Baker Library. Michael Stevenson, a Business Information Analyst in the Library, kept us well supplied with material to read. Finally, Dale Abramson played an instrumental role in our own production process, which involved many drafts and revisions.

As researchers we depend upon our colleagues for both criticism and encouragement. We got large amounts of both in ways that were extremely helpful from Joseph Bower, John Gabarro, Pankaj Ghemawat, Samuel Hayes, Paul Lawrence, Jay Light, and Jay Lorsch of the Harvard Business School; from Harrison White of Columbia University; and from Seth Klarman of The Baupost Group. Jay Lorsch, who demonstrated an uncanny ability to identify the parts of the manuscript most in need of improvements, and Harrison White, who continually challenged us with a different perspective, were especially diligent in commenting on drafts of the manuscript.

Jeffrey Bradach, a doctoral student in the Joint Organizational Behavior Ph.D. program at Harvard, provided multifaceted help during the project. He did some of the data analysis as a research associate; he was an insightful reader of chapter drafts and revisions; and he wrote the Union Carbide case, which is chapter 1 of the book. Substantial financial support was made available to us from the Harvard Business School.

We also appreciate the tolerance and good humor of our wives, Anne and Loretto, and families during the course of this project. During the data collection phase our schedules resembled those of the investment bankers we studied, and we spent as much time with them in New York as we did with our families in Boston. This physical absence was transformed into a mental absence during the analysis and writing phases of the project, when we retreated to our word processors. Now that our book is done, it is time for us to strengthen our own internal ties.

The completion of this book does not signal the end of our interest in the investment banking industry. In fact, we look forward to seeing how this rapidly changing industry and the firms in it will evolve over the next few

years. The management practices that prove to be effective will be the basis
for extending the theory presented here.

Robert G. Eccles   Dwight B. Crane
December 1987   December 1987
Lexington, Massachusetts   Belmont, Massachusetts

—— 1 ————————————————————

THE UNION CARBIDE DEAL

> Everything at the meeting was choreographed. I had spent two solid
> months of sixteen-hour days working on putting this deal together. It
> was the most intense work experience of my life. I knew every answer
> cold. Since then I have replayed it in my mind a dozen times. It was
> great.
>
> Bruce Jamerson
> Vice President, First Boston
> Account Manager for Union Carbide

On November 3, 1986, after a three-hour board of directors meeting, Union
Carbide decided to accept First Boston's proposal to embark on a $2.5 bil-
lion recapitalization program. Jamerson and his associates' efforts had paid
off. Jamerson had reason to be excited: He had changed a weak relationship
between First Boston and Union Carbide into one that would generate tens
of millions of dollars in revenues for his firm. In the highly competitive
world of investment banking, it was a particularly sweet victory, since First
Boston had won the business from Union Carbide's traditional banker,
Morgan Stanley.

Union Carbide and Its Investment Banks

In 1983, Carbide had revenues of $9.1 billion and was ranked 37th among
the *Fortune* 500. Petrochemicals, industrial gases, and metal and carbon
products were historically Carbide's bedrock product lines. The future
growth of the company, however, lay elsewhere. As Warren Anderson,
chairman of the board and chief executive officer, reported in his "Letter to

Stockholders" in the 1983 Annual Report, "Our specialty, consumer and service businesses —the entrepreneurial segments of our portfolio —will play an increasingly important role in the economy of the decade ahead, and in Carbide's future performance." Those business segments included such products as Eveready batteries, Glad bags, and Prestone anti-freeze, and together contributed 45 percent of the company's revenue.

Despite its size, Carbide was not a major player in the capital markets. Carbide had not issued equity since its initial public offering in 1917, and most of its debt offerings were privately placed with institutional investors such as insurance companies, rather than underwritten by an investment bank and sold to the public markets. During the 1970s, some funding and merger and acquisition activity occasionally brought Carbide in touch with the market and with various investment banks. Although Morgan Stanley did most of this work, other firms participated in cases where they possessed needed expertise. Goldman, Sachs, for example, was the dealer for Carbide's commercial paper program. J. Clayton Stephenson, who in 1954 began working at a West Virginia plant and in 1982 was named chief financial officer, summarized Carbide's financial activity through the early 1980s: "We used investment bankers only intermittently."

As Carbide's "relationship bank," Morgan Stanley managed some debt offerings, assisted with some divestitures, and conducted several advisory studies on various aspects of Carbide's financial strategy. Stephenson recollected, "Morgan Stanley had long held a privileged position. It was based largely on close personal relationships between senior managers in the two companies. In 1983, other investment banks felt they were breaking their pick calling on us."

Union Carbide's relationship with Morgan Stanley made Carbide an unlikely business prospect for First Boston in 1983. Nonetheless, account officers were assigned to all major companies regardless of perceived potential, and George Weiksner, a First Boston managing director, was to watch for opportunities at Carbide. (Managing director is the highest position at First Boston, followed by vice president, associate, and analyst.) He was not optimistic about his prospects for generating much business.

In mid-1983, Carbide let several investment banks know that it was accepting proposals on how it might finance the purchase of a ship. Bruce Jamerson and Bob deVeer, vice presidents in First Boston's Project Finance Group, put together a presentation and won the business. The $140 million deal was extremely complex and required working closely with many Carbide administrators. A deal of this size, though, did not necessitate the involvement of senior management at Carbide. Jamerson recalled that "although I didn't get to know any senior people, I worked with the junior treasury people, their lawyers, accountants, and others. In the process I got to know many of the people and, importantly, I got to know the company from the inside."

During the subsequent two years, Jamerson, an eager thirty-three-year-old vice president, willingly invested his time and energy on the account even though no managing director had much hope for it. Because the ship package involved several refinancings, it provided an opportunity for him to keep in frequent contact with Carbide people. Still, First Boston was unable to establish a relationship with the key financial decision maker at Carbide, Clayton Stephenson. His tanned face and silver hair made him look like he stepped out of central casting to play the role of a chief executive officer. And indeed, he was mentioned as a possible successor to Warren Anderson.

Stephenson was involved in virtually all key decisions facing the company. When poisonous gas leaked from a Carbide plant in Bhopal, India, in late 1984, killing two thousand people, Stephenson was one of a few executives charged with managing the crisis. The accident rocked the company and dramatically affected its financial condition. Three days after the disastrous gas leak, an article in *The Wall Street Journal* suggested that the company might declare bankruptcy. Carbide's stock price slid precipitously, and the credit rating on its bonds was downgraded by Moody's from A2 to A3. The litigation generated by the accident haunted every move the company made.

The GAF Takeover Attempt

Eight months after the gas leak, in August 1985, GAF, a company one-tenth the size of Carbide, began purchasing Carbide stock and for the second time in less than a year Carbide's future seemed in doubt. GAF's chairman, Sam Heyman, had a reputation as an aggressive corporate raider, winning control of GAF in a takeover battle two years earlier. Heyman's stake in Carbide grew from 5.6 percent in early August to 9.9 percent by the end of the month. Carbide management was wary and they turned to Morgan Stanley for assistance.

Stephenson recalled that "when we knew there was a raider out there, we put together a team of three: the president, the general counsel, and myself. We involved the board at an early stage, too." The team needed advice quickly "and Morgan Stanley was an easy and practical road to go down; they knew more about us than anyone else. This was not a time for comparison shopping. You go with who you know."

Carbide moved aggressively to defend itself. In the last week of August, an announcement was made that four thousand jobs, 15 percent of Carbide's work force, would be eliminated within a year. Furthermore, plants would be closed, businesses sold, and some of the surplus in the company's overfunded pension fund would be tapped. The cash generated by these actions would be used to buy back 15 percent of Carbide's stock, which would increase earnings per share and support the price of the stock. While Ed Van Den Ameele, a Carbide spokesman, told the *New York Times* (August 1, 1985, p. D7) that "this is a plan we have been working on for quite some time," the GAF threat certainly accelerated its implementation.

During the fall of 1985 Heyman was kept at bay, but his interest in Carbide had not subsided. On December 8, GAF made a tender offer of $68 a share for approximately 70 percent of Carbide's shares. (On August 1, the stock closed at $50 per share. With the persistent rumors of a takeover, the stock had traded up to $63 by December 1.)

The next week the board of directors met to consider the GAF bid. Morgan Stanley outlined the options available to Carbide. After spending a week studying alternatives, the board decided that the GAF offer was inadequate and that the best way to stymie GAF's advances was to offer Carbide shareholders a package of debt securities and cash in return for their shares. Carbide shareholders would thus be able to choose between GAF's cash offer and their own company's exchange offer. Depending on the size of GAF's stake in the company, Carbide was committed to buy back anywhere from 23.5 to 47.1 million shares (approximately 70 percent of the outstanding stock).

Morgan Stanley estimated the value of the exchange offer at $85 per share. For each share of common stock tendered, the shareholder would receive $20 cash and $65 of high-coupon debt. The $65 debt package included three debt securities with intermediate to long maturities and coupon rates from 13.25 percent to 15 percent depending upon the maturity. (Rates would be somewhat lower if only 23.5 million shares were tendered.) The high interest rates were necessary to induce stockholders to tender their securities to Carbide instead of GAF and they also reflected the drop in Carbide's credit rating that issuance of the securities would cause.

In addition to high interest rates, the new debt also contained highly restrictive covenants. Were GAF to succeed in its takeover attempt, the covenants limited its ability to sell assets and use the cash to repay debt GAF was incurring to purchase Carbide's stock. This in turn made it more difficult for Heyman to obtain such financing. Heyman challenged the legality of the covenants, but on December 30 a federal judge in Manhattan dismissed his petition.

After divesting businesses worth over $500 million during the previous year, Carbide surprised financial analysts on January 3, 1986, when it announced its intention to divest its consumer products business, the business that was to be one of the engines for future corporate growth. (This divestiture was exempt from the covenants restricting asset sales.) The consumer products sale was an integral and necessary part of the takeover defense plan. Carbide estimated that the sale would generate over $2 billion. Of this, $1 billion would be used to retire some of the new debt; the rest of the proceeds would be distributed to shareholders. Carbide labored to generate value for its shareholders and fought to keep them from tendering their shares to GAF.

On January 8, after a month of ratcheting up its tender offer price to $78 a share, GAF withdrew its offer. Shareholders who accepted Carbide's exchange offer, including GAF, obtained a substantial profit. Thus, despite failing to obtain control of the company, GAF walked away with an $81 million after-tax profit for its efforts when it took advantage of Carbide's exchange offer.

Carbide, however, had been forced to sell a major portion of its business and had placed itself in a precarious financial position. In the end, Carbide bought back 55 percent of its shares, which resulted in the issuance of $2.5 billion in new medium and long-term fixed-rate debt. Its debt to equity ratio soared from 39 percent to 72 percent. And Carbide paid dearly for the debt. The three debt issues had a weighted average interest rate of 14.2 percent. Carbide's bond rating fell again, this time from A3 to Ba3. The new debt moved Carbide from an "investment-grade" company to a "non-investment-grade" company.

The First Boston Entrée

Soon after the dust settled, Carbide started to chafe under the large debt burden. Stephenson recalled that "while some were celebrating our victory, we knew we were in trouble. We had only completed phase one of a long series of battles. We wanted to be able to run the company as a business, not as an investment banking exercise."

Not only was Carbide hampered by the onerous debt burden, but also the covenants on the newly acquired debt severely restricted its activities. John Clerico, who had been promoted to Carbide's treasurer just the day before Heyman's tender offer, remarked that "we had to pretty much call the bank if we wanted to buy or sell anything." Clerico pointed out that "the financial constraints affected the culture of the company. Managers in different divisions were unable to pursue good ideas, which was counter to the independent, entrepreneurial culture of the company. Financial considerations constrained strategy."

Carbide's first task was to reduce the interest expense. In February 1986, Carbide invited several investment and commercial banks to bid on an interest rate swap advisory. Jim Sawyer, Clerico's assistant, called Jamerson and invited First Boston to make a presentation. (Sawyer and Jamerson were both graduates of MIT's Sloan School of Management and had met there at a First Boston recruiting presentation.) Carbide was betting that interest rates would fall, and wanted advice on how, and at what price, to swap its fixed interest rate obligations into floating interest rates that would decrease if its bet was correct.

Four investment banks (Morgan Stanley, First Boston, Goldman, Sachs, and Salomon Brothers) and two commercial banks (Morgan Guaranty and Bankers Trust) made presentations to Clerico and his staff. First Boston won. Sawyer recalled that "First Boston was the only investment bank that truly understood our needs. We wanted advice on how to price swaps—First Boston understood that. The other banks wanted to *do* swaps with us, which certainly conflicted with our desire to have advice on how to price them." Clerico believed that the loss of the swap deal did not disturb Morgan Stanley too much because it was not an area of strong emphasis for the investment bank.

"I was elated," said Jamerson. He now had something to talk to Clerico about on a regular basis. In Clerico's new position it was crucial that he know what was happening in the capital markets. Jamerson knew that. "I started sending him economic reports, chemical industry surveys, and First Boston Flash Reports on opportunities that he might find useful. If I can help him do his job better—and he looks good to his boss—we both win." The reports, coupled with the ongoing swap program, served Jamerson well in his efforts to develop a working relationship with Clerico. Beginning in February 1986, Jamerson and Clerico talked on the phone once or twice a week. By September, Carbide had swapped over $700 million of its debt.

Jamerson's pursuit of Carbide business complemented his pursuit of promotion at First Boston. In March 1986, Jamerson moved from Project Finance, where he served as product specialist, to the Natural Resources Group, where he was given account coverage responsibility. Along with switching departments, Jamerson received his first customer call list. He asked that Carbide be placed on it, since he had effectively managed that account for some time. George Weiksner had moved to the Technology Group the previous year and Tony Freeman, a managing director, had assumed account management responsibility for Carbide. Freeman agreed to relinquish day-to-day management of the account to Jamerson, although nominally he remained the senior member of the firm assigned to Carbide.

During the spring and early summer, Carbide sought ways to generate cash to reduce its debt burden. At Carbide's request, Morgan Stanley made several presentations to Stephenson and Clerico regarding an equity issue. At the same time Morgan Stanley assisted Carbide in divesting its home and automotive products business, the last divestiture associated with the

GAF takeover defense. On April 22, the business was sold to a group of investors in a leveraged buyout (LBO). The purchase was funded by First Boston's LBO group. Jamerson had nothing to do with the deal; he purposely stayed away from it because in this instance First Boston was working for the buyers of the business and not for Carbide.

Jamerson talked to Clerico several times in the spring about issuing equity or swapping the debt for equity. "I knew there was no way Carbide would stay in its existing financial condition," said Jamerson. The nagging problem of a large amount of high interest rate debt with restrictive covenants remained. A few meetings with Clerico entailed full presentations by First Boston on the impact of an equity offering on Carbide's situation. Although Stephenson and Clerico were interested in doing an equity offering, they were unconvinced that the ideas on the table would solve their problems.

The Carbide/First Boston relationship took another step forward when in July First Boston agreed to finance the buy-back of some of Carbide's high-yield bonds on the open market. The bond buy-back idea emerged out of a conversation between Jamerson and John Kolmer, a managing director and head of First Boston's High Yield Sales and Trading Department. Although in different departments, Kolmer and Jamerson spoke frequently about the bond market and Jamerson's accounts. Kolmer knew that the first call date on Carbide's bonds was three years away, and he believed "there was no way Carbide would be able to wait that long." They both agreed it made sense to purchase some bonds now, since the three issues were currently less expensive compared to other, similar issues. Kolmer also thought interest rates were going down, which would make the bonds more expensive to buy back later.

Clerico was interested in Jamerson's idea. It had added appeal to Clerico because Morgan Stanley had earlier expressed reluctance to provide the same service to Carbide. Kolmer and Jamerson visited Danbury, Connecticut (Carbide's headquarters), the next week and made their pitch. Kolmer said he was certain that he could bring in the bonds at low prices: "I told Clerico I was so confident that I'd sell him the bonds at today's prices." After some discussion, Clerico and Kolmer agreed that First Boston would purchase approximately $200 million of the bonds, hold them in inventory, and Carbide would have the option to buy back the bonds at cost plus accrued interest and a trading commission. Even though the profits on the deal were modest, Kolmer was happy to buy back the bonds. "I knew that this was an entrée deal. I was willing to do it for nothing with the hope that we might get future business."

A few days later, First Boston quietly commenced buying the bonds. No consolidated list of bondholders existed, since most of the bonds had been recycled from the original bondholders (former Carbide stockholders who obtained the bonds in the earlier exchange offer) to institutional investors. At the start nobody knew where the bonds were, but during the six-week buying period Kolmer acquired a substantial amount of market information. By the end of August, First Boston had purchased $207 million of Carbide's bonds, or about 8 percent of the issue.

On September 2, Clerico called Jamerson and said Stephenson wanted to meet with the people at First Boston. After spending many months considering gradualist solutions to their situation, and coming to the conclusion that it would take five to seven years to relieve the debt burden, Robert Kennedy (who was appointed chairman and CEO in April 1986), Stephenson, and Clerico decided to explore "more sweeping and comprehensive ideas," recalled Clerico. Part of the reasoning noted by Stephenson was that "we weren't really getting what we wanted from Morgan Stanley, so we decided to broaden our conversations and to talk with others." In addition, officers at Carbide had been taking a broader look at their use of both commercial banks and investment banks. They concluded that it would be helpful to have more investment banking firms involved in their business, just as they had multiple commercial banks. As Clerico said, "We thought that to get Carbide back on track would require the expertise of many people, not just one investment bank."

A lunch meeting of the Carbide and First Boston people was set for September 10. It was held in a private dining room on the 44th floor of First Boston's midtown Manhattan office. Peter Buchanan, chief executive officer of First Boston, Jamerson, Freeman, and Brian Finn, an associate from the Mergers and Acquisitions Department with expertise on corporate restructurings, attended from First Boston. Stephenson and Clerico represented Carbide. Sitting next to each other in the elegant, wood-paneled dining room, Buchanan and Stephenson discussed Carbide's situation. Stephenson told Buchanan, "There is lots of money to be made here if you come up with a creative solution to our situation." Buchanan's presence at the meeting reflected the magnitude of the opportunity.

Stephenson also let them know that he had asked Salomon Brothers, Morgan Stanley, and Goldman, Sachs for their ideas. Stephenson said they were looking for sketches of proposals, and that they would give all four banking firms access to internal documents and personnel so that they would fully understand Carbide's situation. Once the company decided on a course of action they would pay the chosen investment bank to develop further its ideas. Speed was important. The Tax Reform Act of 1986 had increased the capital gains tax, making financial actions before the end of the year more attractive.

Carbide had three objectives. First, it sought to reduce its interest expense by substituting lower-cost capital for the high-cost debt currently on the books. Second, it wanted the covenants on the debt relaxed in order to have more operating flexibility. The second objective was a problem because covenants were extremely difficult to amend. A change required the consent of 80 percent of the bondholders. Making matters even more difficult was the fact that even though Carbide sought to relax the covenants, they also wanted to ensure that they would not be vulnerable to a corporate raider again.

Carbide's third objective was to give Robert Kennedy a "clean slate." Stephenson noted that Kennedy was "discontented with the capital structure. He was a builder and was working toward building the 'new Union Carbide,' but he was hampered by the financial situation of the company. He provided this entire effort with support and a sense of urgency."

The Proposal

A flurry of activity at First Boston followed the meeting. Suddenly the firm had a good shot at a giant piece of Carbide business. Jamerson met with Dick Bott, a managing director who was co-head of the Investment Banking Group, and requested the necessary manpower. Bott suggested that Jamerson meet with Bob Calhoun, a managing director who had recently formed the Restructuring Group and who was widely respected throughout the firm.

"I had just formed the Restructuring Group a month earlier," said Calhoun. "We were a part-time advisory group made up of a few people from different parts of the firm. Our goal was to serve as a resource to account managers who had clients interested in restructurings." (Calhoun's new group focused on healthy companies that needed to restructure to defend against raiders. There was also an existing reorganization group in the Corporate Finance Department that worked on restructuring of companies in Chapter 11 bankruptcy proceedings.)

By this time, Jamerson also realized that the proposed task extended beyond the scope of a vice president. "This was a big ticket item, and we needed the big bats. I was not too proud to realize that," said Jamerson. One of Jamerson's colleagues remarked, "Not only was it an issue of whether Jamerson was senior enough to deal with the client, it also wasn't clear that he had the muscle to muster all the product groups." Given the substance and the magnitude of the task, Calhoun was the perfect person to serve as the senior account manager. Freeman, who had since been assigned responsibility for calling on industrial clients in the United Kingdom, stepped back into the picture, since he had some experience working with Carbide.

Although Jamerson knew that a managing director should be involved in the deal, he expressed some concern. "You want to be *the* guy, both to the client and internally. You must be perceived to be of that stature to succeed."

In the end, while Calhoun and Freeman offered a guiding hand, Jamerson was responsible for managing the work. It had been largely his efforts that made a nonexistent relationship into one that might yield enormous revenues.

The clock was running and First Boston needed to come up with a proposal. Richard Kauffman, an associate who had recently joined Calhoun's Restructuring Group, was asked to help with the proposal. Kauffman remembered that "it wasn't really clear who was responsible for coming up with a solution. In fact, we didn't have a good handle on the problem." A task of this magnitude cut across organizational boundaries in the bank, and simply getting people together for a meeting was difficult. For several days Jamerson, Freeman, Calhoun, Kolmer, Kauffman, and Mark Lightcap, a managing director from High Yield Sales and Trading who reported to Kolmer, discussed the issue endlessly.

Pressure mounted when Carbide visited First Boston's New York office on September 23 for a follow-up meeting. Carbide officials were disappointed because a formal presentation of ideas was not made. Although the meeting was still productive, it was clear that First Boston would have to have concrete suggestions for the next meeting, to be held a week later on October 1.

The key problem was figuring out how to obtain the consent of 80 percent of the bondholders—the number required to amend the debt covenants. As Carbide's problem came into sharper focus, so did its options: a tender offer to buy the bonds for cash or an exchange offer in which new securities would be offered for the old bonds. John Kolmer was convinced that the only way to get 80 percent of the bondholders to tender their bonds was to offer cash. "I was adamant about this approach. A cash offer had the best, and maybe only, chance of getting 80 percent of the bonds in." Along with the higher probability of success, the cash tender offer had other advantages. First, Leon Kalveria, a vice president from High Yield Finance, worked with outside legal counsel and determined that a cash tender offer would be the quickest approach. Second, the financial impact of the recently ratified tax bill favored the cash tender offer over the exchange offer. Third, the strategy avoided the uncontrolled distribution of equity shares to the bondholders. After its experience with corporate raiders, "Carbide didn't want to have its equity washing around the market," noted Jamerson.

Calhoun concurred, "The cash tender offer was the obviously superior thing to do. To solve the client's problem we had to figure out a way to do it." The difficulty with the approach was coming up with the $3 billion in cash needed to buy back the bonds. This amount was higher than the face value of $2.5 billion, but the market value had risen and some premium would be needed to gain acceptance of the offer. (Part of this $3 billion would be used to buy the $207 million of bonds that First Boston had previously purchased for Carbide, but as agreed, the company would obtain these at First Boston's cost plus commission, not at the tender offer price.)

"We immediately looked at what Carbide's commercial bank financing capabilities were and what it might be able to do in the capital markets," said Jamerson. Jamerson immediately met with Bill Clark, a vice president in the Bank Finance Department. Clark was familiar with the account, since he had assisted Carbide during its swap program. Clark had also worked for several years at Morgan Guaranty, one of the major commercial banks working with Carbide.

Clark told Jamerson he was convinced that the commercial banks would lend Carbide $2 billion. During the most recent negotiations with commercial banks (before the idea of a tender offer was on the table) $1 billion in new bank credit facilities had been offered to Carbide. "I was confident that the banks would lend another $1 billion, as long as specific assets were earmarked to repay the bank debt." Clerico also told Jamerson that, as a part of an overall recapitalization program, Carbide could divest businesses worth approximately $1 billion within a few months. With these assets available, a total loan of $2 billion from the commercial banks appeared to be reasonable.

This left $1 billion to be obtained in the capital markets from a new equity issue and a private placement of securities. Jim Freeman, a managing director and the co-head of Equity Sales and Trading, was involved in early discussions with Jamerson about the feasibility of an equity issue. "Freeman told me that the market could absorb $500 to $600 million in new Carbide equity," said Jamerson. At the same time, Jamerson met with the First Boston Private Finance Department and asked it to determine the amount and type of securities that could be privately placed with institutions. Tom Keaveney and Sean Twomey, a managing director and a vice president, believed they would be able to place between $200 and $500 million of short-term debt securities.

Kauffman was assigned the responsibility of analyzing Carbide's financial position and assessing the financial impact of a cash tender offer. Carbide's recent financial maneuvering had wreaked havoc on their financial statements, leading one banker to comment, "No one had seen clean financials for two years." Kauffman, who was given substantial access to the available data, plowed through Carbide's financial statements line by line, trying to understand what the new, slimmed-down Carbide would look like after a cash tender offer. This torturous process led him to remember the project as "one of the worst I've ever worked on."

"Early on I told Clerico we were leaning toward a cash tender offer," recalled Jamerson. Clerico raised the same issue that First Boston was grappling with: Could Carbide finance such a plan? It appeared that a combination of bank financing, an equity issue, and a private placement of debt could raise the needed $3 billion. But there was still a catch. The equity issue and private placement could not take place until the $3 billion had been spent to repurchase the bonds. Carbide's financial condition prevented it from entering the capital markets until the existing bonds were off the books. Thus another $1 billion of financing had to be found to cover the period between the bond repurchase and the issuance of new securities.

As the informal discussions prior to the October 1 meeting continued, Jamerson and Calhoun raised the idea of First Boston making a bridge loan to Carbide to cover this gap. They and Freeman met with William Mayer, a managing director and one of four senior members of the firm that made up the Executive Committee, to explore the feasibility of making a bridge loan. Mayer's approval was needed for such transactions. As he said, "We don't want salesmen having the ability to commit the capital of the firm." Jamerson explained the Carbide situation to Mayer, emphasizing that in the event of a tie, Carbide would probably give Morgan Stanley the order. The ability to offer financing for the deal would differentiate First Boston.

Mayer liked the idea. Even though First Boston had never made a bridge loan of this size, they had made a number of smaller ones. Mayer noted, "We had the knowledge to execute such a transaction." He was concerned, though, about the particular risks associated with Carbide. "At that time the Bhopal courts were coming out with new rulings weekly and these caused the market prices on Carbide's securities to be incredibly volatile." Mayer assigned several people to do a careful credit analysis on Carbide. They concluded that it was an acceptable credit risk.

Following that, Mayer's primary interest was in assuring the takeout, that is, the financial transactions that would repay the bridge loan. Mayer wanted to be sure of Carbide's ability to access the capital markets after the tender offer. He met with the bankers from the equity department to confirm their market assessments. "I had no desire to see the bridge 'hanging' in the market. The longer the gap between the bridge and the takeout, the greater the risk. I wanted in and out quickly."

Mayer's concern affected the timing of the deal: "We had a small window within which to do the capital market transactions. The tender offer had to remain open twenty business days, which pushed us to the beginning of December. The Christmas lull in the market begins about December 15. In that two-week interval, we had to do the necessary transactions, otherwise we'd be out in the market too long." As a publicly owned company, First Boston also wanted assurance that such a big loan would not be outstanding when it closed its books at the end of the year. Mayer was also worried that such a large loan might affect First Boston's credit rating.

The other issue facing Mayer was whether First Boston had the capacity to lend $1 billion to Carbide. He knew that another bridge loan of over $1 billion was being considered. First Boston was representing Campeau, a

Canadian retailer, in its attempt to buy Allied Stores. Mayer had to be sure that First Boston could handle the unlikely, but possible, occurrence of both bridge loans happening simultaneously. After examining First Boston's own borrowing capacity and the internal capital of the firm, he determined that the firm could commit up to $1 billion to Carbide.

Mayer spoke at length with his three Executive Committee colleagues and the chief financial officer at First Boston, John Toffolon, and they concurred with his assessment. They agreed to make up to $1 billion available to Carbide. Given that a significant percentage of First Boston's funding capacity was at stake, the Carbide bridge was a critical deal. As Mayer later recalled, "For about a two-month period, I spent three to four hours a week on this deal."

A number of activities were under way in preparation for the October 1 meeting with Carbide. Clark, Toffolon, Kauffman, Jim Freeman, Twomey, and Keaveney continued to work on the financing of the cash tender offer. Kalveria worked with outside counsel to propose changes in the debt covenants, one of the major purposes of the restructuring.

In addition, Kolmer and Lightcap worked on the key issue of pricing the cash tender offer. Having purchased $200 million of bonds in the previous month, Kolmer had a good sense of the market. Most of the holders were institutions and Kolmer knew that many of the institutional investors were going to have trouble obtaining their needed performance in the last quarter: "We hoped to lure them with a clear short-term gain." Kolmer settled on premiums over face value of the bonds, ranging from 15 percent to 33 percent on the three outstanding bond issues. Kolmer recalled, "I said I was totally convinced we could get 80 percent of the bonds at these prices. It was a 'trust me' situation, but that's why they pay me." At the prices Kolmer suggested, if 80 percent of the bonds were tendered, the total purchase price would be $2.59 billion; a 100 percent response rate translated into a $3.26 billion outlay.

Calhoun and Jamerson managed the blizzard of activities that First Boston undertook to prepare for the October 1 meeting. Calhoun recalled, "I was working on five or six other projects at the time, but this was certainly the biggest. I probably met with people two or three times a day." Jamerson worked full time on the proposal, spending every other day at Carbide headquarters gathering information. "I worked seven days a week from 8:00 A.M. until 11:00 P.M."

In just a few weeks the contours of First Boston's proposal came into focus. A plan to obtain 80 percent of the bonds was created, the tender offer price was determined, and financing mechanisms adequate for the purchase of the bonds were proposed (see figure 1.1). Help was solicited from several departments or groups within the banking firm, but marshaling resources was not a problem. "Big deals attract a lot of attention," observed Calhoun.

FIGURE 1.1.   The Structure of the Deal

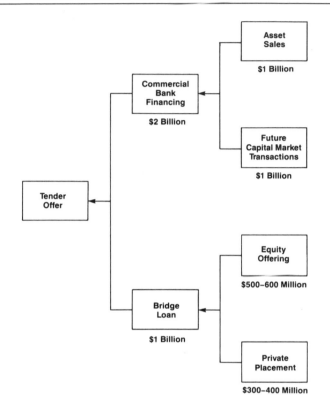

"Once key people are involved—and the deal looks big—you don't have much trouble getting people to help even if they are in different departments."

Winning the Support of Management and the Board

Jamerson, Calhoun, and Kolmer visited Carbide's Danbury headquarters on October 1 and gave their presentation. Dave Batten, a First Boston managing director with substantial new equity issue experience, also took part. Stephenson agreed with their assessment that a cash tender offer was the optimal solution. Most important, First Boston, through its bridge loan facility, offered the means to finance the deal. Stephenson still had concerns about the financial implications of the plan. He wanted to be certain that Carbide would be able to wipe the bank debt and bridge loan off the books promptly and that earnings per share would not be reduced.

At a second meeting on October 13, Jamerson, Calhoun, Jim Freeman, Tony Freeman, and Clark outlined the plan in greater detail. Stephenson was concerned about the size of the premium being paid for the bonds; it would fall directly out of the owner's equity line on the balance sheet. For him "it was vital to hear Jim Freeman say we could take the equity deal to market." Scenario after scenario was examined. The financial analysis was a subject of great consternation because the results depended heavily on an uncertain number, the percentage of the bonds that would be tendered.

The three other investment banks made presentations to Carbide, and each offered entirely different ideas. Goldman, Sachs analyzed several approaches but did not offer a specific recommendation. Salomon Brothers did an extensive analysis of the bond market and told Carbide that the premium necessary to buy back the bonds would be excessive. They recommended that Carbide continue to pursue a gradualist approach and slowly buy back the bonds. Carbide appreciated Salomon Brothers' candor, but disagreed with their view. Morgan Stanley did not believe that Carbide had the resources to make a cash tender offer, so they suggested that Carbide make an exchange offer: swap the existing debt for equity and new, cheaper debt.

After First Boston and Morgan Stanley each made two formal presentations, Carbide management decided it wanted First Boston as the financial advisor on the deal. Calhoun observed that "Carbide wasn't really choosing so much among investment banks as it was choosing among different proposals."

"What clinched the deal was that First Boston could and would put up the necessary money," said Stephenson. "Morgan Stanley clearly had no stomach for this." Though economic reality swayed Stephenson, he was also very impressed with the First Boston team. "They put a very good looking group in front of us with some very good ideas." Stephenson and Clerico were particularly impressed with Bob Calhoun, head of the Restructuring Group. Stephenson remarked that Calhoun "is one of the steadiest and most thoughtful investment bankers I know."

Stephenson emphasized that he was impressed with Jamerson's and Calhoun's ability to put together an integrated package. "They brought all their key functional area people together in one room to be creative and work together. Any of the pieces free-standing made no sense. We had to work with the internal staff at First Boston, and they had to work together to make it all happen. Calhoun and Jamerson had access to the key people and could orchestrate the deal.

"Morgan Stanley was stunned when we told them that we gave the business to First Boston. They were obviously very distressed," Stephenson went on.

The most senior managing directors at Morgan Stanley contacted Stephenson to discuss the matter. Stephenson recalled that, after some reflection, "Morgan Stanley agreed that they had not followed up the account appropriately; they had not worked aggressively to solve Carbide's predicament."

Stephenson insisted that Morgan Stanley be a co-manager on some of the capital market transactions. First Boston sought to lead manage all the capital market transactions associated with the deal. As Jamerson remarked, "We were putting nearly $1 billion at risk. It was only reasonable that we be in control of the transactions associated with the repayment." Stephenson understood this, but he had no intention of terminating Carbide's relationship with Morgan Stanley.

The decision to recapitalize the company was not one Carbide management could make alone. Carbide management and First Boston had to make a formal presentation to the Carbide board of directors and win its approval. The next two weeks were hectic. Each First Boston team had to lay the groundwork so that as soon as the board approved the proposal, the plan would immediately go into effect.

Even though Stephenson was impressed with the organizational capabilities of First Boston, there was actually some confusion below the surface. The three leaders—Calhoun, Jamerson, and Tony Freeman—formed an amorphously structured management team. "It wasn't entirely clear who was in charge," said one banker associated with the deal. Once First Boston received the order from Carbide management, Calhoun reduced his involvement: "I spent about an hour a day on it." Freeman and Jamerson, however, worked full time on the deal. Freeman was responsible for "implementation" and Jamerson was accountable for the "day-to-day orchestration" of the deal. More than one team member mentioned the fact that the distinction between Jamerson's and Freeman's jobs was vague.

Kauffman and Randy Hazelton, an analyst, continued to work with Carbide's financial staff between October 15 and November 3, the date of the board meeting. Kauffman was responsible for the financial analysis and the management of the equity offering, which involved doing due diligence and preparing the "red herring," the preliminary prospectus for the equity offering. A two-day due diligence meeting was held in Danbury, Connecticut, in late October. Lawyers and bankers from First Boston and Morgan Stanley (the latter was to co-manage the equity deal) conferred with senior management and lawyers from Carbide to ensure that the preliminary prospectus adequately and accurately described Carbide's situation to potential investors.

The cornerstone of the recapitalization plan was the tender offer to be made to bondholders. Dick Bott assigned Cliff Gookin, an experienced associate, the task of managing the tender offer process. When Jamerson de-

scribed the tender offer to Gookin, Jamerson told him, "You'll e
hero or a goat."

Because First Boston sought to make the tender offer immediately following the board meeting, all the necessary SEC paper work had to be in
place. Gookin worked day and night for two weeks with First Boston's
lawyers, learning the technical details of how to execute a cash tender offer
and then drafting the offering document. The document included an analysis of the financial impact of the restructuring, discussion of the proposed
covenant changes, and detailed legal terminology about the rights of the
present and future bondholders. The number of meetings and phone calls
among various groups at First Boston was particularly large because the
documents required for each transaction had to include the details of each
of the other transactions. Kauffman and Gookin spoke frequently, since
Kauffman was working closely with Carbide to generate the financial analysis required for the equity prospectus.

At the same time Gookin and Julien Mininberg, an analyst, were arranging the tender offer, Bill Clark was writing up the term sheet to be used in
the negotiations with the commercial bank. Clark was confident that the
commercial banks would loan Carbide $2 billion to buy the bonds, but
Clerico was somewhat skeptical. "We spent a lot of time discussing the
issue," remembered Clark. Clerico wanted to offer evidence to his board of
directors that a $2 billion loan was obtainable. Clark, Clerico, and Jamerson
made presentations to Morgan Guaranty, Manufacturers Hanover, and
Credit Suisse. After a few days of negotiation the three banks agreed, in
principle, to loan Carbide $500 million each, and to syndicate the balance,
$500 million, to other banks.

While Gookin and Clark were laying the groundwork for their portions
of the deal, the people involved in the equity issue and the private placement
were busy. Nancy Stearns, a vice president in Equity Capital Markets, prepared to market and sell the equity. "Our department organizes and controls the process from the 'after getting pregnant' stage—i.e., getting the
order—to having the baby," she explained. While Kauffman was doing due
diligence and writing the equity offering documents, he worked with
Stearns to create the internal sales documents. "A package of information
was created to explain the deal to our sales force." The package included
sections entitled "Outline of Recapitalization," "Salespoints," "Comparable
Companies," and "Equity Analyst Report."

Stearns was the conduit between the equity sales force, the traders, and
the investment bankers. She had to ensure that the equity sales force and
traders had all the information they needed about the offering, and she was
the person who obtained answers to their questions. The marketing and
selling of the equity required close coordination with Kauffman and fre-

quent discussions with Jamerson, Stephenson, and Clerico. Jamerson closely monitored the equity offering: "Equity is not a technical offering; instead, you are selling a story. We wanted to know and manage the story."

Keaveney and Twomey worked with Clerico and his assistant, John Fitzpatrick, hammering out a term sheet for the other immediate capital market transaction, the private placement. Carbide did not want any covenants on the privately placed debt to limit its flexibility. "We ended up with a very liberal term sheet. The buyers weren't getting terms. The primary incentive to buy this security was yield," remarked Twomey. Scott Phillips, an associate in Investment Banking, put together the offering book that would go to potential institutional investors.

On November 3, the special board meeting to consider management's recommendation to pursue First Boston's course of action was held. Jamerson, Tony Freeman, Jim Freeman, Calhoun, Kolmer, and Buchanan attended the meeting. It was unusual for Buchanan to attend such a meeting but everyone felt it was important for him to tell the board he had confidence in the proposal and that they ought to "do it now." With $1 billion of his firm's money on the line, Buchanan had more than a casual interest in the subject.

Stephenson began the meeting by describing the recapitalization proposal. Jamerson then outlined the details of the plan. Clerico presented the term sheets for each of the proposed transactions. Board members asked questions for nearly two hours. Their concerns focused on how confident First Boston was of getting 80 percent of the bonds tendered and whether the equity offering could be successfully introduced to the market. "One director thought the tender price was too low, and another thought it was too high," said Kolmer. "That told me I was probably on target." Freeman assured the board that the equity could be sold in the existing market. Based upon this presentation and discussion, the board voted unanimously to accept management's proposal.

After finally winning the business, Jamerson went home and slept—no celebration, no partying. He knew that the next month would be one of the busiest of his life. Given the proposed schedule, the last two pieces of the deal, the common stock offering and the private placement, would be completed on December 16. There was no slack and the tender offer still made him uneasy. But he would soon find out whether they could obtain 80 percent of the bonds. The next day (November 4) Carbide issued a press release announcing its plan.

Execution

On Thursday, November 6, two days after the plan was announced, the tender offer was officially opened. The offer would remain open for twenty

business days, as legally required. Now it was a matter of talking to the
bondholders, finding out what they planned to do and, if necessary, per-
suading them to tender. Gookin recommended that Carbide hire the Carter
Organization, a proxy solicitation firm, to assist in canvassing bondholders
and disseminating information about the offer. At the same time, Kolmer
and the members of his High Yield Sales and Trading Department were in
contact with many of the bondholders. Gookin managed these information
flows and made sure that First Boston knew all the bondholders' intentions.

Gookin's job was not limited to managing the information flows to and
from the bondholders. Since all of the refinancings were contingent on the
tender offer succeeding, everyone at First Boston and Carbide constantly
wanted to know the status of his efforts. Potential equity and private placement buyers also wanted to know how things were going, so Gookin got
calls from Kauffman and Twomey. He received calls for status reports directly from Stephenson and Clerico as well as John Toffolon, the chief financial officer at First Boston. A smile crossed Gookin's face when he recalled the excitement of the tender offer: "It was terrific. I had all the
information. The first couple of weeks I just silently worked away at my
job. The last few weeks I was the most popular guy at First Boston."

On November 17, two weeks into the tender offer, an apparent catastro-
phe occurred. A judge in Bhopal signed an injunction putting a restraining
order on the entire deal. The Indian government was concerned that the
recapitalization and any associated asset sale would reduce the pool of cash
available for an eventual settlement with the disaster victims. Sawyer spent
a week in Bhopal educating Carbide's lawyers there on the details of the
deal and preparing a briefing for the judge. Clerico flew to Bhopal for the
hearing with the judge. Carbide argued that the recapitalization plan was
not a liquidation but a move that would strengthen the company's overall
financial position. After two weeks of anxiety at Carbide and First Boston,
and extreme volatility in the market for Carbide's bonds, the judge lifted
the restraining order on November 30. Also in November, although it did
not affect Carbide directly, the Ivan Boesky insider trading scandal shook
the bond market.

An unintended but positive consequence of these two scares was that the
bondholders became more skeptical about the future of the junk-bond market and of Carbide's bonds in particular. Even though the two events were
initially thought to have damaged the chances of successfully executing the
tender offer, Kolmer believed that "in the end it helped. People decided it
was a good time to let go of the bonds." Furthermore, speculators who
might have held the deal hostage by trying to prevent Carbide from obtaining 80 percent of the bonds of any of the three outstanding bond issues were
scared away.

Calhoun remembered that his greatest concern during this period was the tender offer. "I talked to Kolmer frequently, since he was closest to the market. Market intelligence was key. I wanted to know what people's sentiments were: Did people think the deal would work? I also wanted to know the locations of the big blocks of bonds."

Gookin spent the last week of the tender offer in a hotel next to the office. "Each night I spent hours preparing for the next day. Everyone wanted to know where we stood. I had to assimilate all the information that had come in to that point, and figure out what other information we needed and who we needed to call."

With the tender offer in motion, Carbide had to finalize its borrowing agreements with the commercial banks. As with the tender offer, the Bhopal injunction preventing asset sales caused the banks to be concerned. It was not until December 3, after the injunction was lifted, that Clerico wrapped up the agreement with the banks. Carbide would pay the banks up to $1.1 billion in proceeds from asset sales. The balance of the $2 billion loan would be repaid with proceeds from future issues of securities.

At the same time, Jamerson, Tony Freeman, and Toffolon negotiated the terms of the bridge agreement with Stephenson and Clerico. Although First Boston had agreed in principle to provide up to $1 billion, the terms had not been finalized. Stephenson remembered that "hammering out the bridge loan was the most difficult part of the deal." Jamerson had a similar sentiment: "It was extremely difficult to be negotiating the protection of First Boston's capital at the same time we were giving Carbide advice on the recapitalization." The final agreement between Carbide and First Boston stipulated that the bridge loan would be refinanced immediately by two capital market transactions: an equity offering and a private placement. In the weeks preceding the close of the tender offer, Toffolon was in constant contact with Jamerson and Gookin so that he could stay apprised of the status of the tender offer. The amount of First Boston money needed for the deal would be determined by the percentage of bonds tendered.

The equity and private placement transactions attracted unusual interest at First Boston, since they were the source of the bridge loan repayment. On November 4, the red herring (preliminary prospectus) for the equity offering was delivered to the SEC. It announced that twenty-five million shares of Carbide stock would be issued. On the same day, the sales binders Kauffman and Stearns had created were distributed to the equity sales force at a presentation that described the deal. Sixty members of the sales force in New York attended and the presentation was broadcast worldwide on First Boston's private communication system. Jim Freeman was the keynote speaker. Kauffman noted that "Freeman used to be the head of research, so he had lots of credibility with the sales force." But it was not just out of respect for Freeman that they listened. "They wanted to hear what was happening anyway. They're on commission, so it means money in their pockets," said Stearns. The Equity Capital Markets staff passed out golf balls, pens, and hats to the sales force—"we wanted to get people psyched," said Stearns. (It was customary to distribute products associated with the client to stimulate interest in the offering, but given Carbide's product line, alternative gifts had to be used.)

With the official announcement, salespeople could now call their accounts and build a book (a list of investors who indicate an interest in the issue). To stimulate demand for the equity issue and explain the deal directly to institutional investors, two teams took a "road show" around the United States. Stephenson and Jamerson covered the East Coast—with Kennedy attending a few of the key presentations—while Anderson, the former chairman and CEO, Clerico, and Kauffman met with investors on the West Coast. Using two corporate jets, "we spent four days having breakfast, lunch, and dinner in several cities a day," said Jamerson. "Many of the investors wanted one-on-one meetings with Carbide executives so the schedule was grueling." Since four million shares of stock were to be sold in Europe, Stephenson spent two days meeting investors there.

On December 10, Stearns told the sales force that the book would close the next day at noon. By the deadline the book contained orders for over thirty-three million shares. "We felt we had a good book. You always want an issue to be oversubscribed, and we had that. We also thought that most of the buyers would hold onto their shares," said Stearns. It was important for demand to be strong and to limit the shares going to "flippers" (buyers who would immediately try to sell the stock at a profit); otherwise there could be downward pressure on the stock price. First Boston wanted to avoid having to counter this downward pressure by purchasing shares on the open market.

After Stearns and her assistants allocated the stock to the accounts that placed orders, the deal was ready to be priced and offered. At the close of the stock market on December 11, Stephenson, Clerico, the First Boston people, and representatives from Morgan Stanley met at First Boston's offices. Jim Freeman and Nancy Stearns, speaking for the co-managers of the deal, conducted the pricing meeting. As was typical, they advised pricing the issue at the day's last sale price prior to the market close, $22.50 per share. The strength of the book led them to recommend that the offering be enlarged to twenty-seven million shares and Stephenson readily agreed. (In addition, First Boston had a "green shoe," an overallotment option that would allow the firm to issue an additional three million shares if there was demand.) Finally, after some negotiation, Stephenson agreed to a gross spread (i.e., fee paid to investment bankers) of $0.80 per share. Then First Boston determined how the gross spread would be divided among the underwriting fee, management fee, and sales concession.

Immediately following the meeting, Nancy Stearns ran upstairs to the trading floor. "Everybody was standing around waiting to hear the price," she recalled. Most important, "they wanted to know what the sales concession would be—that is, how much money they [the sales force] would make." Meanwhile Kauffman rushed the final prospectus to the printers, so that the SEC would have a copy before the markets opened the next morning. On December 12, the following morning, the sales force called their accounts and offered the stock. Within five business days, most of the final proceeds, $675 million, were in hand.

While the equity people were creating the book, Jamerson, Keaveney, and Twomey visited major buyers of private placements such as Prudential, Equitable, and New York Life. "Because of the complexity of the deal, we wanted to sell it in major pieces—$20 million chunks," said Twomey. First Boston contacted twenty different institutions before they "circled," or obtained commitments for, $300 million. The coupon rate and terms were negotiated with the lead buyer, who had $100 million of the deal, and the buyers of smaller pieces went along. When it occurred, the Bhopal injunction also alarmed the institutions that "circled" a piece of the private issue. (After yet another review of the Bhopal case, Stephenson noted that "the Bhopal situation has probably been examined by more lawyers than any other event in history.") In accordance with industry practice, the lenders took a "fresh look" at the deal. The lead institution cut its participation to $75 million and three of the other lenders backed out. "Through skill and luck," said Twomey, "we were able to keep most everyone in after that." These events reduced the size of the placement from $300 million to $200 million.

Each piece of the puzzle fell into place by year-end. Ninety-six percent of the bonds were tendered at a cost of $2.976 billion to Carbide. The commercial banks loaned Carbide $2 billion and First Boston made a loan of $976 million. The equity offering and private placement yielded $875 million, which immediately went to pay down the First Boston loan, to $100 million. Also before year-end, divestitures totaling almost $900 million had been closed by Carbide's own internal Acquisitions and Divestitures Group, the proceeds of which paid down a portion of the commercial bank debt. By early January 1987, work had already begun on the remaining capital market transactions that would repay the balance of the First Boston bridge loan and the commercial bank loan.

Reflections

In three months, Carbide's entire capital structure was altered: a nascent idea in early October had developed into a set of deals that gave the company an entirely different balance sheet by the end of the year. With the help of First

Boston, Carbide achieved its goals of lower debt, reduced interest expense, and less restrictive covenants. It could approach the future with new flexibility and vigor.

First Boston also met its objectives. With the completion of the equity and private placement offerings, First Boston's bridge loan was paid down from nearly $1 billion to $100 million in just a few weeks. The package of transactions garnered revenues to First Boston exceeding $70 million, and it was in a strong position to do future business with Carbide: "We finally established a strong relationship with Union Carbide," said Jamerson.

Virtually all the First Boston bankers agreed that the Carbide deal was a great experience. With characteristic flourish, Tony Freeman remarked that "this was the Olympic Games of investment banking." In discussing the deal with Jamerson six months after it occurred, we could not help being swept up in his enthusiasm. He would leap from his chair and reenact the meetings associated with the deal.

Even though the financial rewards for individuals at First Boston were significant, the sense of having participated in something "big" was the most salient memory people had of the deal. Although Kauffman possessed a rather jaundiced view of the experience because of the long hours and grueling detail, even he conceded that "there was a certain sense of excitement involved in doing the equity deal." Six months after the deal he moved from Investment Banking to the Equity Capital Markets Group: "My experiences on the Carbide deal enabled me to meet these people and I was impressed with them." Twomey confessed that the one-month period during which the deal was happening "generated a lot of stomach acid. But that is what this business is all about. I wouldn't want a steady diet of these but one or two a year are great."

Gookin was even more ebullient about his experience. "This was a great deal—the biggest tender offer ever done, the biggest bridge ever done, and a Christmas tree of refinancing transactions. I also became an expert on debt tender offers." On a more personal level he said, "This was a great credibility builder for me. I got to work with a multitude of organizations within the firm." He also developed relationships with the Carbide people. "I now regularly call on several people who work for Clerico."

Stephenson believed that the recapitalization was a success. "The president of the company was able to go to the shareholders with a clean slate in 1987." In a June 1987 *Corporate Finance* article (p. 54), Stephenson described the plan as "a surgical, quick, neat, trim, clean silver bullet sort of solution." That same article concluded that "for Union Carbide shareholders, it is without a doubt a most successful restructuring."

As for whether First Boston earned its fees, Stephenson responded, "I think they did given the fee structure that obtains in the industry." His satisfaction with First Boston's work, however, did not lead to the conclusion that it was now Carbide's exclusive "relationship" bank. "Carbide's aggressive financial strategy attracted the attention of many investment banks," said Clerico. "Now a number of them are quick to call on us with new ideas." Still, Carbide's investment banking relationships, old and new, endured. "Morgan Stanley has a very strong person assigned to the account, and things are back on course," said Stephenson. Clerico's assessment was similar: "Morgan Stanley and First Boston are equal runners on anything that comes down the road."

— 2

THE NETWORK NATURE OF
INVESTMENT BANKING

The Union Carbide deals done by First Boston illustrate some of the management practices used by investment banks. Although there are differences among firms' management practices, there are also some important similarities in how investment banks formulate strategy, design organizational structures, use management control systems, determine bonuses, and manage relationships. The management practices that are effective in the investment banking business have their roots in the underlying nature of the business. The practices result from the function of the firms, their economic characteristics, and the production process involved in doing deals. Changes in the industry over the last several years, such as increased size of firms, product diversification, and geographical dispersion, have made it more difficult to use these practices. The changes by themselves, however, are not reason to depart from management practices that have proven to be effective. Such trends in the industry make it harder to implement these practices, but unless there are important changes in the function, economic characteristics, or production process of the business, they will remain relevant to the management of investment banks [see Figure 2.1].

Function

The function of investment banking, the first determinant of management practices in the industry, is to mediate the flow of assets between "issuers" and "investors." We define *issuers* more broadly than usual to include companies (and other entities) that sell assets, such as stocks, bonds, and even parts or all of the company itself. Investors include companies, institutions, and people who buy these assets. Although issuers can and sometimes do

FIGURE 2.1. Network Nature of Investment Banking

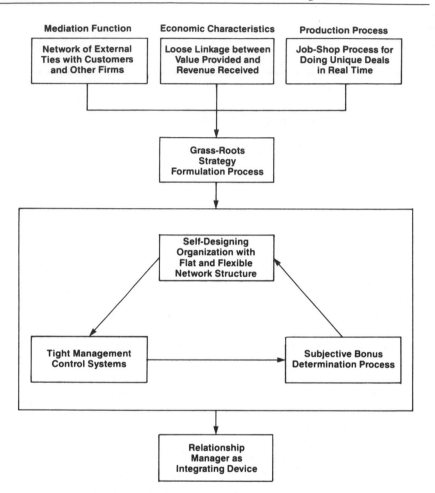

sell assets directly to investors, in most instances the exchanges involve an investment bank. The large number of issuers, investors, and types of assets that they sell makes it difficult for these exchanges to take place directly, especially given the large amount of information needed for efficient transactions.

Investment banking is a specialized function (performed not only by investment banks but also by commercial banks and other institutions) for collecting information on issuer needs for investors and on investor needs for issuers, for pricing and structuring transactions that satisfy the needs of both sides of the market, and for distributing and making markets in securities. In the deals it did for Union Carbide, First Boston performed all of these tasks. The knowledge it gained about which investors held Carbide's bonds during the bond buy-back program, for example, helped tremendously in the bond tender offer.

As they mediate asset flows, investment banks develop a network of *external ties* with issuers, investors, and their competitors. In the past, when a typical issuer had one investment bank that was represented by a senior generalist banker, ties between issuers and investment banks were few in number and simple to describe. The number and complexity of ties with issuers, however, has increased because of the growing number of product specialists with customer contact. As is common, a relationship manager and numerous product specialists at First Boston developed ties with Union Carbide's treasurer and members of his staff, the chief financial officer (CFO), the chief executive officer (CEO), and ultimately the board of directors. The complexity of ties between issuers and investment banks has also increased because a large number of companies use several firms. From 1984 to 1986, for example, 124 companies used 5 or more investment banks to lead transactions.[1]

On the investor side, fixed-income and equity salespeople, research analysts, and, to a lesser extent, traders maintain ties with portfolio managers, analysts, and traders at investor customers. Because of the variety of products and large numbers of people involved in investment decisions, large investors have even more complicated networks with investment banks than do frequent issuers. Between a large investor and a large investment bank, over one hundred people can be involved in ties.[2]

The network of ties between investment banks themselves can also be quite large because of the deals they do together. Although the size of syndicates has been decreasing, syndicates for underwriting and distributing securities create ties between the lead manager and co-manager and other members of the syndicate. From 1984 through 1986, for instance, Merrill Lynch and Salomon Brothers each served as a co-manager in more than 15 percent of the security issues led by the other firm, so the ties between them were particularly strong. Ties also form between the firm representing the buyer and the firm representing the seller in merger and acquisition (M&A) transactions. In the same three-year period, Morgan Stanley and Goldman, Sachs were on opposite sides of the table at least twenty times. Finally, securities trading leads to numerous ties among investment banks.

These external ties lead to a complex network of *internal ties* as the people within an investment bank who form the ties with issuers, investors, and other investment banks also form ties with each other.[3] Within the investment banking function the relationship managers and product specialists who share issuing customers have ties. (There is some ambiguity in the term *investment banking function,* since it is used in the industry to refer both to the firm as a whole and to the individuals who work with issuing customers. Whether the broad or narrow definition of investment banking is being used in this book should be clear from the context; in most cases it will refer to that part of the firm dealing with issuers, including customers involved in merger and acquisition transactions.) Similarly, ties exist among the salespeople, traders, and research analysts who share investing customers. For example, since markets move in relation to each other, ties among traders are used to communicate market information. Ties must also exist among the investment banking and the investor functions of sales, trading, and research. At First Boston, a great deal of communication took place between the head of the High Yield Sales and Trading Department, John Kolmer, and members of Investment Banking, such as Bob Calhoun and Bruce Jamerson.

The management practices of investment banks are fundamentally grounded in the need to manage this network of internal ties—creating, maintaining, and changing them as needed. All organizations are made up of an internal network of ties, but the network in investment banks is distinctive.[4] Because of their role in mediating the flow of assets between issuers and investors, and because of their economic characteristics and production process described below, investment banks have an internal network that is unusually flat and flexible. This is in contrast to many other organizations that have a more hierarchical network of ties in which communication occurs primarily up and down a relatively rigid organization rather than across departmental lines.

The complexity of deals, the speed with which many of them are done, and the financial stakes involved, especially on large deals, require a high level of coordination among the people in an investment bank across both functions and hierarchical levels. In the Carbide deal, a First Boston vice president was able to call upon the help of more senior managing directors and departmental lines were readily crossed as numerous specialty and functional areas in the firm cooperated to obtain and complete the deal. Any attempt to restrict information flows to official reporting channels would make it impossible for the necessary informal and rapid coordination to take place.

Furthermore, changes in external ties occur often and these changes require that internal ties adapt. Both on a deal-by-deal basis and more generally, the particular issuers, investors, and other investment banks involved in the flow of assets change over time. The increased sophistication of corporate financial staffs and the growth in the number of financing products have required changes in the internal organization of the investment banking function and how it relates to the trading function. For example, the new tax code adopted in 1986 fundamentally affected the issuers of and investors in municipal securities, again affecting firms' internal network of ties. Finally, as the mortgage-backed securities market developed, new external ties were developed to originate transactions and to sell the securities. Internally, new ties to link the mortgage finance, sales, and trading operations sprang into being. These examples illustrate the formation of new ties, but the process also works the other way. As certain external ties dissolve, the people in the firm who maintain these ties will dissolve the corresponding internal ties.

Thus an investment bank can be regarded as a complex and changing network of internal ties between various functional specialists. Even though many investment banks have become larger and more dispersed firms, there is still an important need for management practices that encourage a network of internal ties that adapts to changes in the external ties. Perhaps a more hierarchical organization with a more precise definition of roles and responsibilities will become more relevant in the future, if the financial markets become more stable and product innovation decreases. Under these conditions, the network of ties between customers and investors would also be more stable and simpler, so that the mediation of ties would be more amenable to bureaucratic principles.

Economic Characteristics

The second determinant of effective management practices in the investment banking industry is the economic characteristics of the business. The most distinctive of these is the loose linkage between value provided to customers and fees earned.[5] Investment bankers provide information, advice, ideas, and studies, much of it unsolicited, to both investors and issuers without the firm receiving any direct compensation. Investors compensate the firm for the research product through "soft dollar payments," that is, future trading commissions that are only loosely based on the value and cost of the service provided. Similarly, issuers compensate the firm only when a deal is done. Bruce Jamerson at First Boston sent John Clerico at Union Carbide a steady stream of information and talked to him on a weekly basis for many months before his firm got any financing business.

Nearly all of the investment bankers we talked to about this practice expressed little interest in changing to a fee arrangement similar to that of consulting or law firms—an hourly or per diem rate. They were willing to bear the risk of uncompensated services in return for what they felt were the higher fees they could earn on a deal basis. This was particularly true in M&A, where compensation was based on a percentage of the value of the deal.

Future payment for current advice is not an industry practice that could be easily changed; it is based partly on an important economic paradox. The value of advice is not known before it is given. Once it is provided, though, it is too late to enforce payment because the customer already has the advice.[6] In the investment banking business, the value of the advice becomes apparent over time as it is studied and compared to other ideas, and as events related to the advice unfold. In awarding transactions, customers take into account their assessment of the value of uncompensated services already received from investment banks.

In the past, when an issuing customer had a relationship with one investment bank, such as Union Carbide had with Morgan Stanley, the loose linkage between value provided and compensation received was not a problem; the firm was certain of getting the order on the next deal. Moreover, before shelf registration and other environmental changes that have made the business more competitive, the investment bank was more likely to make money on the deal. Because of the close relationship it had with its investment bank, the customer would be inclined to share confidential information about corporate strategy to get the firm's advice on what financial strategy was most appropriate. And because it knew that it would receive the fees on the next deal, the investment bank had an incentive to provide assistance. The investment bank also knew that while it might do some marginally profitable or even unprofitable business, it would also do the customer's more profitable deals. Finally, because its customer shared substantial information, the investment bank was able to provide financing and acquisition ideas that truly met the customer's needs, thereby using the time spent with a customer efficiently.

The breakdown of the model in which a company used only one bank turned the loose linkage into a problem. With companies shifting to multiple relationships, as Union Carbide did in adding First Boston, an investment bank has only a probability of getting the next deal. The problem is exacerbated when the margins on the deal are very small, such as a "plain vanilla" debt deal for an investment-grade customer. Thus investment banks face considerable uncertainty about the timing and amount of compensation they will receive for the information, advice, and ideas they provide to their customers.

Compounding the loose linkage problem is the fact that customers have less incentive to share information with several investment banks. One reason is that doing so takes time, and there are limits to how much time the CEO and members of the financial staff want to spend educating investment bankers on their strategy and objectives. A more serious problem is that concomitant with the growth of multiple relationships has been a decrease in the amount of trust between customers and investment banks. Customers are not always sure that the latter have their best interests at heart. On the other hand, investment banks are fearful of customers' taking ideas to another firm that will do the deal for less money.

The ironic result of increased uncertainty about getting the next deal and more restricted information flow between customers and investment. is increased interaction and product innovation. One way investment banks learn about a customer's needs is to present them frequently with various acquisition and financing ideas. Clayton Stephenson, the CFO at Union Carbide, noted that once his company had made it clear that they were no longer a one-investment-bank company, other firms were "quick to call on us with new ideas." Even though the particular idea may not be of interest to the customer, and the investment bank may strongly suspect this going in, it is a way of initiating a discussion through which the investment bank may learn better what would be of interest. This can improve the firm's probability of getting the next deal. Such a discussion is also an opportunity for the investment bank to tell the customer about other capabilities of the firm beyond the ostensible purpose of the conversation.

Product innovation also contributes to increasing the interaction between investment banks and both issuing and investing customers. By inventing "new" products to solve client problems, even if some are only slight variations on an existing product, investment banks hope to get customers to talk to them, to help them stay on the leading edge of financial engineering technology. Obviously, there is a cost to developing a new product, and the economic advantage of being first deteriorates rapidly as new ideas are imitated.

There are two important consequences of loose linkage, particularly for firms attempting to serve the needs of sophisticated frequent financers in a multiple relationship world. (Niche firms seek to avoid these consequences by explicitly going after only a limited number of "high value-added" products where they believe they can successfully compete.) First, at the time of our study, there was a common belief that diversification was important. If a firm cannot do a certain type of deal, it lowers its chances of getting the next deal, making it even harder to solve the loose linkage problem. Furthermore, talking with customers about even low-margin commodity products, such as commercial paper, elicits information that increases the chances of the firm getting the next and possibly more lucrative deal.

Commodity products especially lend themselves to this use because customers have little reason to use more than a few firms for products whose price is easily known and whose characteristics are uniform. Companies typically have only one or two commercial paper dealers, for example, and change them infrequently. This makes it difficult for new investment banks to break in, but it is a good continuing source of information for the designated dealers. Goldman, Sachs was legendary in the industry for having used this strategy to its fullest benefit.

Another reason for diversification is that margins vary significantly between new and mature products, and some products, especially M&A, are much less price sensitive than others. The margins on products can also vary cyclically. It is especially important for a firm to have capabilities in the higher-margin products because the loose linkage problem may simply not be solvable within a low-margin product. Most recently, M&A had been such a product. Customers were aware of the subsidy aspect of M&A and used it in this fashion. Thus although many customers think M&A fees are excessive, if not outrageous, particularly on the very large deals, the fees are expected to pay for uncompensated services or to subsidize other products, such as investment-grade debt underwriting.[7] The concentration of profitability in a few products is so great that a common phrase we heard during the course of our interviews was that "without M&A, trading, and mortgages, the Street as a whole would be losing money."

Variations in the profitability of products and functions are so wide that in some cases the activities are, for all practical purposes, viewed more as a cost center, or service unit, than as a profit-making business. For example, this is obviously the case for research, which all investment banking firms treated as a cost center. A more subtle example is a mortgage finance unit that acts as an origination "service" to generate mortgage products for sales and trading. At the time of our study, most money in mortgage-backed securities was made in secondary trading, rather than in the origination or issuer side of the activity. Although market forces help determine whether an activity is profitable on its own, an important component of an investment bank's strategy is the choices it makes about which activities are "services" and which are "businesses."

A final reason for diversification is that markets move in relation to each other. A lack of information about one market, such as the domestic U.S. Treasury market or securities traded in London or Tokyo, may put a firm at a competitive disadvantage in other securities, such as domestically traded corporate bonds. By serving various markets, defined both in terms of products and geographical locations, the firm protects and enhances its position in all of its markets.

The second consequence of loose linkage is that high market share is important, both in terms of the various products and at the individual customer level. This has less to do with the kinds of scale economies found in manufacturing industries than with the positive relationship between information and market share. The greater a firm's market share in a particular activity, the more extensive its information about both sides of the market interface concerning potential deals. It is colloquially called "being in the deal stream." Being in the deal stream improves a firm's pricing and distribution capabilities, which lower the risk of an underwriting and increase the profit potential on the deal. A high market share also contributes to trading profits and, to a certain extent, is a useful marketing tool when a firm's volume of activity places it high in league table rankings published by *Institutional Investor, Investment Dealers' Digest,* and other publications.

Market share is even important in M&A, since it enables a firm to gain knowledge useful in asset valuations.

With individual customers, a high market share is also beneficial. Not only are lead positions in deals more profitable than co-manager or other positions, but also a large share of a customer's business leads to a closer relationship with a corresponding increase in trust and information. More information enhances the investment bank's ability to provide good ideas and recommend appropriate transactions. Furthermore, with a large share of the customer's business, the firm has a better chance of winning the next transaction, so that the loose linkage problem is minimized.

Just how much market share firms need in a product varies by market and over time. In some markets, each incremental improvement in league table rankings may lead to increased competitive advantages. In other markets there may be a minimum market share above which little advantage is gained, and it is even possible for diseconomies to appear at some point.

For the full-service firm, the perceived importance of diversification and market share, when taken together, have a clear implication: It is best to have a large market share in many products. Within limits, the special bracket firms follow this strategy. The obvious constraints on the strategy are the capital and people requirements; even the largest firms are finding themselves stretched in these areas. It seems clear that these firms will have to make choices that involve market share objectives for certain products or markets and for certain geographical locations.

Another reason why diversification may take place less casually than in the past is that top management in the largest firms is becoming increasingly cost conscious in what has, for a long time, been described as a "revenue-driven business." Because of the size of fees and the large proportion of total costs that are, at least in theory, variable (since they are paid out in performance bonuses), investment banks have historically been more concerned with increasing revenues than with controlling costs. The vastly increased cost bases in the largest firms, not the least of which is the growing importance of the operations functions, have, however, led to more concern with controlling costs. John Gutfreund at Salomon Brothers received kudos from his competitors when he announced a hiring freeze in August 1987.[8] Clearly, Gutfreund was prepared to make choices about the array of markets in which Salomon would compete and he was followed by several other firms.

The economic characteristics of investment banking reinforce the complex internal networks. The loose linkage between value provided and fees earned, the disparity in profitability across products, and the number of products that can be involved in a complicated deal reinforce the need for cooperation among the people who constitute the network that is an investment bank. People have information that is useful to others. Even though the information was obtained at some cost and the revenues might go to another department, which eventually does a deal with the customer, it is important for the information to be shared. Consequently, everyone must be willing to do what is best for the firm as a whole even if the benefits do not accrue directly to him or her. John Kolmer, head of High Yield Sales and Trading at First Boston, expressed this attitude when he described the modest fees earned on the bond buy-back effort for Union Carbide: "I was willing to do it for nothing with the hope that we might get future business."

The need for a complex network of internal ties makes it difficult to decentralize an investment bank into the fairly autonomous profit centers that are found in conglomerates. The units in an investment bank are not nearly so separable, and instead form what one investment banker called a "seamless web" of activities. As long as loose linkage exists, along with the interrelatedness of markets and variations in product profitability, the economics of the business reinforce the kind of internal networks created by its function. If payments for services provided were direct and markets were less related, a firm could be divided into separate businesses. Increased size and complexity from diversification, however, are insufficient reasons to create highly autonomous units. Rather, while making it more difficult, large size and complexity only reinforce the necessity for cooperation, so that the firm as a whole can solve the loose linkage problem.

Production Process

The third determinant of the industry's management practices is the production process used in doing deals. Two rather obvious characteristics of deals are of fundamental importance. First, a deal is a service performed in real time by people in interaction with customers. Second, each deal is unique; investment banking uses a job-shop production process.[9]

These two characteristics reinforce the network nature of investment banking created by its function and economic characteristics. In performing the service, external ties are created with customers that involve many people in the firm. And because the deals are unique, exactly who is involved varies from deal to deal. This results in a large number of internal network ties.

The service nature of investment banking, both in originating deals with issuers and in distributing to and trading for investors, means that a large proportion of the professionals in an investment bank are directly involved with clients. In the Carbide case, at least eighteen First Boston people, ranging from two analysts to eight managing directors to the CEO, had direct contact with the company. Some of these people also had contact with investors; a number of debt and equity salespeople had contact only with the investor. Because so many people are involved in ties with customers, the boundaries of the firm are extremely porous. Porosity enhances the flow of information into the firm, so that changes in customer needs or the environment are rapidly felt. Thus internal networks must be flexible enough to adjust quickly, ensuring that the right people communicate and work with each other on a timely basis.

Another consequence of the service nature of the business is that deals are not a manufactured product that can be put in inventory and then delivered in finished form to a customer when needed. Although deals can be somewhat backlogged until a market opportunity opens, buffer inventories cannot be created to help smooth out production requirements. (The bridge loan to Carbide was a form of buffering in that First Boston held the assets until the new securities were sold, but this was a major commitment of capital for the firm, which is atypical of most transactions.) Since all deals in the pipeline have priority status and are based on market opportunities that may disappear unexpectedly, there is continually an air of crisis, an urgency to get deals done, especially when business is booming. First Boston was under great pressure to complete the debt tender offer before the end of the year in order to take advantage of the tax code and to avoid the Christmas lull in the markets. It also wanted to complete the takeout financings as expeditiously as possible in order to both minimize its risk on the bridge loan and remove it from First Boston's books for the year-end closing of its own financial statement as a public corporation.

The first response to time pressure is to expand capacity by working longer hours, which reinforces the atmosphere of constant crisis. Several people at First Boston reported spending seven-day weeks of fifteen or more hours per day proposing and executing the transactions for Union Carbide. When the strong demand continues for some time, it cannot be solved by simply working harder. Firms face the dilemma of forgoing business while keeping capacity at a level appropriate for leaner times or of staffing up to meet demand. In the first case, opportunities for earnings and market share are lost and efficiency is preserved. In the second case, earnings and market share are won at the cost of lower efficiency and higher risk from the rapid growth, as well as potential overcapacity when market conditions weaken. At the time of our study, firms were in the boom part of the cycle and with a few exceptions, such as Dillon, Read and Lazard Frères, all of them had been growing rapidly for several years. Four of the major firms doubled in size in the five years from 1981 to 1986 (First Boston Corporation, Morgan Stanley, Salomon Brothers, and Goldman, Sachs).

Because long lead times are not needed in investment banking, capacity can be increased as rapidly as employees can be hired and trained. (Some newer products, such as varieties of asset-backed securities, which involve extensive software development, do have longer lead times for building production capacity.) When almost all of the firms in an industry are trying to increase staffing levels rapidly, escalation in compensation is inevitable. At the time of our study, not only were most U.S. investment banks growing rapidly, but U.S. commercial banks and foreign financial institutions were also aggressively attempting to make inroads into the business. Not too surprisingly, senior executives in the industry bemoaned the somewhat astonishing salaries and bonuses being paid to very young people. Nevertheless, they remained willing to pay six-figure salaries in order to get what they perceived to be the best people. In return, college graduates and M.B.A.'s lined up for the opportunity to participate. A much-discussed article in the *New York Times,* "Feeling Poor on $600,000 a Year," reflected how those outside the industry looked upon its compensation levels with a mixture of envy, disbelief, and anger.[10]

At the time, money was one of the most important incentives motivating investment bankers, partly because of its purchasing power and partly because it provided a quantitative measure of success. The amount involved made investment bankers willing to live with the ambiguities, stress, tensions, and conflicts inherent in a complex and crisis-ridden internal network where, to a greater or lesser extent, everyone is dependent on everyone else. Although such structures are especially effective in investment banking, they have costs for the people who work in them. Six and seven figure salaries for people in their twenties, thirties, and forties have made them willing to bear the costs.

Independent of the compensation involved, investment bankers are also strongly motivated by the desire to get and do deals and tremendously enjoy the competitive nature of the business. The excitement at First Boston about the Union Carbide deals persisted from the early competition for them through the completion of the debt and equity offerings, and was still remembered by the people involved for months after the deals were done.

The desire to beat one's competitors (wresting business from a company that had a strong relationship with one of its archrivals was an especially sweet victory for First Boston), together with the compensation at stake, has made investment bankers notoriously aggressive. Customers have mixed feelings about this. It can lead to high levels of customer service. It can also lead to great annoyance when an investment bank demands an explanation for why it did not get a particular deal.

The second production characteristic is that each deal is unique. A common phrase in the industry is that "every deal is different." (Managers in the construction industry, another project-based business, are fond of saying that "every job is different." Not too surprisingly, some interesting parallels in organization can be found between construction and investment banking, such as flexible and complex networks.)[11] Each deal is distinctive in terms of the issuers and investors involved; the amount of assets exchanged between them; the form (equity, debt, lease, or merger or acquisition), structure, and price of the assets; the timing of the deal; what other deals are in process within the firm; and market conditions at the time the deal is done. Thus each deal represents a unique configuration of internal resources in terms of who, how much, and when each person is involved and what their particular contribution is to the deal. This requires an organization that can mobilize the necessary resources from disparate parts of the firm, often at short notice for high stakes, and make trade-offs when there are competing resource demands from other deals. Flexible networks combine resources into teams for processing deals and then disband them when the deals are done.

The uniqueness of deals has consequences for the loose linkage problem. On any given deal, certain people (and the departments they represent) will contribute more than they will receive relative to others. This creates an array of debits and credits representing who owes what to whom. These debits and credits form the basis for cooperation and make the necessary coordination possible. Someone who has benefited from the efforts of others on an important deal has an obligation to reciprocate on later deals for which no direct or immediate compensation is received. Failure to do so risks having others refuse to help in the future when their input can be crucial to getting a deal done.

The production process in investment banking reinforces the management practices required by its function and economic characteristics. If a way could be found to standardize deals, which is happening to a certain extent, and, less likely, to inventory them (thereby buffering the production function and reducing the porosity of the firm's boundaries), there would be less need for practices that create flexible and adaptive organizations. More stable bureaucratic management principles could be usefully applied. But as long as the technology of investment banking is based on doing unique deals as a real-time service in interaction with clients, this will not be the case, regardless of the size or complexity of the firm. If anything, even more flexibility and adaptability are required to manage this production process in especially large and complex firms.

Management Practices

We have argued that the function of investment banking, the economic characteristics of the business, and the production process for doing deals require that management put in place a set of practices that emphasizes flexibility, adaptability, and cooperation. Mediating the network of flows of assets between issuers and investors requires that investment banks form external ties with them and with other investment banks. These external ties form the basis for a network of internal ties within the investment bank. Changes in external ties require corresponding changes in the internal ties.

A firm's strategy determines its particular network of external and internal ties. The process that determines this strategy is one of five management categories in our theory of management in investment banking: the *strategy formulation process*. The other four categories are *organizational structure, management control systems,* the *bonus determination process,* and *relationship management*. These four practices are determined by strategy and in turn influence its development.

Investment banking firms use the five categories to manage the opposing but interdependent requirements for specialization and coordination within the network of internal ties. To be efficient in both marketing and execution, some specialization is required, as in First Boston's formation of a sales and trading department for high-yield securities and a corporate restructuring group. It is also necessary, however, for the specialized groups to coordinate their activities, as did the groups at First Boston involved in the Union Carbide deals.

In their influential theory of management, Paul Lawrence and Jay Lorsch described companies' needs for both differentiation and integration.[12] Our objective is to extend their insights into the practices of a particular industry. When people specialize, the result is differences in objectives, attitudes, behaviors, and time frames. Traders, for example, have time frames and behavior patterns that are quite different from investment bankers calling on issuing customers. When specialists must work together, substantial cooperation is needed to integrate their efforts. The greater the specialization (differentiation), the more necessary but the more difficult the required cooperation (integration). Managing differentiation and integration means managing a network of internal ties. As investment banking has become more specialized and the need for integration has continued, resulting in extremely complex networks, it has become perhaps the most extreme form of the differentiation and integration problem Lawrence and Lorsch described over twenty years ago.

Investment banks have strategies that influence the amount of business done in certain markets and products, and that result in the pattern of deals done by the firm. Senior managers express their strategies through choices they make about areas in which to specialize. Some investment banks, for example, have set up a high-yield finance group as a specialized unit, whereas others use the regular investment banking department to develop and execute high-yield business. In addition, senior managers make strategic choices about which activities are businesses and which are services that act in support of business units. Finally, senior managers determine how these specialties and other activities will be linked together. Although flexible networks are meant to facilitate whatever ties are necessary to get a deal done, the reality is that some ties are stronger than others. Strategy both influences the strength of ties and results from the pattern of ties that exists within the firm.

Although top management has an obviously important role in formulating the firm's corporate strategy, most strategy formulation for specific businesses occurs lower in the firm. The number and complexity of the markets in which investment banks operate mean that those closest to the markets are in the best position to make decisions about business strategy. The process of *grass-roots strategy formulation* requires a *self-designing organization* in which organizational structure is determined by those who develop the business strategies within the broad parameters of organizational design established by top management.

Because the organization needs to respond to short-term pressures as well as adapt to longer-term environmental shifts, the structure is loose and flexible. Certainly top management has a role in changing these structures, especially to meet the broader environmental changes, but it is the people in the firm dealing directly with issuers and investors who are in the best position to determine how to organize in order to serve them effectively. Consequently, they must take responsibility for a constant organizing process. Thus, to a significant extent, the network structure is self-designing. And to be effective, the internal network of ties must be flexible and adaptive, not a precisely defined chart that moves from one steady state to another. As long as change is a constant condition of the markets, continuing change in the network of ties is a constant as well.

Structures used to implement current strategies constrain the development of future strategies. Changes in the network of ties change the patterns of information collection and dissemination. This helps to expand the range of perceived opportunities, as well as the perceived means to take advantage of them. Because the extent to which the network is changed through self-designing capabilities is limited, however, top management needs to complement these reorganizing efforts through episodic and major changes in strategy, structure, and personnel. Between the shake-ups, the grass-roots strategy formulation process, and the self-designing capabilities of the organization largely determine the strategy and structure of the firm, respectively.

The loose and self-designing networks form a flexible endoskeleton for the firm. In effect, they provide the means to accomplish the investment bank's objectives. But despite the obvious virtues of the self-designing organization, it does have its flaws. In particular, it may be too loose, too flexible, and provide people with too many choices. There is the risk that people will dissipate their efforts through a lack of focus. Furthermore, on their own they may not adequately integrate their efforts with others by establishing ties of appropriate strengths.

Thus, complementing the loose network structure of the self-designing organization, top management imposes tight *management control systems,* such as call reports, reports on deals done away, customer evaluations, internal cross-evaluation surveys in which members of different groups evaluate one another, and measures of financial performance. The systems form an exoskeleton for specifying objectives and measuring outcomes. By establishing individual and unit accountability, the systems provide a focus for action, and indicate which ties should be stronger than others. But, like all systems, those used by investment banks can create problems as well. Because systems are social artifacts, they are necessarily imperfect and subject to manipulation by those affected by them. Some people will always do what is necessary to produce the right numbers rather than what is right for the firm. Local optimization that is suboptimal for the firm as a whole occurs most often when the control system measures are perceived as important for the bonus determination process.

A bonus determination process that emphasizes the contributions a person makes to collective as well as unit outcomes can overcome these tendencies. The process necessarily requires managers to exercise a substantial amount of subjective judgment, using data from systems and a number of other sources to reward people for activities—marketing to potential customers, recruiting, training, and internal management responsibilities—that cannot easily be related to current revenues. Bonuses based on an assessment of a person's contribution to the short- and long-term performance of the firm as a whole, or at least to a large unit within the firm, reinforce the integrative nature of loose and flexible network structures.

Conversely, such structures also help to compensate for a potential weakness of the bonus determination process. Because the process contains a large element of subjective judgment, there is always the danger that some people will think that bonuses are unfair. Given the large amounts of money involved and the difficulties inherent in balancing internal equity with external labor market prices, this perception is understandable. The information transmission capabilities of complex network structures provide top management with the data it needs to make reasonably accurate assessments of people's contributions to collective outcomes.

In implementing strategy through structure, systems, and bonuses, investment bank managers determine how the resources of the firm are used. Ultimately, resources are applied on a customer-by-customer basis. Ideally, the people involved with each customer will balance what is in the overall best interest of the customer with what is in the overall best interest of their own firm. Because of the limitations inherent in using the organizational level practices of strategy, structure, systems, and the bonus process to determine this balance, managers in investment banks have developed the *re-*

lationship manager as an integrating device. Especially common in large firms with many customers and many product specialists who are involved with customers, the relationship manager most often interacts with issuing customers. At the time of our study, however, there were pressures for assigning relationship management responsibilities for investors as well.

Relationship managers are responsible for how the resources at their disposal (getting them depends to some extent on their powers of persuasion) are used in relation to the customers to which they have been assigned. In allocating resources, a relationship manager may encourage a product specialist to contribute in ways that are largely to the benefit of other specialists. The relationship manager must also ensure over time, even though the linkage between value to the customer and fees earned by the firm is loose, that fees are fair compensation for services rendered. In fulfilling these responsibilities, the relationship manager is acting as an agent for the investment bank's CEO: he or she is taking a firmwide perspective on balancing the use of resources and the needs of particular customers. The agency role provides a level of integration that the overall structure, systems, and bonus process cannot.

To be effective at resolving inevitable organizational squabbles, the relationship manager needs to be, in a sense, outside the organization. It is a help, therefore, if the relationship manager does not have product responsibilities. But without a product, it can be difficult for the relationship manager to establish credibility with the customer and with product specialists in the firm. The dilemma is inherent in the relationship manager's role.

Another dilemma is the degree to which the relationship manager should exercise control over the customer interface. When control is high, coordination is high as well, but opportunities for the firm may be lost because product specialists may not have enough access to customers to be knowledgeable about their needs. Responsiveness can be improved by reducing the relationship manager's control and letting product specialists have more freedom in dealing with the customer. In this case, coordination is sacrificed.

Just as the internal network of ties is influenced by the external ties, the dilemmas inherent in the role of relationship manager are a result of outside forces. Increased emphasis on transactions by customers creates pressures for the relationship manager to have transaction expertise as well and to exercise minimal control over the customer interface. Yet the desire of nearly all customers for some relationship is best met by a relationship manager acting solely as an agent of the investment bank's CEO, without his or her own product objectives, who has a high level of control over the customer interface.

The shift from single to multiple investment bank relationships has greatly increased the complexity of a firm's network of external customer ties and consequently the network of internal ties. In developing a theory of management for investment banking, one must begin with an understanding of the consequences of this shift.

3

CONSEQUENCES OF MULTIPLE
BANK RELATIONSHIPS

Because of the function, economic characteristics, and production process in investment banking, firms in the industry are managed from the outside in. The shift from single to multiple bank relationships has been one of the most important external changes and has had a profound effect on the management of investment banks.

Senior investment bankers and corporate officers speak fondly of earlier days when most customers had a strong tie and a professional relationship with only one investment bank. Several bankers, for example, mentioned that at one time the relationship between General Motors and Morgan Stanley was so strong that other investment bankers did not call on the company. These same bankers, though, were quick to point out that times have changed. From 1984 through 1986, General Motors and its subsidiaries used a total of sixteen firms to lead manage at least one transaction. Although Morgan Stanley still led more of these deals than any other firm, its share was only 22 percent. And General Motors is not an isolated case. Many active corporate customers and other issuers of securities normally use more than one investment bank. In the 1984 to 1986 period, 87 percent of the five hundred most active companies used more than one investment bank to lead a transaction; the average was almost four per customer.[1]

The shift to using several investment banks is partly a result of corporations' wishes to take advantage of increased opportunities. For example, to take advantage of the growth of international markets and the resulting availability of financing in different geographic markets, companies need particular knowledge and placement skills. They also need to manage corporate assets and liabilities more actively to manage risk and take advantage of opportunities in more volatile markets. In a record-setting ten-year swing, U.S. corporate bond rates almost doubled, from a low in January

1977 to a high in September 1981, and then by late 1986, fell back close to
their previous low. Furthermore, facing new competition from U.S. commercial banks and foreign banks, investment banks are now competing
more actively for business. A changing regulatory environment, such as the
adoption of Rule 415, allowing shelf registration of securities, has assisted
this push.

As companies have shifted from using one investment bank to having
multiple relationships, the responsibilities and sophistication of the financial
officers and staff who deal with investment bankers have increased.[2] A series
of surveys sponsored by Donaldson, Lufkin & Jenrette documents the shift.
In 1967, for example, chief financial officers (CFOs) were involved in the
decision to select a new underwriter in only 11 percent of the companies.
By 1986, according to a survey of corporations conducted by Collins and
Goss, the figure had increased to 72 percent. The data show a sevenfold
increase in the percentage of companies in which the treasurer and CFO
were involved in the selection of a new investment bank to underwrite securities. As the role of financial officers has expanded, the role of the board
of directors has decreased: from 62 percent to 37 percent over the same
period.[3]

Because the increased roles of the CFO and the financial staff have been
encouraged by the shift to multiple investment banks and have contributed
to the shift, cause and effect are difficult to untangle. As new opportunities
and more active management of assets and liabilities have led to the use of
more than one firm, companies have needed more active and sophisticated
financial officers to manage the transactions and deal with the investment
banks. Viewed from the opposite perspective, as their level of sophistication
increases, financial officers are more inclined to be critical of proposals and
to negotiate aggressively on price. Consequently, they are likely to encourage solicitations from more than one firm. Furthermore, they are interested
in receiving and are able to evaluate innovative ideas that can save their
company money and contribute to their reputation, both within the company and in the broader financial community.

Investment banks benefit from the shift to multiple bank relationships as
well, particularly those that do not have longstanding ties with major corporations. The willingness of customers to do business with more than one
investment bank has created opportunities for firms to attack the customer
bases of their competitors. Through aggressive pricing and innovative
ideas, an investment bank can improve its competitive position. In the past,
firms were more passive and their competitive positions were largely a
function of the frequency and types of deals their customers did over a
period of time. Several investment bankers we talked to recalled that in the
past because it was considered ungentlemanly to initiate business with one's

own customers, let alone approach a competitor's, they waited for the telephone to ring.

Whatever the reasons, the shift to multiple bank relationships and the increased roles of the CFO and financial staff have important consequences for the nature of the ties between customers and their investment banks. People in firms and companies we talked to described the change by saying that the investment banking business had shifted the emphasis from relationships to transactions. This statement contains some truth, but it does not reflect the fact that virtually all the customers and investment bankers we talked to insisted on their desire to have relationships. Nor does the statement convey the full range of consequences that result from the shift to multiple bank relationships. The shift has exacerbated problems that stem from the loose linkage between the services provided and revenues received. These linkage problems have had important consequences for the way customers and investment bankers perceive each other, for the amount of information they exchange, for the rate of product innovation, and for the level of tension and distrust between them. Underlying all of these issues is a paradox in the assertions that investment bankers and their customers make about each other concerning transactions and relationships.

The Relationship Paradox

Investment bankers we interviewed commonly observed that "customers have become more transactional." That is, in order to obtain a good price on each transaction, issuers encourage competition among investment banks. When asked what their strategy was for coping with this change in customer buying behavior, without exception investment bankers responded that their strategy was to build relationships. The customers we interviewed also acknowledged that the world had become more transactional, but from their point of view this was largely because of investment bankers' changed behavior. Although there was a range in how these customers managed the purchasing of investment banking services, they generally agreed that even though they, the customers, valued relationships, their investment banks were more interested in simply doing transactions.

Thus while investment bankers want relationships, they perceive their customers as transactional. At the same time the customers claim that they also want relationships and it is the investment bankers who are transactional. How can this paradox be explained? The answer lies in the fact that both customers and investment bankers want the advantages of relationships *and* the advantages of a more transactional orientation.

Customers define a relationship in terms of what they get out of it, and the reference point they use is the traditional one-investment-bank-per-customer model. When asked what a "relationship" means to them, customers emphasize the importance of the investment bank understanding the company and its needs, knowing something about the industry or industries the company competes in, and its competitive financing and acquisition strategies. In the 1986 Greenwich Associates survey, an understanding of the company's needs was the criterion customers cited most often as important in evaluating the lead manager of a domestic bond or Eurobond offering. Similarly, 60 percent of the companies in the survey said the single most important factor in determining the effectiveness of an investment banker's presentation was an understanding of the company and its industry. Forty-eight percent cited credibility with the company's senior management, a factor that is probably dependent upon having the same understanding.[4]

To the customer a "relationship" also means receiving useful ideas based on an understanding of its needs. In a particularly strong relationship, the customer expects to get a look at potential acquisitions or new financing techniques before other customers. When conflicts arise in an M&A transaction, the customer expects the firm to represent it. Although it does not expect to pay the investment bank for services received between deals, a customer in a relationship wants information on the markets, ideas, and advice from the investment bank on a continuing basis. Payment is made when a deal is done.

Instead of ideas that are based on an understanding of the company's particular situation, however, customers feel that investment bankers often present them with products that they or the industry are currently emphasizing. Customers frequently complain that investment bankers have a "Deal of the Week" mentality.[5] Several people we interviewed pointed to large piles of blue books and other documents they had recently received from investment banks, complaining that they were irrelevant to their needs.

Customers complain that investment banks are only really interested in them when they are working on a deal and that between deals they receive poor service. The Collins and Goss survey found that personal service and attention was one of the top three areas in which customers felt improvement was needed.[6] Customers assume this lack of attention occurs because the investment bank is busy seeking opportunities with other customers who are getting ready to do a deal. Intense interest during a transaction, which wanes until the next one, leads the customer to conclude that the investment bank is more interested in transactions than in relationships.

Customers are also concerned about possible conflicts of interest between it and its investment banks. Especially worrisome is the possibility of a hostile takeover attempt in which its investment bank represents the acquiring company. This creates an incentive for customers to withhold information from its investment banks for fear that it might be used against them. Conflicts of interest can also arise when the investment bank is looking for deals in which to invest its own capital and gives itself first look at potential deals before showing them to customers.[7] In the customer's eyes, these conflicts are further proof that the primary concern of investment banks is to do transactions, even if they are not in the best interest of the customer.

This perception by the customer is especially interesting in light of the great feeling with which investment bankers expressed to us their interest in building relationships with their customers. Not unexpectedly, investment bankers define a relationship in terms of what they get out of it, and, like customers, their reference point is also the one-investment-bank-per-customer model. They emphasize that in a good relationship they get all the customer's deals they can handle, or at least the right of first refusal. As several expressed it, "You get the first call." Because the margins and risk vary substantially depending on the type of deal, getting all deals is especially important.

Investment bankers emphasize the role of financial advisor and the deals that follow when a strong relationship exists. They also emphasize the amount of information made available to them when they have a strong relationship with a customer. When an investment bank has access to detailed financial statements beyond what is publicly available, it is better able to propose ideas for deals that the customer will accept. The information cycle—deals generate information, which in turn generates more deals—is especially strong when a relationship exists.

Finally, investment bankers emphasize that a relationship includes close personal ties based on trust with key company executives that lead to extensive information sharing, more deal assignments, and better deal structures

Despite their interest in relationships, however, investment bankers complain that customers are interested in transactions only and do not want to use them to build relationships. As evidence, they cite the customer's desire to pay the lowest price possible. "Loyalty is a basis point" is a common phrase in the investment banking industry. Probably no deal was ever lost simply because a bid was literally one basis point (.01 percent) worse than the competition's, but the phrase captures investment bankers' sense of the environment and grows out of the perception that customers will sacrifice the relationship for the sake of the transaction.

Further complicating the paradox is an inherent ambiguity in the terms *relationship* and *transaction* that is based on a false dichotomy. When speaking about the nature of the customer and investment bank interface these terms are often used to denote opposite ends of a continuum that runs from very "relationship oriented" to very "transaction oriented." Posing the issue in these terms implies that there is a choice between relationships and transactions. But since a relationship is based upon a series of transactions, the former cannot exist without the latter. A transaction can take place, however, without a relationship and a transaction may or may not be the beginning of a relationship.

A relationship implies continuity over a series of transactions. In a world of one-bank relationships, doing a transaction with a firm is an implied promise to do the next one as well. But when the customer can choose from among a group of investment banks, a profound change takes place in the expectations each has about the future. Before, it was a *certainty* that the investment bank with the relationship would do the next deal. When several firms are used, doing the next deal becomes a *probability.* The customer does not know itself which bank it will use on the next deal. Because a relationship is based on both transactions and the *expectation* of future transactions, uncertainty about the future diminishes the quality of the relationship. This is especially problematic in light of the loose linkage between services provided and revenues earned. In order to increase the probability of capturing fees for these services, investment bankers have become extremely aggressive, which to the customers appears to be a strong transaction orientation.

The customer's unwillingness to share information with the investment bank beyond what is necessary to do a particular deal further diminishes the quality of the relationship. When interaction between deals decreases, the relative significance of transactions increases, further reinforcing the perception of an increased transactional orientation on the part of the customer. This withholding of information makes it difficult for the investment bank to respond to customer needs because it understands the customer less well and therefore finds it difficult to provide the kind of service the customer desires. It is also frustrating to be expected to perform this service, typically for free, without any guarantee for future deals. To the investment banker, between transactions the customer appears to want the advantages of a relationship without the costs.

The relationship paradox can be summarized as follows. Both customers and investment bankers want the advantages of relationships, defined in terms of the one-bank model, but perceive that the other party is more interested in simply doing transactions. This perception is based on the reality that each party's desire for the advantages of multiple relationships makes it necessary for the other to have a more transactional orientation. The increased emphasis by each party on transactions that are not necessarily embedded in relationships reinforces this transactional orientation in the other. Both customers and investment bankers need to accept that there are both costs and benefits in shifting from single to multiple relationships.

Product Innovation

When customers used only one investment bank, both the customer and the investment bank had a strong incentive to stay informed of one another's needs and capabilities. Since the investment bank knew it would be doing the next deal, it was willing to expend the resources necessary in order to stay informed about its client's corporate and financing strategy. For its part, because of the close professional relationship it had with its investment bank, the customer was willing to be open with information—strategies, plans, and detailed financial results. Since it was only dealing with one investment bank, it could spend a substantial amount of time with it. This greatly contributed to the investment bank's ability to be responsive to the particular needs of the customer and to provide services appropriate to its customer's circumstances.

Given the increased complexity of today's capital markets and the plethora of financial products available for serving clients, the need for investment bankers to understand their customers is perhaps greater than ever before. But it is harder and harder for investment bankers to do so. Because it is now dealing with two or more investment banks, the customer has less time to spend with any given one. As E. Stanley O'Neal, general assistant treasurer at General Motors, put it, "Investment banks are well informed about the market, but naive about the company's business. This is understandable because they get less information from the company than in the days when they were the one investment bank." Even if time limitations could be overcome, a customer believes it has to be careful about how much information it makes available to any investment bank. To put this in its starkest terms, customers believe they cannot be sure that the firm will use information for them rather than against them.

By not committing to do the next deal with an investment bank, the customer faces the possibility that the investment bank will be representing someone else in a competing transaction. In September 1987, for example, Citicorp asked First Boston to step down as a co-manager of a forthcoming equity issue because the firm was also serving as lead manager on an equity issue for Manufacturers Hanover Trust Corporation. First Boston denied a conflict of interest, but Citicorp apparently felt it was not worth the risk of having information about the timing of its issue in the hands of its competitor's lead underwriter.[8] The change in managers occurred even though First Boston and Citicorp had a longstanding relationship and the firm had led a substantial share of Citicorp issues. Even worse than the issue of competition is the possibility that the firm could be on the opposite side of the table in an M&A transaction.

As customer concerns about confidentiality lead to a reduced flow of information, investment banks must find ways to replace it. One way of doing this is to find opportunities to meet with the client or to at least have discussions over the telephone. The most natural way for creating these opportunities is to present a regular stream of "innovative ideas" to customers. As Neil Osborn stated, ". . . as much as anything else, it's the bankers who are the engines of change. Not that they've had much choice: This is a world where more and more corporate financial officers put less and less stock in traditional banking relationships, a world where bankers are obliged to scratch and scramble for business with escalating ferocity. One way to get a hearing from a stony CFO is to show him a new technique that may pique his interest."[9]

By seeing how the customer responds to these ideas, the investment banker hopes to learn more about what the customer's needs really are and the kind of deals it really does want to do. The resulting dynamic has a certain gaming character to it: the customer controls the flow of information, attempting to reveal its needs without revealing too much.

Because of the substantial profit potential of new ideas and their use in generating information from customers, investment banks devote considerable resources to new product development. Almost all the major firms, for example, have formed research groups with key phrases like "fixed-income research" and "financial strategies group" in their names. Staffed with quantitatively oriented people, or so-called quants, these groups search for new ways to arbitrage markets or solve a problem issuers or investors face, such as the need to hedge certain kinds of interest rates or foreign currency risks.[10]

The great majority of new products, perhaps 80 percent to 90 percent, result from working with issuing or investing customers. Max Chapman, now president at Kidder, Peabody, observed, "New products come from serving clients and they develop in an evolutionary, not revolutionary way." Wesley Jones, vice president and head of new product development at First Boston, also emphasized the importance of customers in generating new ideas: "In my mind we don't come up with anything new. Everything we come up with is in response to a request from a customer. It's a matter of clarifying questions."

Which ideas turn out to be viable depends in large part on whether the other side of the market (issuers or investors) can also benefit from the product. Money-market preferred stock, for example, benefits corporate investors because 85 percent of the preferred dividend is tax-free. The preferred stock product, however, went through several earlier forms before an effective design and marketing mechanism was developed to share the tax benefits between issuers and investors.[11]

The need to link issuers with investors requires that substantial information flow throughout the firm. A new idea resulting from work with investors must be developed within sales and trading, then sold to investment bankers within the firm and then to issuing customers. Similarly, an idea originating on the issuing side of the firm must work its way in the other direction from investment banking to sales and trading to investors. In order to test ideas and revise them to better meet the needs of both issuers and investors, a mechanism is needed to collect information from a number of people in the firm.

With varying degrees of formality, all of the large firms we studied, and some of the smaller ones as well, had formed new product development groups to perform this integrating function.[12] Wesley Jones provided an apt metaphor for his integrating role: "Sometimes I feel like a telephone switchboard. We're a home for unconventional questions." His counterpart at Smith Barney, Edward Glickman, described his new product development role: "I'm the investment bank's investment bank." Just as clients received ideas from and generated them for Smith Barney's bankers, so did the firm's bankers obtain ideas from Glickman and provide him with thoughts for potential products.

Given the role of customers in the innovation process, "lead users" are particularly important clients.[13] Investment bankers pointed to a small number of frequent issuers—including Citicorp, General Motors Acceptance Corporation (GMAC), Student Loan Marketing Association (Sallie Mae), and the World Bank—as responsible for a disproportionately large number of new products.[14] Because of their roles in generating new ideas and their help in refining new products, these customers received a lot of attention from investment banks.

Don Howard, CFO for Citicorp, was well aware of his company's role as a lead user: "We lead the market in many products or structures. Investment banks that do business with us can take the ideas to other customers." The benefit to Citicorp from its lead user position was that investment banks brought new ideas to the company early in the design of the product, giving Citicorp an early look. Howard was quite willing to help evaluate such products. He noted, "Almost all ideas are biased toward the issuer or the buyer because they are developed to solve a specific problem. We help bring them back into balance by playing the devil's advocate for the other side."

The costs to the investment bank from the information-gathering game played with product innovation are numerous. In addition to the direct cost of research and new product development groups, the firm must spend a substantial amount of time marketing its capabilities and specific ideas for deals to potential customers. The investment bank also runs the risk that a customer will take its new idea and conduct the transaction with another firm. If this happens, not only does the first investment bank lose out on the revenue from the transaction, but also the customer will have enhanced the capabilities of a competitor.

It is difficult to document the extent to which customers execute with one investment bank ideas that were given to them by another. Customers are aware of their investment bankers' concerns and described to us various mechanisms to protect ideas. Allen Harrison, assistant treasurer at Exxon in charge of investment banking relationships, for example, kept a detailed log of the ideas that were presented to him during each telephone call and visit. Furthermore, since creative people at all firms are observing the same changing opportunities in the capital markets and are likely to identify similar customers' needs, it should be expected that two or more investment banks will develop similar ideas at about the same time.

This is not the only reason that similar products appear. One of the jobs of research and new product development groups is to "reverse engineer" new products offered by competitors to quickly develop a version for their own firm. Sometimes this can lead to a certain amount of embarrassment, which happened to First Boston. One article reported: "In the prospectus of First Boston Corp.'s first offering of Dutch auction preferred stock, for example, there was even wording copied from the American Express transaction which was only appropriate if the issuer was the parent of the underwriter. First Boston officials did not delete that wording when photocopying the Shearson Lehman documents."[15]

An innovator's first-entry advantage does not normally last very long. Investment bankers use clever acronyms—CATS (Certificate of Accrual on Treasury Securities), TIGRS (Treasury Investment Growth Receipts), and LYONS (Liquid Yield Option Notes) to name some in the feline family—to develop a brand identification that might last after the product is copied.

The cost to customers of playing the information game is that they must consider numbers of "Deal of the Week" proposals. Investment bankers from numerous firms will bombard the companies—particularly larger, more active companies—with a flow of ideas in an attempt to gather information. In fact, the increased calling effort is well under way. As reported in the 1986 Greenwich Associates survey, the average number of investment banks soliciting business from the *Fortune* 100 increased from 11.8 in 1982 to 16.0 in 1986. Although the number of solicitations grew more slowly, the investment bankers did not ignore the next 400 *Fortune* companies. The average number of solicitations among these grew from 8.8 to 9.2 investment banks in the same period.[16]

There is also the cost of excessive innovation. We have no evidence documenting unnecessary innovation, either in terms of transactions that were not really needed or innovations that were not really innovative. Several officers and bankers noted, though, that most new products were minor variations on existing products, and expressed the view that there was too much product proliferation.[17] There is also the possibility of misguided product proliferation by investors as well as issuers. One banker noted that portfolio managers were often primarily concerned with the "yield to my departure" characteristics of a new security.

Finally, there is also the possibility that the high rate of product innovation in the investment banking industry is to a certain extent self-defeating.[18] The ease with which new products can be copied makes it difficult in most instances for a firm to sustain a competitive advantage for very long. Yet in an effort to obtain this advantage, firms invest even more money in product innovation and take ever-larger risks. In their competitive struggle, investment banks push each other to invest more and more in product innovation that has diminishing returns for themselves if not for their customers.[19]

Tensions in the Relationship

The information game, in which customers attempt to limit information flowing to investment banks, which in response seek information through proposed deals, is just one example of the increased tension between customers and firms that the shift to multiple bank relationships has caused. Tensions are further exacerbated by the increased role of the financial staff in managing investment banking relationships because of the increased sophistication of corporate financial officers. The ties between company financial officers and investment bankers constitute a complicated network of relationships that contain both adversarial and collaborative elements. Michael M. Thomas, a former investment banker at Lehman Brothers, takes an even more extreme view: "Where I once believed the relationship between the investment banker and his corporate client to be founded on a commonality of long-range interest and purpose, I am now inclined to see it as basically adversarial."[20] As is true of any buyer-seller relationship, people at the customer and at its investment banks need to protect their own self-interests while at the same time working together.

A common example is the negotiations over the pricing of a debt deal. The customer's financial officers want the interest rate and other costs of the issue to be as low as possible, consistent with a successful sale of the security. A lower cost is better for the customer, and it enhances the reputation of the financial officers within the company. From the opposite perspective, investment bankers will push for an interest rate high enough to provide assurance that the deal will sell successfully and for fees that compensate them for the risk they take.

The adversarial element needs to be balanced against the need for sufficient collaboration in order to have a successful offering. Both the company and the investment bank suffer if the deal is priced incorrectly.[21] If the deal does not sell because the pricing is unattractive, the company will be concerned about the market receptivity to its next security issue. If the market price is so attractive that the security moves to a large premium after issuance, the investment bank will lose credibility, at least in the eyes of the customer. Although the presence of other investment banks bidding for the same transaction swings the balance of power in the negotiations toward the issuers, there is still the need to collaborate for a successful deal.

The shift to multiple bank relationships and the resulting competition between investment banks have exacerbated the adversarial aspects of the relationship. Several customers recounted stories of feeling pressed by investment bankers who, when bidding for a deal, cited the help they had provided the customer in the past at no cost. In addition, investment bankers act adversarially with customers when they squabble about placement of the investment bank's name in the "tombstone" for a new security issue. The treasurer at a large manufacturing company remarked, "They'll kill for the right place on the tombstone. I can't believe it. We've gotten callous and just tell them what to do in terms of size, lettering, and so forth." His callousness grew from an experience on a particular deal: "We were arguing about this at four o'clock in the morning. I said to myself, 'I don't believe we're doing this.'"

In contrast, innovation is an area of likely collaboration. As we have noted, investment bankers are clearly interested in pushing new product ideas to generate a transaction or gather information. Financial officers also have an incentive to do an innovative deal that reduces costs or limits the interest rate or foreign currency risk. Such innovation can potentially enhance the professional reputation of both the financial officers and the investment bankers. Some would argue that the innovative aspect of the transaction is even more important in this regard than the cost savings or risk reduction. (Witness the trumpeting of new deals in trade journals such as *Investment Dealers' Digest, Institutional Investor,* and *Corporate Finance.*) Saving five basis points through sheer negotiating aggressiveness on a "plain vanilla" deal yields much less glory.

Much of the tension between customer officers and investment bankers concerns control of the interface. Financial officers at the customer have a clear desire to control the relationships with investment banks. Their stature in their company and their profession is enhanced if they control the company's contacts with investment bankers and if they select the firm used for particular transactions. Their position is also strengthened if they have authority to make decisions to reward firms for past service or withhold reward for poor service.

For their part, investment bankers want to establish and maintain contact with all relevant decision makers within the customer company. They like to have ready access to all decision makers, particularly the CEO, since he or she is typically the ultimate decision maker on the high-margin M&A and equity products. In contrast, lower-margin debt products are typically purchased by a member of the financial staff, down to an assistant treasurer or even cash manager, and this decision has minimal CEO involvement. Thus investment bankers need direct contact with those purchasing debt underwriting. It is also easier to have more frequent contact with them than with the CEO which has advantages for information gathering.

The CEO will surely be involved in selecting an investment bank for major transactions that affect the business or financial structure of the company, as in the Union Carbide restructuring. In addition, a CEO also knows more about the future strategy of the company than anyone else. A direct conversation with a CEO, for example, might yield a hint that the company would be receptive to an offer for one of its businesses. The CEO might not have even mentioned the idea to the financial staff. This possibility leads to a considerable effort to get access to the CEO. Customers recounted numerous instances in which investment bankers refused to talk to anyone but the CEO on certain issues, such as M&A advice.

CEOs are caught up in the tension as well. They do not want to be bothered by investment bankers unnecessarily, and so delegate considerable authority to financial officers. Among frequent financers, it is quite common for the CEO to completely delegate decision-making authority on standard debt issues to financial officers. Don Howard reported that a twenty-nine-year-old vice president at Citicorp had authority to commit to financings up to $500 million in size and thirty years in maturity on the telephone. Such delegation, Howard explained, enabled Citicorp to "hit markets that are only available for an hour" when he was not immediately available to approve the deal.

On the other hand, CEOs do not want to be completely isolated from their investment bankers. They may want confidential advice on such matters as a potential sale of a major company asset, an evaluation of the company's financial strategy, or feedback on the performance of the CFO and the staff. At times, the CEO may also want to influence the behavior of the financial staff and may find it convenient to do so through an investment banker with whom he has a close relationship. For instance, CEOs can use their personal ties with a senior investment banker to suggest a particular type of deal or a particular structure for a deal. The senior banker can pass the suggestion along to a more junior banker who is working directly with the CEO's financial staff. Such indirect influence is especially effective when the investment banker lets the financial officer take credit for the idea in front of the CEO, who in turn acknowledges the important contribution of the financial staff to the company.

Of course, members of a financial staff are not unaware of how a CEO can use an investment bank to control them. One defense is to do business only with investment banks that do not have officers with close personal ties with the CEO. Struggles for control within a company make it necessary for investment banks to carefully manage their relationships at all levels. If they focus exclusively on the CEO, they risk alienating the financial staff and losing business that the CEO does not get involved in, such as debt deals. If they permit the financial staff to completely control the interface, however, they lose access to the CEO and information that would be helpful in obtaining more lucrative advisory and M&A deals.

The Implicit Contract

The vast disparity in compensation between investment bankers and their customers exacerbates the tensions between them. When asked how he decided how much to pay people at his firm, Tom Unterberg, then CEO of L.F. Rothschild, Unterberg, Towbin, replied, "I figure out what somebody is worth and then add a zero." This only partially facetious explanation is a rough indication of the difference in compensation between investment bankers and their customers. An article in the March 1987 issue of *Corporate Finance* reported that in 1986 the average total annual compensation (including bonuses) was $374,000 for CEOs, $220,000 for COOs, $140,000 for CFOs, and $81,000 for treasurers.[22] In the same year, newly minted M.B.A.'s were receiving compensation packages worth $100,000 (including bonus) at major firms. Associates and vice presidents four to six years out of business school, typically between the ages of twenty-eight and thirty-five, frequently made between $200,000 and $600,000. More senior vice presidents and managing directors often made well over a million dollars.

That such handsome earnings are a fairly recent phenomenon, and unlikely to persist for long, does not alleviate the animosities financial staff members feel toward investment bankers who make five to ten times what they do. It is difficult to explain the differences in rational economic terms. Instead, investment bankers and their customers have developed an implicit contract based on rhetoric and behavior that enables each side to rationalize the differences in income among people performing similar tasks but on different sides of the transaction.

The basis of the contract is that investment bankers are trading quality of life for money. Both they and their customers emphasize how hard investment bankers work, both in terms of total number of hours and a willingness to have these hours interfere with their personal lives, to serve the customer and get the deal done. Stories of "all nighters," weekends in the office, canceled vacations, abandoned families, divorces, heart attacks at a young age, and burnout contribute to the belief that investment bankers make substantial and dreadful sacrifices to earn their lavish compensation. To the extent that these things happen, investment bankers rationalize them by accepting the view that they have traded quality of life for money and the excitement of doing deals. After all, when so much money can be made in such a short period of time, one need not do it for long before retiring or moving on to something else at an early age.

The stories may well be exaggerated in their telling: the greater the extent to which customers believe investment bankers work under combat conditions, the less concerned they will be about differences in income. Customers can rationalize the discrepancies by telling themselves, "No amount of money is worth this kind of sacrifice."

The sacrifices do contribute to fast responses to customer needs, however extensive and short the period of time in which they must be met, with nary a complaint to the customer. Some customers seem to take delight in making highly compensated people act obsequiously, but investment bankers believe such rapid response is important in providing good "customer service."

The other major sacrifice investment bankers make is a feeling of acceptance by and affiliation with their customers. In a world in which most customers use more than one investment bank, the investment bankers trying to bring in deals to the firm hear no a lot more than yes. They are constantly in a position of asking for business, giving the customer the satisfaction of controlling whether or not they get the deal. Ego strength is necessary in order to keep asking for deals, to withstand rejections, to push for access to the CEO, and to make decisions involving high levels of risk under great pressure and in a short time.

John Thorndike, a senior banker at Merrill Lynch, described the kind of persistence necessary to get business. He was assigned a large Pennsylvania company that did not use Merrill Lynch as one of its investment banks. "I called the CFO twenty times," Thorndike recalled, "and never got past his secretary or received a return phone call. I kept sending him materials between calls. Finally, on my twenty-first call early one morning he picked up the phone himself. I told him I wanted to see him and he said no. Now I've been there, but there is no business yet. I expect to get some. We simply have too much to offer."

Sometimes someone finally says yes. Thorndike recounted that he had called on another company, Hospital Corporation of America (HCA), for three years before getting any business. William McInnes, vice president of finance at HCA, said, "He stayed after us. He stayed on top of us. He did a good job of building a relationship block by block through making his calls. Whenever he got on a plane and came down here he always had something interesting to show us."

Although there is no denying that investment bankers work hard, there are industries, such as some high-technology industries, and occupations, such as research scientist, where people work equally hard if not harder but do not earn as much money. An interesting example can be found in the book *The Soul of a New Machine* by Tracy Kidder, which describes the hours and intensity worked by engineers developing a new computer.[23] Although the people on the project received modest bonuses, it wasn't the money that drove the team members, but the opportunity to work on the next exciting project. The participants described this in terms of "pinball"—the chance to play again. In the investment banking business, the pinball effect is also at work. Investment bankers we talked to were clearly excited about their business and the thrill of doing deals. They also made a lot of money, so it is difficult to separate the two effects.

The pinball effect and money came up often in conversations with customers and investment bankers, but each group used a different terminology. Both groups commonly stated that investment bankers are motivated by "ego and greed." Ego gratification comes from the feeling of being involved in big deals of crucial importance to the success of their customers. Even young investment bankers can be involved early in their career in big deals involving the highest levels of corporations. One thirty-year-old investment banker waxed eloquent about flying around the country with the future CEO of a large company in the corporate jet while they discussed restructuring plans for the company. "It's pretty heady stuff," he said.

The "greed" portion of an investment banker's motivation is the opportunity to make a lot of money very quickly. And although the amount of money they make is a source of tension, it creates a symbiosis between investment bankers and their customers. Investment bankers, who are relatively indifferent if not opposed to moving up a managerial hierarchy, increase their income by doing more and bigger deals. In contrast, to make more money, members of a company's financial staff *need* to be promoted up a managerial hierarchy. By helping members of the managerial staff get promoted, investment bankers can also improve their chances of getting more and more lucrative deals, and thus more money.

The rhetoric about a superior quality of life does not reconcile corporate staff to the enormous wage differences. Both investment bankers and their customers need to believe that they are different in fundamental ways in order to justify the differences and the anomalous fact that the power balance favors the customer.

This belief is created and sustained mainly through differences in dress and behavior, which convey differences in status. Investment bankers are artists at managing image and presentation of self by wearing expensive clothes and the ubiquitous suspenders, traveling first class, demanding access to the CEO, simultaneously conveying an impression of aggressive self-confidence and obsequious servitude, and demanding an explanation from a customer for why another firm got the deal.

Reflecting on the image-building devices, the treasurer of one company concluded that investment bankers are "masters of psychology." Their mastery lies in knowing how to serve while at the same time being accorded a superior status that justifies their incomes. The treasurer also commented about how much he liked to watch them in action.

Through these devices, investment bankers seek to cultivate an image of competence and quality, which is especially important in a competitive professional service business in which the purchase is made before the service is delivered. Since a customer knows the quality of the service only after the deal is done, unlike a tangible good, which can be examined before being purchased, the buying decision is based on reputation and past experience and the degree to which the image conveyed by the investment bank creates confidence in the customer.

Of course, the more firms that are successful in creating such an image, the less of a competitive advantage it becomes. Joe Perella, co-head of Investment Banking and Mergers and Acquisitions at First Boston, recognized this when he commented about the major firms in the industry: "They all have the good looks, the suspenders, and the blue books. It's all B.S." Nevertheless, such image management mechanisms may still be useful if they enable customers to tolerate differences in earnings with equanimity.

The need for investment bankers to construct an image introduces a large element of theater into doing deals. One customer we interviewed referred to this as the "Hollywood set" nature of investment banking. And while he appreciated and enjoyed it, he noted that "the scenes look great but when you look behind them you see a lot of clutter and devices."

The Decline of Trust

Skepticism about the interaction reveals the fundamental source of tension between customers and investment bankers—a lack of trust. As the competitiveness of the industry has increased, to a large extent because of the customers' own actions, and as investment bankers aggressively use theatrical techniques to distinguish themselves and justify their ample compensation, customers have simply come to trust their investment bankers less.[24] A suspicion that investment banks are putting companies in play in hostile takeovers in order to generate fees for defending them or for taking them over and a growing emphasis by investment banks on principal transactions have diminished customers' trust even further. Although investment bankers deny that they work against the interests of their customers, it is a very real fear among corporate executives.

At the same time that CEOs and financial officers expressed to us their concerns about sharing sensitive information with investment banks, investment bankers continued to speak about establishing "trust and credibility" with their customers. But to confront one another would threaten the carefully constructed game in which both parties participate. The failure to do so, however, only heightens the tension and level of distrust.

Underlying the distrust is the loose linkage between services provided and revenues earned. When customers use only one investment bank, this loose linkage actually helps to manufacture trust between customers and investment banks, since obligations are incurred and eventually paid off. The crucial word here is *eventually*. What distinguishes a relationship from a transaction that is not embedded in a relationship is that in the former both parties do not feel the need to keep the debits and credits in perfect balance at all times. Trust is developed when debts are willingly incurred and carried for some time before being paid off. This trust is ultimately expressed in the personal relationships between corporate officers and investment bankers who perceive themselves as being treated fairly by the other.[25]

Multiple relationships interfere with the development of trust. Because of the uncertainty faced by investment banks about whether or not they will get the next deal, and uncertainty faced by the customer about whether an investment bank will be working for or against it on a future transaction, each has an incentive to limit the degree to which the other is in its debt: the uncertainty about if and when the debt will be repaid. This creates pressure to ensure that the costs and benefits of doing business together are in reasonable balance at all times, which in turn inhibits opportunities to build trust. When both parties perceive the need to equate costs and benefits with each transaction, it becomes more difficult to build a relationship in which transactions are embedded.

Investment bankers and their customers avoid discussing the tension between them because of their mutual dependency.[26] However much they dislike some of the consequences of dependency, each party needs the other to accomplish its objectives and both are reluctant to stop playing the game. Contained within their dependency is a certain hostility. Investment bankers believe that customers are somewhat dull witted and unappreciative, more concerned with low prices and free services than with building a long-term relationship, and, at times, inclined to do deals that make no sense. Customers believe that investment bankers are arrogant, obnoxiously aggressive, and more interested in getting deals to make themselves wealthy than in understanding and satisfying customer needs.

Clearly one cannot totally blame these problems on the attitudes and behavior of investment bankers. In the end, it is customers who decide to engage in acquisitions that may have questionable economic benefits. It is also customers who retain investment bankers for takeover defense, perhaps at times out of fear for the personal consequences to the company's senior executives. Furthermore, no customer is forced to engage in an innovative, complex, and risky financing. Customers make the ultimate decision to proceed on a deal.

It is the aspirations of both customers and investment bankers that contribute to the excesses that each party deplores. To discuss this with one another, however, would threaten the game from which each benefits. As long as the benefits outweigh the costs, it is unlikely that either side will initiate any changes.

The tensions and distrust that have developed in investment bank relationships are disturbing to customers and bankers, but they are an inevitable result of the shift to multiple investment banks. At the time we did our study, companies were trying to achieve a balance between the benefits of close relationships and the advantages of a free flow of ideas and competitive prices from several investment banks.

4

HOW CUSTOMERS MANAGE
INVESTMENT BANKS

Companies that have made the decision to do business with more than one investment bank use either of two basic models. In the *dominant bank model*, the company has a very strong relationship with one investment bank but uses a number of others. With this approach, the company attempts to preserve the advantages of the one-bank model while also securing the benefits of having more than one supplier of investment banking services. The second model is the *core group model* in which the company has roughly equal relationships with a small number of investment banks but uses others as well.[1] Although this approach also attempts to preserve some of the advantages of a relationship, it sacrifices them to a certain extent to obtain the advantages of a more transactional orientation. These models are two ways to find a new equilibrium between the historical one-bank model and a purely transactional orientation in which no relationships exist.

An important determinant of which model a company chooses is the extent to which it is a buyer of investment banking services. Because they do not have enough business to sustain strong relationships with more than one firm, companies that do few deals tend to use the dominant or one-bank model. In contrast, more active financers (using this word in its broadest sense to include M&A activity) are more likely to use the core group model.

The level of a company's investment banking activity does not, however, completely explain the total number of firms used or the choices of a model. Historical circumstances and personal preferences of key company executives and board members also play a role in determining how a company manages its investment banks. Many companies that have enough investment banking business to economically justify using the core group model have chosen not to do so. Although these companies have chosen to seek the benefits of a closer relationship with one dominant bank, we believe that the complexities of the capital markets and competition within the investment banking industry will continue to encourage a shift to the core group model by companies that have sufficient investment banking business. In this chapter we explore these issues more fully. How the customer manages these firms is one of the environmental factors that determine the management practices within investment banks.

The Dominant Bank and Core Group Models

In a world in which some transactions are embedded in relationships and others are not, the rhetoric of transactions versus relationships obscures more than it clarifies. Rather, the interface between a company and the investment banks it uses can be described in terms of a pattern of ties, some of which represent relationships and others of which do not.[2]

A comparative example best illustrates the differences between the two models. During the three years from 1984 through 1986, Illinois Power Company and Monsanto Company each did fourteen transactions and each used four investment banks to lead their deals. But the pattern of ties between these companies and their investment banks was quite different. Monsanto used one of its four lead firms, Goldman, Sachs, to lead 79 percent of its deals. Illinois Power allocated its business more broadly; First Boston and Salomon Brothers led the most deals for this company, but each led only 36 percent of the transactions. Goldman, Sachs was in a dominant bank role in the case of Monsanto. First Boston and Salomon Brothers formed a core group of two investment banks for Illinois Power.

In the *dominant bank model,* the company allocates a majority share of its business to one investment bank, which thus dominates its investment banking business. In addition to this *dominant* bank, the company may give other firms, including one or more *significant* investment banks, a good share of its business. It will only include these other firms if there is a sufficient number of transactions to justify them. In addition, the customer may also have *transaction* banks that it has used for an occasional deal in the past and would use again if the need arose. Finally, the company has a set of *conversational* banks with which it is willing to talk about ideas.

The strength of the tie between the customer and an investment bank depends upon which of the four categories the bank is in. The customer has a very strong tie with the dominant bank, a less strong tie with its significant bank, and a still weaker tie with its transaction banks. From the customer's point of view, it has relationships only with its dominant and significant banks. With its transaction banks it does transactions that are not embedded in a relationship, although one may develop. A customer's conversational banks have yet to do a transaction at all or have not led one in recent history.

The customer's very strong tie with its dominant bank is based on a close relationship in which it freely shares information in return for advice and counsel on a regular basis. The dominant bank leads a majority of all deals and plays a particularly important role in key transactions, such as mergers and acquisitions.

Although it is easy to pick out the dominant bank relationship in a pattern of transactions, it is not so easy for an outside observer to tell the difference between significant and transaction banks. Especially if the customer is not a frequent financer, it may use firms in both categories for only occasional transactions. If the company desires a relationship, however, it can take steps to create one in several ways, such as soliciting advice and sharing confidential information. Customers do not use transaction banks in this way, and give them business only if they offer an extremely attractive price or a unique idea. In doing the deal, the customer often explicitly tells the firm that it should not interpret the transaction as the beginning of a relationship. Despite these warnings, however, in some instances relationships do emerge that give investment bankers the hope that they will develop with other customers as well.

Hope also explains why investment bankers from conversational firms will call on customers and submit proposals for financing and M&A ideas. Although this tie is only based on information sharing rather than deals, the investment banker hopes that eventually this information sharing will lead to a deal and an upgrade in the firm's status to a transaction bank, from which base it can then attempt to create a relationship.

Many of the customers using the dominant bank model are small or middle-market companies. Large companies that do not undertake many transactions and cannot justify several relationships also use this model. Numerous large, active companies, however, also use the dominant bank model. Dow Chemical, for example, between 1984 and 1986 used Smith Barney to lead 54.5 percent of its twenty-two transactions. The second-ranked firm, Goldman, Sachs, led only 13.6 percent of the deals, and six other firms led one or two each. Smith Barney was clearly the dominant bank. We cannot tell from these data whether Dow Chemical perceived that it had a relationship with Goldman, Sachs. If so, Goldman, Sachs was a significant bank, whereas the remaining six investment banks appear to have had only transactional ties with Dow Chemical.

Because it contrasts sharply with other leading companies in its industry, Ford Motor Company provides a particularly interesting example of a company taking a dominant bank approach. Over the three-year period, 1984 through 1986, Ford and its subsidiaries did seventy-eight transactions that were captured in the Securities Data Company (SDC) database. Although

Ford used twelve investment banks to lead deals, Goldman, Sachs was the lead manager for 70.5 percent of these transactions. First Boston Corporation led 6.4 percent as the second leading bank and Salomon Brothers led 5.1 percent of the deals. Nine other banking firms led one, two, or three deals. Goldman, Sachs was the dominant bank with a very strong tie to Ford. First Boston, Salomon Brothers, and possibly one or two other investment banks had significant ties with Ford, and the remaining firms seem to have had transactional ties.

The *core group model* represents the second pattern of ties. Instead of a dominant bank, the customer uses a small core group of roughly equal investment banks, each of which receives a significant amount of business and has a relationship with the company. The tie between each member of the core group and the customer is strong, but it is generally not as strong a tie as the one between a customer and its dominant bank. For example, the customer shares information with its core banks, but it is more difficult to have a close, confidential relationship when several firms are involved.

Although the amount of business the customer allocates to each of its core investment banks may not be exactly equal, the investment bank it uses most often does not dominate other firms that have a relationship with the company. Although the investment banks in the core group compete with each other, the customer actively works at treating each of these firms fairly and keeping a roughly equal relationship with each. Sometimes the customer deliberately shares its business among the core firms by, for example, rotating responsibility for running the books on security issues or spreading small M&A deals around.

The number of core banks a company uses depends primarily on the amount of business it has to allocate. Having a core group at all requires that a customer have a sufficient amount of business to maintain the interest of at least two investment banks. Below a certain point the investment banking revenues are spread so thinly that it is impossible to maintain more than one strong relationship. The maximum number of core banks is probably four to six. To justify this many relationships, a company would have to do frequent and large transactions.

Three other factors limit the number of investment banks in the core group. First, the people in the company who deal with investment bankers have a limited amount of time and energy to devote to this activity. Because frequent financers have large financial staffs, this capacity constraint is inversely related to the amount of business. Second, a company needs only a small number of core banks to get a high level of price competition and broad exposure to a number of ideas. And third, only a limited number of investment banks can do the deals of the size and complexity frequent financers require.

As in the dominant bank model, the core group model contains *transaction* and *conversational* investment banks, defined in the same way as above, neither of which has a relationship with the company. Conceivably, the customer could have a relationship with a firm it uses for infrequent transactions and consider it a significant bank, as in the dominant bank approach, but it is more likely that the customer has all the banking relationships it needs within the core group of banks.

The core group model is found most frequently among the very active investment banking customers. General Motors provides a good illustration of such a customer as well as an interesting contrast to Ford. They are both large global firms in the automobile industry, and they are both very active customers that used a dozen or more investment banks to lead transactions. In the three years from 1984 through 1986, General Motors and its subsidiaries did seventy-eight investment banking transactions captured in our database (the same number as Ford) and used sixteen investment banks to lead these transactions. In contrast with Ford, none of these firms received even close to one-half of the General Motors business. Morgan Stanley led the most deals with 21.8 percent of the transactions. It was followed by First Boston Corporation, Merrill Lynch, and Salomon Brothers, each of which led 16.7 percent of the deals. Each of the twelve other firms led one to five transactions, and the majority were non-U.S. banking firms used for international transactions.

From the viewpoint of General Motors, the twelve other firms appear to be transaction banks, whereas the four leading firms formed the company's core group of investment banks. E. Stanley O'Neal, general assistant treasurer, explained, "We used to use Morgan Stanley for everything. Then after shelf registration, we went to the other extreme, getting bids on everything. But it became clear for the long term that it is better to have a few relationships. We've chosen a few banks—basically four—and concentrate on them for our business."

By making a quantitative assumption to distinguish between the dominant bank and core bank approaches, one can estimate the number of customers who use each of these models. Since a dominant bank should have a large share of a customer's business and should dominate the second-ranking firm, a customer is defined as using a dominant bank model if its most-used bank led at least 50 percent of its transactions *and* if this firm led at least twice as many deals as the second-ranking firm. Many companies would meet this definition, including Monsanto, Dow Chemical, and Ford. Although selection of a particular cut point to separate the dominant and core group approaches is arbitrary, companies not meeting these two criteria, such as Illinois Power and General Motors, in fact seem to be using the core group model. (It is theoretically possible that some customers might

use a third model, which is a highly transactional approach with no relationships. But, we could find no examples of this approach among active
customers.)

Among corporations generally, the great majority use the dominant bank
approach. Even among the five hundred most active customers in 1984 to
1986, 55.6 percent used a dominant investment bank, including the 13.0
percent that used only one firm. (Although the dominant bank model developed out of the one-bank model, the latter can be considered a reduced
form of the former in which there are no significant or transaction banks.
In most instances there will be conversational banks, since even one-bank
customers are reluctant to refuse to even listen to free ideas from other
investment banks. Maintaining conversational ties is also a cheap and easy
way to apply competitive pressure to the company's investment bank, since
it creates a viable threat to do business with others without suffering the
consequences of doing so.) The one hundred most active of these customers, however, tended to use the core group model, with only 44.4 percent
using the dominant bank appproach.

It is easy to see why small and less active companies prefer the dominant
bank model. Some customers shift from the one-bank model to receive
more competitive prices and because they need capabilities other firms provide. But most of them do not have enough business to sustain two or more
equal relationships. In order to preserve the advantages of a relationship
they must concentrate much of their business in one investment bank. Less
active financers also tend to have smaller financial staffs and to be somewhat
less sophisticated than active investment banking customers. The former
often need basic financial advice that a dominant investment bank familiar
with the company can best give.

It is also easy to see why the majority of large and active customers prefer
the core group model. They have enough business to share among a small
group of roughly equal firms and thus can get the increased information
flow and ideas from multiple relationships. These customers are important
enough to each of their core relationship banks for the firms to invest considerable resources in providing service. They also have much greater in-
house financial capabilities and are, consequently, more interested in being
exposed to new ideas than in receiving basic financial advice. Don Howard,
CFO for Citicorp, which used the core group approach, noted: "We know
more about the debt markets of the world than any one investment bank,
since we talk to them all on a daily basis."

In the view of such customers, the total value received in information and
competitive prices is greater when their investment banking business is
spread across a small group of firms than when it is concentrated in one.
They believe that other investment banks are less likely to bring them new
ideas and submit attractive bids if they think the customer retains a primary

commitment to a dominant bank. Any one investment bank can only have so many ideas.

Although a majority of the very active customers use the core group model, a substantial minority use the dominant bank approach. These customers are aware of the potential disadvantages of using a dominant bank, but want the benefits of a close relationship with an investment bank in which the latter's foremost concern is doing what is best for the client. The firm knows the customer well, brings new ideas to it before taking them to others, and provides personal service and attention between deals. In the view of these customers, by having a dominant bank they avoid the "Deal of the Week" phenomenon and other problems that lead to tensions in the relationship.

A critic might argue that these customers may not be getting competitive prices on deals. On the other hand, a dominant bank would be foolish not to provide attractive prices and a high level of service. At a time when most active customers maintain multiple bank relationships, a company can credibly threaten to include other investment banks if the dominant bank does not provide good service or pricing.[3] (Such a threat did not exist to the same extent when most customers had one-bank relationships.) Because of an active customer's importance, the customer has substantial leverage in dealing with its dominant investment bank. More than one investment banker in the dominant bank position complained to us about the amount of effort it takes to keep customers happy.

Managing Investment Banks

There is a direct relationship between the amount of investment banking business a customer does and which of the two models it uses for managing its investment banks, as well as the total number of investment banks it uses on deals. As the number of deals a customer does increases, so does the number of lead investment banks it uses (see table 4.1). At the same time, the proportion of companies using the dominant bank model decreases. Less than 15 percent of the companies that use eight or more investment banks in a lead role use the dominant bank model. When the lead-management role is spread across a number of firms, it is very difficult to maintain a dominant relationship with one.

Two other indicators of amount of investment banking activity are the number of services used and the fees paid in a year. Data from Greenwich Associates confirm that as each of these measures increases, so does the number of investment banks with which a company does deals. Companies using one service used an average of 1.5 investment banks and companies using more than ten services used an average of 9.7 firms.[4] Companies using

TABLE 4.1. Use of the Dominant Bank Model, 1984–1986

Customer Characteristics			% of Companies in this Category
Number of Lead Investment Banks Used	Average No. of Deals	% Using Dominant Bank Model	
1	6.6	100.0	13.0
2	6.6	78.9	22.5
3	7.5	57.1	22.1
4	9.5	42.4	18.1
5	10.5	21.4	8.3
6	13.4	25.9	5.3
7	22.1	23.1	2.6
8	21.5	14.3	2.8
9	22.0	8.3	2.4
10 or more	44.8	6.7	100.0

NOTE: These data include the 507 customers doing five or more deals.
SOURCE: Securities Data Company database.

only one investment bank paid on average $522,000 in fees, compared to the average of $7,599,000 in fees paid by companies that used more than ten firms.[5]

Although the Greenwich data do not provide another way of estimating the use of dominant and core group models, they do show the importance of being a relationship bank. Of all companies in the sample, the most important investment bank received 65 percent of total fees, and the second most important bank received 35 percent.[6] Thus even though most companies use more than one investment bank, these companies concentrate most of their business in a few firms.

Despite the strong correlation between amount of investment banking business and number of firms used, the relationship is not strictly linear. The net benefits from adding more investment banks diminish quite rapidly. By threatening to add another firm a customer can generate price competition as well, or almost as well, as if it actually added another firm. Similarly, as it adds more firms, the incremental value of market information and new ideas it receives decreases. The rapid diffusion of product innovations reduces the number of firms needed. Furthermore, because more company time is required, the cost of dealing with investment banks goes up and, more important, confidential information about the company is shared with more firms. As a result, companies tend not to add to the number of investment banks they use in proportion to the growth in the number of deals they do.

There is a diminishing return from adding more investment banks (see figure 4.1). We examined the number of lead firms used by the 1,167 companies that did three or more deals during the three-year period. On average, a 100 percent increase in transactions led to a 61 percent increase in the number of investment banks used.[7]

Even though the statistical relationship is significant, it only explains roughly half of the variation in the number of firms used. Similarly, the amount of investment banking business a company has does not completely explain which of the two models the customer will choose. Beyond a minimum level of business, a company has the choice between the dominant bank and core group models.

The personal preferences of the CEO, members of the financial staff, and a company's board of directors influence the choice of how a company manages its investment banks. A financially sophisticated CEO, for example, may perceive less need for general financial advice and may want to stimulate the flow of ideas from a number of firms. (To the extent that this is true, the increasing number of CEOs with a strong financial background is itself another cause of the shift to multiple bank relationships.)[8] A comparison of two high-technology companies of similar size, Burroughs (later renamed Unisys when it merged with Sperry Rand) and Digital Equipment Corporation, illustrates this point.

FIGURE 4.1.   Number of Lead Banks Used, 1984–1986

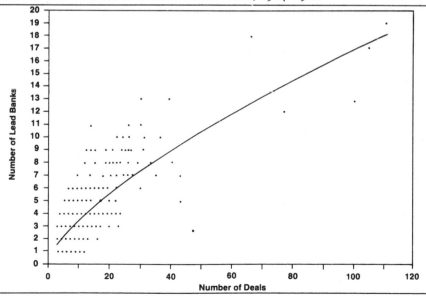

NOTE: These data include customers doing three or more deals.
SOURCE: Securities Data Company database.

Michael Blumenthal, the CEO of Burroughs at the time of our study, was a former professor of economics, secretary of the treasury in the Carter administration, and CEO at Bendix. Blumenthal was personally involved and a key decision maker in selecting, adding, or dropping an investment bank. In M&A transactions, Blumenthal's involvement was extensive in all aspects of the investment banking relationship.

Historically, Burroughs had been a one-bank company using Kidder, Peabody. This changed when Blumenthal became CEO. For a variety of business reasons Burroughs dropped Kidder and, partly because of a set of personal relationships, added Lehman Brothers (later Shearson Lehman). Roger Altman, the Burroughs account manager at Lehman, was Blumenthal's deputy secretary of the treasury, and Pete Peterson, who at that time was CEO of Lehman, was also well known to Blumenthal. Lazard Frères and Goldman, Sachs were also considered to be part of the core group of relationship banks. Blumenthal had a personal relationship with Felix Rohatyn at Lazard and valued his firm's M&A expertise. Goldman, Sachs managed the Burroughs commercial paper program and had led other deals.

In addition, Burroughs retained the boutique firm of James D. Wolfensohn & Co. as a financial advisor. The use of Wolfensohn illustrates how some companies deal with the confidentiality problem that arises when using a core group of firms. Burroughs felt that because his firm did not engage in underwriting, Wolfensohn could offer objective advice. James Unruh, senior vice president of finance at Burroughs, explained, "James Wolfensohn is a think tank in a sense. We will share more with him than with anyone. The concept is to have a close relationship, since we don't do transactions with his firm." Burroughs used Wolfensohn to perform confidential analyses and to help the company manage its other investment banks. For example, Wolfensohn's advice was used when Burroughs selected Drexel Burnham Lambert for a bond underwriting, an unusual choice, since Drexel was not known for its investment-grade debt capabilities.

Whereas Burroughs had three core group investment banks and had done deals with others, Digital Equipment Corporation (DEC) had a historic and very close, exclusive relationship with Shearson Lehman Brothers and its predecessor firms. Lehman handled DEC's initial public offering and had lead managed every public security offering since then. The account manager, William Osborne, had been involved with DEC since the beginning and still helped manage the relationship even though he had retired from Lehman Brothers. While Shearson Lehman Brothers was clearly the dominant bank, DEC had engaged in occasional private transactions with a few other firms, including Goldman, Sachs and Morgan Stanley. In addition,

DEC had regular conversations with these two firms and First Boston Corporation.

The board of directors at DEC was much more involved in management of investment banks than was the Burroughs board. Georges Doriot, who had provided venture capital funds to DEC and had been a member of the board for many years before his death in 1987, was particularly involved. Paul Milbury, DEC's assistant treasurer, noted that the board's philosophy was not to put deals up for bid, even if some basis points could be saved by inviting other firms to compete: "The board expects us to analyze the pricing and services we receive from Shearson Lehman Brothers. If some problem arises, the board's view is that we should talk with the firm about the problem. Only if it could not be resolved, would they be willing to get another investment bank."

Will companies that prefer the close, confidential relationships provided by the dominant bank model, such as DEC, tend to select an investment bank known for its relationship orientation? Correspondingly, will active companies choosing the core group approach tend to select investment banks known for their transaction skills? Even though there are undoubtedly companies that fit these models, an analysis of the data indicates that there is little correlation between the choice of a dominant or core group approach and the choice of an investment bank.

To study this issue, we identified the primary investment banks for each of the five hundred most active issuers in the 1984 to 1986 period. For this purpose, the primary bank of a customer was defined as the firm that led the most deals in the period. Investment banks that were tied in the deal count were considered co-primary. Secondary and co-secondary banks were defined in a similar manner.

Salomon Brothers was the primary (or co-primary) bank for seventy-five of the most active customers, more than any other investment bank (see table 4.2). Consistent with Salomon's security underwriting reputation, its customers also did more deals on average than other firms' customers. Forty-eight percent of Salomon's customers, however, used the dominant bank approach, with Salomon as a dominant bank. This was the second-highest percentage of dominant bank relationships among the special bracket firms, belying the transaction-oriented image that many people have of this firm. Salomon Brothers had a high share of dominant bank relationships even though on average its customers were the largest, most active customers and they used more investment banks to lead transactions than other companies, practices that generally lead customers to use the core group approach. Thus even though competitors uniformly mentioned Salomon Brothers to us as the most transaction-oriented firm, it was apparently quite effective in managing close relationships.

TABLE 4.2. Customer Characteristics, 1984–1986

Primary Investment Bank	No. of Comp.	Avg. No. of Deals	Avg. Sales	Avg. No. Lead Banks Used	% Dominant
Salomon Brothers	75	13.4	8,435	4.7	48.0
Goldman, Sachs	69	11.4	6,166	3.7	53.6
First Boston	61	12.2	5,733	4.5	47.5
Drexel	51	7.3	1,930	2.5	72.5
Shearson Lehman	49	9.4	3,798	3.7	40.8
Morgan Stanley	43	9.1	6,153	4.0	44.2
Merrill Lynch	38	11.8	5,276	4.2	44.7
Kidder, Peabody	34	8.2	1,731	3.5	55.9
PaineWebber	30	9.4	3,904	3.4	33.3
Pru-Bache Securities	15	6.4	859	2.8	60.0
E.F. Hutton	14	7.6	1,306	3.4	64.3
Smith Barney	12	10.8	4,546	4.0	33.3
Dillon, Read	9	8.2	6,585	4.0	44.4
Lazard Frères	4	10.5	5,724	4.8	25.0

NOTE: These data include the 507 companies doing five or more deals. Average sales figures do not incorporate entities that do not report normal sales figures, such as insurance companies.
SOURCE: Securities Data Company database.

Among the special bracket firms, Goldman, Sachs had the largest share of customers who used it as a dominant bank, 53.6 percent, consistent with its relationship image. Its share of customers who had a dominant bank, however, was smaller than the average of the five hundred most active customers (55.6 percent). It was only moderately higher than Salomon Brothers in this regard. Like its major competitors' customers, the Goldman, Sachs customers in the most active group were large and very active, with almost half including the firm as one of a core group rather than as a dominant bank. Goldman, Sachs apparently provided competitive and effective transactions in spite of its reputation as a relationship-oriented firm.

As this comparison of two firms with very different reputations shows, effective relationship management and transaction expertise are interrelated. Without transaction expertise, relationships will diminish. Strong relationships encompassing many transactions contribute to transaction expertise.

Whereas the special bracket firms had customers whose dominant or core group profiles were similar, the customers of the other investment banks varied substantially. These differences resulted from a combination of each firm's position in the customer marketplace, as well as customers' use of a portfolio approach in their selection of investment banks. Customers that used Prudential-Bache Securities and E.F. Hutton as primary banks, for example, tended to be smaller, less active companies that naturally tend to concentrate their business with one firm. Among the top nineteen investment banks, we found a high correlation between customer choice of dominant bank or core group approach and the level of customer activity (see figure 4.2). (Because they are highly correlated, level of activity is also a proxy for customer size.)

Drexel is a particularly interesting example. Almost three-quarters of its customers used it as a dominant bank, the largest share among the major firms. With its strength in high-yield bond underwriting, Drexel had brought many companies to the market. Maintaining a close relationship with these companies, Drexel had captured a large share of each customer's business.

In managing their investment banks, customers also pay attention to their portfolios of firms. They often establish ties with a set of firms, in which each firm brings a particular area of strength to meet the customers' needs. One pattern in a portfolio structure is for companies to use a "niche" firm, particularly one strong in M&A, along with one or more large investment banks that are better able to handle large underwritings. For example, six of the twenty-one companies we interviewed used Lazard Frères largely for

FIGURE 4.2.   Customer Profile, 1984–1986

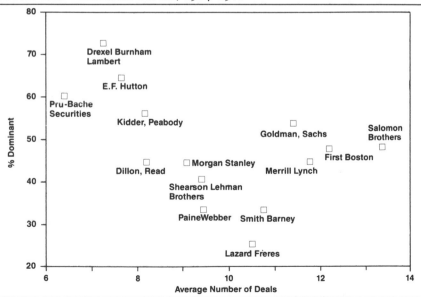

NOTE: These data include the 507 companies doing five or more deals.
SOURCE: Securities Data Company database.

M&A advice and execution, along with one or more special bracket firms that handled their financing needs.

Another type of portfolio includes investment banks that are roughly comparable, but have different strengths. Customers who used Morgan Stanley as their primary bank did a relatively large number of M&A transactions, particularly compared to customers of the other special bracket firms (see table 4.3). But these companies also did a substantial number of investment-grade bond issues. This suggests that several of Morgan Stanley's customers used the firm as one of a portfolio of firms to take advantage of the firm's noted M&A strength, but also used other investment banks to add bond underwriting strength. (Although Morgan Stanley's market share in bond underwriting had improved in recent years, in the early 1980s, following the introduction of shelf registration, it had slipped.)

A comparison of primary and secondary relationships among investment banks supports this conjecture (see table 4.4). Given Morgan Stanley's reputation in M&A and Salomon's stature in bond underwriting, one would expect that active companies would often pair them in primary and secondary relationships. Our data confirm this. Customers who used Morgan Stanley as their primary bank in the 1984 to 1986 period used Salomon Brothers most often as their co-primary or secondary bank. The opposite was also true; when Salomon was primary, Morgan Stanley was most often the co-primary or secondary bank.

TABLE 4.3. Product Profile of Customers, 1984–1986

Primary Investment Bank	Inv. Grade	Non-Inv. Grade	Equity	Intl. Bonds	Tax-Exempt	M&A
Salomon Brothers	31.6	25.0	10.4	10.4	9.7	14.3
Goldman, Sachs	27.0	1.9	13.0	8.5	8.7	16.3
First Boston	25.5	2.0	10.9	10.3	7.1	15.9
Drexel	3.8	23.1	19.1	0.6	3.1	15.8
Shearson Lehman	24.5	3.3	16.5	6.0	9.6	10.5
Morgan Stanley	23.1	3.9	13.9	7.9	13.1	22.8
Merrill Lynch	33.6	1.3	5.9	6.4	18.9	13.1
Kidder, Peabody	18.1	3.5	19.3	2.9	21.4	11.5
PaineWebber	10.1	6.1	14.7	1.4	9.8	9.1
Pru-Bache Securities	8.0	7.6	15.9	1.0	5.7	10.1
E.F. Hutton	12.4	3.8	13.9	3.7	27.1	6.1
Smith Barney	27.2	11.7	10.2	1.3	14.2	11.6
Dillon, Read	25.8	1.9	4.0	17.9	0.0	34.3
Lazard Frères	20.6	0.0	14.2	4.8	5.0	49.4

NOTE: These data include the 507 companies doing five or more deals. To illustrate the entries, 27 percent of the deals done by customers for which Goldman, Sachs was the primary bank were investment-grade debt deals.
SOURCE: Securities Data Company database.

TABLE 4.4. Primary and Secondary Bank Relationships, 1984–1986

Primary Investment Banks	Co-Primary or Secondary Investment Banks								No. of Primary Positions
	Salomon Brothers	Goldman, Sachs	First Boston	Drexel	Shearson Lehman	Morgan Stanley	Merrill Lynch	Other or No Second Bank	
Salomon Brothers	—	11	13	0	5	16	12	55	75
Goldman, Sachs	17	—	13	1	6	7	6	46	69
First Boston	18	7	—	0	5	9	6	47	61
Drexel	4	4	3	—	3	4	4	45	51
Shearson Lehman	5	8	5	1	—	6	8	36	49
Morgan Stanley	9	5	5	2	5	—	8	38	43
Merrill Lynch	4	5	5	2	5	7	—	38	38
Kidder, Peabody	3	4	3	3	3	5	8	25	34
PaineWebber	5	2	4	6	3	0	2	20	30
Pru-Bache Securities	1	2	0	0	4	1	1	12	15
E.F. Hutton	4	1	0	0	1	2	2	13	14
Smith Barney	2	2	0	1	0	3	2	6	13
Dillon, Read	1	1	3	0	0	1	2	7	9
Lazard Frères	2	0	0	0	0	1	0	2	4
Other Banks	10	11	9	2	10	10	10	65	86
No. of Secondary Positions	85	63	63	18	50	72	71	455	591

NOTE: These data include the 507 companies doing five or more deals.
SOURCE: Securities Data Company database.

It is also interesting to note that Salomon had a relatively low-ranking position with the customers using Drexel as their primary bank. Similarly, when Salomon was the primary bank, Drexel was never the secondary firm for this set of customers. When companies choose a portfolio of firms, they need strength in either investment-grade debt or noninvestment-grade debt issues, but not in both.

Although many company portfolios include investment banks that differ in relative strengths, some active customers adopt the opposite approach and deliberately select firms that offer comparable services across most of the customers' needs. Competitive prices and a large number of ideas are ensured by having at least all (or most) of its relationship banks compete for every deal. Citicorp, for example, had strong ties with First Boston, Salomon Brothers, Merrill Lynch, Shearson Lehman Brothers, and Goldman, Sachs, firms with substantial strengths in nearly all major product categories. A number of other companies use this particular portfolio approach; as a result, the major firms are often paired with each other as the primary and secondary banks (see table 4.4). Of the seventy-five customers using Salomon Brothers as a primary bank, for example, 60 percent also used other special bracket firms as co-primary or secondary banks.

From the Dominant Bank Model to the Core Group Model

At the time of our study the dominant bank model (including its reduced form version, the one-bank model) was the preferred model for 55.6 percent of the five hundred most active users of investment banking services. As we noted, however, only 44.4 percent of the one hundred most active corporations used this approach. For firms that do sufficient investment banking business to have a choice, it is likely that they will shift to the core group model. This will result from the competitive vulnerabilities of dominant bank relationships and the difficulties of shifting in the opposite direction, that is, from the core group model to the dominant bank one.

At first glance, it might appear that it is easier for a transaction bank to break into a group of core banks and establish a relationship with the customer. After all, such a customer already has proven itself to be open to multiple relationships and a new firm simply needs to get the customer to add one more. But if the customer already has as many core banks as it can sustain with its present level of investment banking business, the company's position vis-à-vis its firms is in equilibrium unless one of the core banks commits a serious mistake or demonstrates sustained inattention to the customer.

Furthermore, the larger the number of firms a customer has in its core group, the less is to be gained by increasing this number by one. There may actually be disadvantages in doing so. Additional time and attention need to be paid to managing a new relationship. Even if the company has enough business to justify adding an additional relationship, it will come at the expense of all members of the current core group if the company wishes to retain all of its existing relationships. If the business allocated to the core group is to be evenly distributed, each firm in the group must give up a significant fraction of its business. There is always the risk that the costs of these diminished relationships will exceed the benefits from adding another firm.

Opportunities for firms to create fairly strong relationships with customers are greater with active financers who are using the dominant bank model. When a large number of deals are going to one investment bank, it is easier for the customer to allocate a few deals to another firm. Competitors of the dominant bank can present persuasive arguments to the customer that it can better serve its interests and those of its shareholders by broadening its investment banking relationships. Even better, the argument continues, the customer can do so without disrupting its acknowledged valuable relationship with a dominant bank that has served it well over the years. Thus a transaction bank can be upgraded to a significant bank, which can in turn be upgraded to membership in a core group, at the same time that the dominant bank is downgraded to core group status. This occurred, for example, at Union Carbide, which went from a one-bank model with Morgan Stanley, to a dominant bank model with Morgan Stanley, to a core group model with Morgan Stanley and First Boston.

Although the dominant bank will certainly complain when it sees the strength of its relationship diminish in favor of a competitor, it is unlikely to do more than this. When a firm is getting most of a customer's business, it can lose a substantial fraction of it while still getting enough to keep it as a responsive vendor of investment banking services. It is even possible that at least in the short term, the sharpness of its prices and the amount and quality of its service may actually increase in an effort to halt or even reverse the deterioration in the relationship. Even if there is some decline in the level of service, a former dominant bank will be reluctant to sever the relationship because of the loss of revenues and loss of face that would ensue.

In this model, upgrading the status of other firms comes at the expense of only one relationship, not many. This makes it possible for the customer to add a significant relationship while retaining the dominant bank, or even to shift to a core bank approach. When transaction banks are upgraded to significant banks, the hierarchy of ties according to their relative strength is maintained. Thus although it may take more time and effort for a firm to penetrate an active customer with a dominant bank relationship, the long-term opportunities are greater.

Finally, a dominant bank is more vulnerable than is a firm in the core group. A dominant bank that performs poorly on one or more deals, or violates the customer's trust by divulging confidential information or by using such information against it, creates opportunities for competitors to establish strong relationships with its customer, or to replace it completely. In contrast, it is less likely that a customer will become dissatisfied with all of its core group banks at once.

The same reasons that make it difficult for an investment bank to break into a core group, particularly one of more than three firms, make it unlikely that customers who have adopted the core group model will shift to a dominant bank model. If a customer concentrates its business in one firm, the other members of the core group may adopt a more transactional approach and invest less in maintaining a relationship. Furthermore, the advantages of the core group model are difficult to give up. Maintaining more than one relationship exposes the customer to a broader array of ideas and different ways of thinking about financing and acquisitions. The resulting increased sophistication of the customer that comes from managing more than one relationship becomes a determinant in its own right in favor of the core group model. Shifting to a dominant bank model may decrease opportunities for the customer to sustain its level of financial sophistication. It certainly increases the company's dependency on, and reduces its control over, the relationship.

The current shift by a greater number of customers to the core group model assumes that the capital markets will remain at least as complex in the future as they are today. A relatively simple market favors the advantages of a dominant bank relationship; a complex capital market favors the core group model for active customers of investment banks.

___ 5 _____

STRUCTURE OF THE INDUSTRY

The external ties between customers and their investment banks are an important part of the structure of the investment banking industry. Each investment bank occupies a certain position in the industry, defined by the products it offers and the customers to whom it offers them. In addition, a unique and important feature of this industry is the extent of ties among the investment banks themselves. They share customers, work together to underwrite deals, and negotiate with each other in M&A transactions. These relationships are a part of and affect the overall industry structure.

Contacts between firms, which result in the formation of ties, take several forms. The most structured are the syndicates formed for a securities underwriting. Prior to Rule 415 and bought deals, these syndicates were one of the most dominant features of the industry landscape. Although their importance for distributing securities has declined, syndicates have not disappeared. Over time, patterns of ties develop between firms from these syndicates, enabling information to flow between firms and facilitating the movement of employees between them.

The hierarchical syndicate structure given in tombstones—with its categories of special (or bulge) bracket, major bracket, major out of order, and submajor or regional firms—reinforces the positions occupied by the firms in the industry.[1] (A typical example is the announcement of the new issue of Union Carbide stock with First Boston as lead manager and Morgan Stanley as co-manager [see figure 5.1]). There is a high correlation between a firm's volume of underwriting business and its place in the industry's hierarchy. Because this hierarchy is defined and legitimized by the participants themselves, it acts as a mobility barrier to firms trying to shift their position. Since a firm's hierarchical position is based partly on its volume, and the volume of securities it gets to underwrite and sell is based on its hierarchical position, syndicates are a conservative force, stabilizing the industry structure.

This is reflected in the often-heated arguments about a firm's place in a tombstone advertisement. High-status firms want to reinforce their status by maintaining the rank order, whereas lower-status firms seek to improve their status by moving up. As Kenneth Gilpin observed, "Wall Street's 'tombstone' ads may look stately, but the politicking that goes on before they ever appear in print can get downright undignified."[2] In some cases, firms will not participate in a deal rather than have themselves listed below other firms they consider of lower status. This occurred with a $2.4 billion bond offering of the Farmers Home Administration; the tombstone listed thirteen regional and small minority-owned firms ahead of ten much larger firms.[3]

A firm's position in the underwriting hierarchy is, at best, an incomplete description of its position in the industry. A more useful way to understand the structure of the industry is to identify "strategic groups" of firms that occupy similar competitive niches.[4] Two key dimensions that help define such groups are the product diversification of each firm and the nature of its customers as reflected in their size and amount of investment banking activity. One strategic group of firms, for example, contains investment banks that are highly diversified and serve large, active companies.

Defined in this way, competition among firms in the same strategic group is especially intense, since they are competing for the same customers along the same product dimensions. Each firm seeks to further distinguish itself from the others in its group. This is difficult to do in a deal-based service business, particularly when the characteristics of a deal are determined as much by the customer as by the investment bank, and when products are easily imitated. Thus investment banks attempt to create positive reputations to distinguish themselves from their competitors. The reputation a firm desires, or its self-concept, often differs from its actual reputation or image. Firms seek to take advantage of the negative aspects of their competitors' images. This entails some risk if customers do not share these perceptions and a firm underestimates the strengths of its competitors.

Patterns of Ties among Investment Banks

The most visible ties among investment banks are the syndicates formed to underwrite and distribute a security offering. Under the direction of the firm acting as lead manager, each firm in the syndicate takes on the risk associated with underwriting (i.e., guaranteeing to purchase) a certain minimum number of shares or bonds. Just how many securities it actually gets to distribute to investors is determined by the lead manager.

These ties contain both adversarial and collaborative elements. They are

FIGURE 5.1.

NEW ISSUE   December 15, 1986

27,000,000 Shares

Union Carbide Corporation

Common Stock
($1.00 par value)

Price $22.50 Per Share

These securities are being offered in the United States and internationally.

United States Offering

23,000,000 Shares

The First Boston Corporation   Morgan Stanley & Co.
                                                    Incorporated

Goldman, Sachs & Co.   Salomon Brothers Inc   Bear, Stearns & Co. Inc.   Alex. Brown & Sons   Dillon, Read & Co. Inc.   Donaldson, Lufkin & Jenrette
                                                                        Incorporated   Securities Corporation
Drexel Burnham Lambert   Hambrecht & Quist   E. F. Hutton & Company Inc.   Kidder, Peabody & Co.   Lazard Frères & Co.   Merrill Lynch Capital Markets
Incorporated   Incorporated
Montgomery Securities   PaineWebber   Prudential-Bache   Robertson, Colman & Stephens   L. F. Rothschild, Unterberg, Towbin, Inc.
                         Incorporated   Securities
Shearson Lehman Brothers Inc.   Smith Barney, Harris Upham & Co.   Wertheim & Co., Inc.   Dean Witter Reynolds Inc.
Allen & Company   Oppenheimer & Co., Inc.   Thomson McKinnon Securities Inc.   Advest, Inc.   Sanford C. Bernstein & Co., Inc.
Incorporated   Incorporated
Butcher & Singer Inc.   Cowen & Co.   Dominion Securities Corporation   Eberstadt Fleming Inc.   Furman Selz Mager Dietz & Birney
Gruntal & Co., Incorporated   Interstate Securities Corporation   Raymond James & Associates, Inc.   Janney Montgomery Scott Inc.
Ladenburg, Thalmann & Co. Inc.   Cyrus J. Lawrence   Legg Mason Wood Walker   McLeod Young Weir Incorporated   Morgan Keegan & Company, Inc.
                                                      Incorporated
Moseley Securities Corporation   Neuberger & Berman   Richardson Greenshields Securities Inc.   The Robinson-Humphrey Company, Inc.
Tucker, Anthony & R. L. Day, Inc.   Wheat, First Securities, Inc.   Wood Gundy Corp.   Craigie Incorporated   Fahnestock & Co. Inc.
First Albany Corporation   First Manhattan Co.   Johnson, Lane, Space, Smith & Co., Inc.   Johnston, Lemon & Co.   Josephthal & Co.
                                                                                              Incorporated   Incorporated
Laidlaw Adams & Peck Inc.   Mabon, Nugent & Co.   Needham & Company, Inc.   W. H. Newbold's Son & Co., Inc.   Anantha Raman & Company, Inc.

International Offering

4,000,000 Shares

Credit Suisse First Boston Limited   Morgan Stanley International

Banque Bruxelles Lambert S.A.   Banque Nationale de Paris   Banque Paribas Capital Markets Limited   Cazenove & Co.
Commerzbank Aktiengesellschaft   Goldman Sachs International Corp.   Salomon Brothers International Limited
Swiss Bank Corporation International Limited   S. G. Warburg Securities   Yamaichi International (Europe) Limited

adversarial in that a fixed number of securities must be allocated among the members of the syndicate. Firms also struggle for recognition by the customer. It is not uncommon for the co-manager to make subtle, or even blatant, remarks about how the lead manager is handling the deal. At the same time, the members of the syndicate must collaborate with each other in order for the offering to be distributed to desirable investors in a timely manner.

These syndicates form large, complex networks among numerous investment banks, including the lead manager, co-managers, other members of the underwriting group, and firms that are part of the selling group but have no underwriting obligation. The importance of syndicates has declined as the business has become increasingly concentrated in a few large firms. The result is that external ties have been replaced by internal ties. Thus as the largest firms have built up their distribution capabilities, the number of ties between investment banking and sales has increased while the number of ties with other firms has decreased. (There is some controversy about the extent to which Rule 415, shelf registration, is responsible for this concentration. In their study of shelf registration, Joe Auerbach and Sam Hayes concluded that "there is no dramatic trend in overall industry concentration as a result of the shelf phenomenon." Yet a study by the Securities and Exchange Commission concluded the opposite.)[5]

The lead manager and co-manager pairings among the special bracket firms during the period from 1984 to 1986 indicate the role of interfirm networks (see table 5.1). Lead managers and co-managers do the bulk of the distribution. They also work most closely together in the underwriting, and these data therefore indicate the most important ties.

From 1984 to 1986 the six special bracket firms (First Boston, Merrill Lynch, Morgan Stanley, Salomon Brothers, Shearson Lehman Brothers, and Goldman, Sachs) lead managed 6,327 domestic security issues (excluding tax-exempt issues), according to the SDC database. Of the co-managers on these deals, 60.4 percent were other special bracket firms. Thus, as a result of the security issues they do together, there are strong ties among the major firms. Goldman, Sachs, Salomon Brothers, and First Boston relied most heavily on other special bracket firms as co-managers, using them for 60.4 percent to 72.3 percent of the co-manager positions. The other three firms, Shearson Lehman Brothers, Merrill Lynch, and Morgan Stanley, used special bracket firms for 51.9 percent to 53.2 percent of their co-manager positions.[6] A partial explanation of the difference between the two groups is that a larger share of the deals led by the second group, particularly Merrill Lynch and Shearson Lehman, were security issues in which regional firms were used as co-managers to get more retail distribution.

Some of the ties reflect the distribution reputation of firms. Merrill Lynch and Salomon Brothers, known for their retail and institutional distribution,

TABLE 5.1. Lead Banks and Co-Manager Banks, 1984–1986

Lead Bank	Co-Manager Banks							Total Co-Manager Positions
	Goldman, Sachs	Salomon Brothers	First Boston	Morgan Stanley	Shearson Lehman	Merrill Lynch	Other Firms	
Goldman, Sachs	0.0%	18.8%	12.3%	9.4%	8.8%	11.0%	39.6%	100.0%
Salomon Brothers	11.9	0.0	15.6	7.1	8.3	23.5	33.7	100.0
First Boston	18.8	14.0	0.0	14.5	11.8	13.2	27.7	100.0
Morgan Stanley	10.4	16.9	11.8	0.0	3.8	10.2	46.8	100.0
Shearson Lehman	11.5	11.9	15.2	4.3	0.0	9.0	48.1	100.0
Merrill Lynch	6.9	17.9	14.3	4.7	9.2	0.0	47.1	100.0
Other	2.9	4.5	4.2	1.1	5.4	5.4	76.5	100.0
Total	8.1%	9.4%	8.9%	5.1%	6.7%	9.9%	51.9%	100.0%

SOURCE: Securities Data Company database.

respectively, were used the most as co-managers (see table 5.1). Morgan Stanley, known more for its historical strength in origination than for distribution, was least used as a co-manager by other special bracket firms.

As reflected by the number of deals done together, the tie between Merrill Lynch and Salomon Brothers was particularly strong. When Merrill Lynch led transactions, Salomon was most often the co-manager (17.9 percent of the co-manager positions), and when Salomon was lead manager, Merrill Lynch was most often the co-manager (23.5 percent). These two investment banks worked together much more than would be expected if all ties were of equal strength. (Tests of statistical significance are provided in the Appendix.)

It is also interesting to note that Merrill Lynch was relatively underutilized by the other special bracket firms. Even though Merrill Lynch was the most used co-manager overall, it ranked fourth among the co-managers working with First Boston, fourth with Morgan Stanley, fourth with Shearson Lehman Brothers, and third with Goldman, Sachs. Perhaps this indicates how difficult it is to shed a "wirehouse" image and move into the leading investment banking group. Shearson Lehman shared a similar fate, ranking last or next to last as a co-manager with every special bracket firm except Merrill Lynch.

Ties are also formed when banks work together on M&A deals, with one firm representing the seller and the other representing the buyer. These ties contain adversarial and collaborative elements as well. They are adversarial because each investment bank is representing the interests of one party in a negotiation that involves bargaining over price and terms. But collaboration is important as well in order for the deal to be consummated. An exception to this is a hostile takeover, which can be a purely adversarial transaction.

We examined the number of deals completed from 1984 to 1986 in which each of nineteen leading firms represented an acquirer (buyer) or target (seller); we included only deals with an investment bank on both sides of the transaction. These nineteen firms worked on 1,338 M&A deals with another investment bank on the other side (see table 5.2). (As described in the Appendix, a number of smaller deals are not included in the database.)

The M&A data indicate that investment banks occupy different niches according to their emphasis on advising buyers or sellers. Representing buyers is often a more aggressive role, particularly when the buyer is attempting a hostile takeover. Drexel Burnham Lambert stands out for doing the largest proportion of its M&A deals for acquirers (63.7 percent). However, other major firms, including Merrill Lynch, First Boston, Morgan Stanley, Lazard Frères, and Donaldson, Lufkin & Jenrette (DLJ), represented acquirers in more than half of their reported deals. On the other side, Goldman, Sachs had an announced policy of not representing acquirers in

TABLE 5.2. Merger and Acquisition Activity of the
19 Leading Investment Banks, 1984–1986

Firm	Acquirer	Acq. % of Total	Target	Targ. % of Total	Total
Goldman, Sachs	65	34.0	126	66.0	191
Morgan Stanley	79	53.4	69	46.6	148
First Boston	68	54.0	58	46.0	126
Shearson Lehman	56	46.7	64	53.3	120
Drexel	72	63.7	41	36.3	113
Merrill Lynch	62	58.5	44	41.5	106
Salomon Brothers	40	37.7	66	62.3	106
Kidder, Peabody	35	37.2	59	62.8	94
Lazard Frères	37	52.1	34	47.9	71
Bear, Stearns	24	46.2	28	53.8	52
DLJ	19	52.8	17	47.2	36
Dillon, Read	14	38.9	22	61.1	36
Smith Barney	11	39.3	17	60.7	28
PaineWebber	13	48.1	14	51.9	27
Alex. Brown	8	29.6	19	70.4	27
Pru-Bache Securities	11	47.8	12	52.2	23
E.F. Hutton	7	36.8	12	63.2	19
Dean Witter	4	33.3	8	66.7	12
L.F. Rothschild	2	66.7	1	33.3	3
Total	627		711		1338

NOTE: Repurchase of stock is not included in the figures.
SOURCE: Securities Data Company database.

a hostile takeover, so it tended to represent targets (66.0 percent). Kidder Peabody, known for its early development of the takeover defense business, also was naturally oriented toward working with target companies. Other investment banks in this niche included Salomon Brothers, Dillon, Read, and Smith Barney, all of which did more than 60 percent of their M&A deals with sellers.

As in underwriting syndicates, M&A transactions often involve two or more special bracket firms working on opposite sides of the table, but the factors determining the combination of firms are quite different. In underwriting syndicates, the lead manager, working with the customer, has some influence in the selection of co-managers and the other firms included in the underwriting group. The lead manager will try to include firms that bring the needed distribution skills and with which it has a good working relationship. Since large security issues require substantial capital and distribution ability, it is often necessary for the lead manager to ask several special bracket firms to work with it.

In contrast, when special bracket firms appear on opposite sides of the M&A negotiating table, the firm on one side most often has no say about the selection of the investment bank representing the other party. For example, Goldman, Sachs frequently represented the target in deals when Morgan Stanley was advising the acquirer (see table 5.3). This pairing occurred because both firms were very active in the M&A business, most often advising the target and acquirer, respectively. Thus, the frequency of M&A pairings tends to reflect the amount of M&A business of the firm and its strategy, rather than other factors linking or separating particular firms.

Finally, ties are also formed when investment banks compete for business from the same customer. As reported in chapter 4, for example, Goldman, Sachs and Salomon Brothers were often competing for the same customer as primary and secondary banks. These ties are competitive in nature, since one firm gets the deal at the expense of others. (Some customers told us that when two or more firms submit prices very close together, they made the winning bidder the lead manager and encouraged the firm to include the others as co-managers on the deal. When this occurs the competitive ties between these firms become syndicate ties, with their mixture of adversarial and collaborative elements.) They are also indirect ties, which are mediated by a common customer who controls the information each firm has about the other, such as ideas on how to structure a deal.

Ties formed for the purpose of doing deals and those formed when firms compete for a customer's business can serve other functions as well. They create opportunities, not always intended, for information to flow between firms, giving each one glimpses into the strategy and management of the other. They also provide information to firms about particular people in their competitors, which may lead to an effort to hire them away. For example, several people we interviewed who had changed firms said they had been approached for a job by their current employer after having worked on the opposite side of an M&A deal with them.

Although we do not have hard measures, a striking characteristic about the investment banking industry during the 1980s has been the high degree of interfirm mobility reported in such publications as *Wall Street Letter, Corporate Financing Week,* and *Investment Dealers' Digest.* The mobility extends to entire departments: moving a department from one firm to another is one way the hiring firm can enter a business or increase its presence in a dramatic way. For example, the eleven-person, fixed-income research group at Donaldson, Lufkin & Jenrette went to Smith Barney, Harris Upham, and most of E.F. Hutton's mortgage-backed securities group was hired away by L.F. Rothschild.[7] Dean Witter hired a number of key municipal bankers from Salomon Brothers when the latter left the business.[8] These moves can even involve several steps. For example, the commercial paper group at Becker Paribas moved to PaineWebber when Becker was

TABLE 5.3. Advisor to Acquirer and Advisor to Target
Six Leading Investment Banks, 1984–1986

Acquirer's Investment Bank	Target's Investment Bank							
	First Boston	Salomon Brothers	Goldman, Sachs	Merrill Lynch	Shearson Lehman	Morgan Stanley	Other	Total
First Boston	1	3	13	6	5	10	30	68
Salomon Brothers	2	0	8	4	0	3	23	40
Goldman, Sachs	5	9	6	2	6	6	31	65
Merrill Lynch	6	7	7	3	7	7	25	62
Shearson Lehman	4	2	12	4	4	6	24	56
Morgan Stanley	6	6	20	4	8	0	35	79
Other	34	39	60	21	34	37	248	473
Total	58	66	126	44	64	69	416	843

NOTE: Repurchase of stock is not included in the figures.
SOURCE: Securities Data Company database.

acquired by Merrill Lynch, and then moved to Citicorp.[9] The high-technology group at Kidder, Peabody left for Drexel Burnham Lambert and then moved on to PaineWebber.[10]

The underlying cause of this interfirm mobility has been rapid growth and the efforts of firms to enter new businesses, but it is facilitated by the information made available to employers and employees through the ties formed between firms that do deals together. There are other facilitating factors: many of these people work in New York City, live in the same communities, belong to the same social and philanthropic organizations, and went to the same schools, particularly for their M.B.A.'s

Patterns of Competition

To further understand the structure of the investment banking industry it is helpful to identify the dimensions of strategy along which the firms compete and then see how the firms differ in terms of their position on these strategic dimensions. This mapping of firms enables us to identify different *strategic groups* within the industry. According to Michael Porter, "a strategic group is the group of firms in an industry following the same or a similar strategy along the strategic dimensions."[11] Firms within the same strategic group are especially competitive with each other because they generally are seeking the same customer base and using a similar strategy. Each group, however, seeks to create mobility barriers between it and other groups, barriers that make it difficult for firms outside the strategic group to compete successfully against its members.

There are a number of dimensions along which an investment bank's strategy can be defined; four are especially important. The first concerns the customers that the firm serves. Some investment banks target large, relatively sophisticated companies that are frequent financers or active in merger and acquisition transactions, or both. Others concentrate more on medium-sized companies that are less sophisticated and more inclined to have a close relationship with a dominant bank. Still others focus on small, emerging companies that will be active in the equity market. Other customer approaches are also possible, such as a combination of the market segments above or a focus on particular industries, such as Keefe, Bruyette & Woods in commercial banking and Hambrecht & Quist in high technology, or geographic regions such as Legg-Mason and Wheat, First Securities in the southeast.[12]

A second key dimension concerns the products of the firm and the relative emphasis it places on each of them. Although the strategy of some is to have a full product line and be very diversified, other investment banks have a more concentrated product line. Those with a full product line, such as all six of the special bracket firms, believe that there are strong interdependencies across the various financial markets and that they can serve some customers better by being able to meet all their needs.[13]

Other firms believe that there are viable strategies that involve less product diversification. These firms can be described as niche players, since they concentrate on particular and usually high-margin products, such as Lazard Frères and Dillon, Read in M&A. Between them are firms that have developed enough strength in one or a few products that they appear to have a more focused product strategy but which are actively attempting to diversify, such as Drexel Burnham Lambert, the dominant firm in noninvestment-grade bonds.

The distribution capability of firms is a third dimension of strategy. The most distinctive aspect of this dimension is the size of each firm's retail distribution network. Among the special bracket firms, Merrill Lynch and Shearson Lehman Brothers have developed large retail capabilities. They and other firms, such as PaineWebber and Smith Barney, use their retail brokers as a competitive weapon to seek underwriting business. A second aspect of distribution strategy is one that is less distinctive now than in earlier years. Some firms, such as Salomon Brothers, were known for their strength in the distribution of securities to institutional investors, and others, such as Morgan Stanley, had placed more emphasis on the issuer side of the market. Although these historical differences still have some impact on the strategy of a firm, in recent years investment banks have become less distinctive in this regard as each has worked to build up the "weaker side" of the firm.

Finally, the fourth strategic dimension concerns the decisions investment banks make in regard to the amount of their own capital and funds they put at risk in principal positions, such as bridge loans, equity investments, swaps, and trading. (Investment banks also differ in terms of how much capital they have, but firms with larger capital positions target larger customers, so that amount of capital, per se, is not a completely independent dimension.)[14] Until recently, serving issuers was primarily an agency business in which investment banks collected fees without putting much capital at risk. Capital was at risk in the underwriting of securities, but this risk was tightly controlled and shared with other firms in syndicates. This has changed for firms that have sought to obtain a competitive advantage in M&A and LBO deals by engaging in the so-called merchant banking activities of bridge loans and equity investments. On the investor side, firms also differ in the amount of their own capital they are willing to put at risk in various kinds of trading positions.

If we were to define strategic groups based on just one dimension, the key dimension would be the customer base of each firm. As discussed in chapter 4, firms are distinctive in the extent to which they deal with large active customers as compared to middle-market and smaller companies. There are also natural groupings, such as the special bracket firms and other categories used in tombstone advertisements, with mobility barriers that make it difficult to move up in the standings. As mentioned earlier, lead managers tend to be the special bracket firms and they tend to use other special bracket firms for co-managers, making it difficult for other firms to improve their standing in securities issued.

There are other, more basic economic barriers to mobility. A study by Sam Hayes, Mike Spence, and David Marks found that large corporations tended to use investment banks that had large corporate finance staffs.[15] Such staffs are difficult to build and require a long period of time. They also develop through experience expertise in the many product specialties required to serve the needs of these customers. Similarly, firms that concentrate on emerging growth companies develop a different kind of expertise, that which is required to act as a generalist investment banker to the entrepreneur of a small company with a smaller and less sophisticated financial staff. Each type of customer is also associated with particular types of investors with whom distribution and trading ties need to be established. Evidence that these market segments require distinct capabilities is found in the organization of the firms: firms that serve both often have a separate group that focuses on smaller companies, such as the Emerging Growth Group at Merrill Lynch.

Whatever customer segment a firm focuses on, a choice has to be made about the range of products it will furnish to these customers. Although there is some correlation between size of customer and the number of products used, for any given customer segment choices must be made about which products to offer. Because of its importance and independence with respect to the dimension of customer size, product diversification was chosen as the second dimension for creating a strategic group map.

As with customer size, there are barriers to mobility along the product diversification dimension. It is difficult for a nondiversified firm to become diversified. Product expertise on both the issuing and investing side needs to be developed or acquired. Evidence of the importance of distribution is that in many cases firms attempting a product diversification do so by first building up secondary trading capabilities in the new product in order to learn about its market. Furthermore, some products, such as asset-backed securities, require large investments in hardware and software that also create barriers to these markets. Firms usually try to remove the obstacles to diversification by leveraging off a particularly strong product line that is closely related to the new product in some fashion, such as having a common buyer (e.g., in leveraging a strength in equity to build up in M&A, since both products are purchased by the CEO) or requiring similar resources (e.g., the computer technology developed for mortgage-backed securities may be useful in other forms of asset-backed securities).

It is also difficult to become less diversified; at least until very recently the trend of most firms in the investment banking industry was toward greater diversification. One barrier to reduced diversification is concern about the consequences to customer relationships of not having a full product line. Even low-margin businesses may provide useful information about customers or markets, and many believe a full product line is needed to help solve the loose linkage problem with customers. Because revenue received is only loosely linked to services provided, it is helpful to offer a variety of products to a customer so that revenue in one product area may compensate for services provided by another. Finally, there are the normal political problems of cutting back or eliminating a business: those affected can make strong arguments for keeping it and create obstructions to protect it and their jobs.

The other two strategic dimensions, the distribution strategy of investment banks and their use of capital, are also potentially useful in the identification of strategic groups, but we limited our strategic mapping to the first two dimensions. The availability of a large retail network is undoubtedly a strength when soliciting certain kinds of customers, such as companies with household names that issue equity securities. On the other hand, firms without their own retail network can and do put together syndicates that include retail strength; witness the many times Merrill Lynch was a co-manager when Salomon Brothers was the lead manager. Furthermore, the study by Hayes, Spence, and Marks found that the presence of a retail network was not a factor in the strategic groups serving larger companies.[16] With regard to firms' use of capital, data are simply not available that indicate the extent to which investment banks invest their own funds in principal positions. Looking at the industry through 1986, some comfort can be taken in the likelihood that the number of merchant banking deals using firms' capital was not sufficient to have a major effect on strategic positioning, although this dimension may become more important in the future.[17] On the other hand, there are subtle differences among firms not captured in our strategic group map.

In the strategic group map, the horizontal axis indicates the level of product diversification of each investment bank shown (see figure 5.2). The diversification measure used for each firm is based on its market share in each of twelve broad product categories. Highly diversified firms had similar market shares in all product categories. Less diversified firms had much higher market shares in some product categories than in others. A firm's market share, based on the number of deals it did between 1984 and 1986, was calculated for each of twelve product categories including, for example, investment-grade bonds, privately placed securities, international bonds, convertibles, tax-exempt bonds, common stock, initial public offerings (IPOs), M&A advisor to an acquirer, and M&A advisor to a target. The average market share for the three products in which it was the weakest, that is, its three lowest market shares, was divided by its average market

FIGURE 5.2.   Strategic Map of Investment Banks, 1984–1986

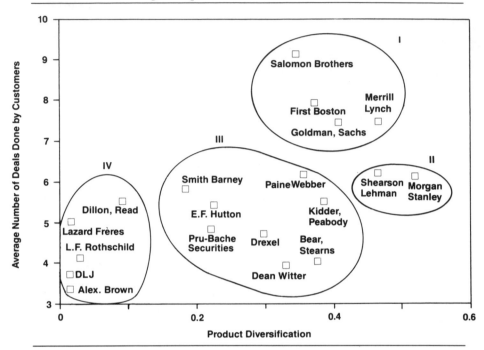

NOTE: These data include the 1,167 companies doing three or more deals.
SOURCE: Securities Data Company database.

share for all twelve products. This diversification measure ranges from zero (0), for firms that did no deals in at least three product lines, to one (1), for firms that had equal market shares in all twelve product lines. (See the Appendix for a more complete description.)

The vertical axis records how extensively each firm's customers use investment banking services. Since the most active customers tend to be large and have experienced financial staff, the axis also reflects the size of customers and their level of sophistication. Customers included in this figure were the 1,167 domestic customers that did three or more deals from 1984 to 1986. Customers were assigned to their primary bank, that is, the investment bank that led the most of their deals. For example, the customers for which Salomon Brothers was the primary or co-primary bank did an average of 9.1 deals per company during the three-year period, and Salomon had a product diversification measure of .35.

There is a substantial dispersion of firms. Identifying strategic groups is a matter of judgment, but based on this map and our interviews, we have identified four strategic groups. The first, Group I, is defined primarily by the number of deals done and comprises First Boston, Goldman, Sachs,

Merrill Lynch, and Salomon Brothers, four of the six special bracket firms. These firms were primary banks for very active users of investment banking services. The customers of each firm averaged more than seven deals from 1984 to 1986. All four firms were also among the most diversified firms, having diversification measures of .35 or higher. In addition, each firm accounted for a major share of the volume of securities underwritten. In 1986, they accounted for a combined market share of 54.6 percent of the securities underwriting volume (see table 5.4).

Salomon Brothers could be regarded as its own strategic group, since it has an especially high number of deals done. With an average sales revenue of $6.6 billion, the customers for whom Salomon was the primary bank were both very large and very active. Salomon's strengths in investment-grade debt and mortgage-backed securities contributed to its number-one league table ranking in 1986, with a 17.8 percent market share. Strength in these two products also made Salomon Brothers the least diversified of the six special bracket firms.

The second strategic group, Group II, comprises Shearson Lehman Brothers and Morgan Stanley, the other two members of the special bracket

TABLE 5.4. Total Corporate Securities Issued in the United States, 1986

Rank	Investment Bank	No. of Issues	$Volume (Millions)	Share of Total Volume
1	Salomon Brothers	446	$50,867	17.8
2	First Boston	408	45,051	15.7
3	Morgan Stanley	280	32,180	11.2
4	Merrill Lynch	309	30,368	10.6
5	Drexel	268	30,355	10.6
6	Goldman, Sachs	265	30,180	10.5
7	Shearson Lehman	268	17,256	6.0
8	Kidder, Peabody	193	10,289	3.6
9	PaineWebber	119	4,975	1.7
10	Bear, Stearns	86	4,168	1.5
11	Pru–Bache Securities	77	4,080	1.4
12	Smith Barney	56	3,315	1.2
13	E.F. Hutton	44	2,564	0.9
14	Lazard Frères	15	2,202	0.8
15	Dillon, Read	26	2,185	0.8
16	Dean Witter	42	2,171	0.8
17	DLJ	39	1,389	0.5
18	Alex. Brown	47	1,340	0.5
19	L.F. Rothschild	31	1,264	0.4
	Total	3,019	276,199	96.3
	Total U.S.	3,765	286,000	100.0

SOURCE: "The 1987 Corporate Sweepstakes," *Institutional Investor* (March 1987), p. 178. Full credit is given to the lead manager.

group, which accounted for 17.2 percent of underwriting market share in 1986. These two firms were even more diversified than those in the first group, reflecting relatively equal strength in all product areas, even their weakest ones. Morgan Stanley, for example, developed a larger market share in noninvestment-grade debt than did firms in Group I.

Compared to those of the first group, customers of these two firms on average made less extensive use of investment banking services. Although customers of Shearson Lehman and Morgan Stanley had about the same level of investment banking activity, there was a significant difference between the two customer bases: Morgan Stanley had much better penetration of large customers. The average sales volume of Morgan Stanley's customers was $4.9 billion, compared to the $3.1 billion for Shearson Lehman Brothers. Morgan Stanley's customers did fewer deals than Group I firms, but their transactions were relatively large. In 1986, the firm ranked third in underwriting volume, with a market share of 11.2 percent, a significant improvement over its sixth place ranking in 1984, when it had a market share of 5.4 percent. Shearson Lehman Brothers' customers were smaller on average because they included more middle-market customers. It ranked seventh in 1986 with a securities market share of 6.0 percent, well behind the 10.5 percent of sixth-ranked Goldman, Sachs.

Group III (Bear, Stearns; Dean Witter; Drexel Burnham Lambert; E.F. Hutton; Kidder, Peabody; PaineWebber; Prudential-Bache Securities; and Smith Barney) comprises less diversified firms (.20 to .40) that largely served middle-market companies. In industry parlance, these firms are second-tier investment banks, the phrase indicating their rank below the special bracket group, both in terms of total revenues and in the size and prestige of their customers. Drexel Burnham Lambert is something of an anomaly in this group. It is well within this group in terms of diversification and customer activity, but that it is not more diversified results from its success in one product, noninvestment-grade debt. This helped give it a fourth-place tie with Merrill Lynch in the league table rankings, with a market share of 10.6 percent, or nearly half of the total market share for the firms in this group.

At the time of our study, most of the firms in this group were attempting to move into the top right-hand or "northeast" part of the strategic group map. They were launching aggressive calling efforts to get business with larger companies that made more extensive use of investment banking services, even though these companies were already receiving a great deal of attention from the special bracket firms, which were competing vigorously with each other for this business. The second-tier firms were also attempting to improve their market shares, particularly in their weaker product lines, which if successful would increase their diversification. Particular strategies for accomplishing this varied from firm to firm. For example,

Drexel was attempting to use profits from its junk-bond activity to establish a presence in the mortgage securities business. Bear, Stearns was attempting to leverage its secondary capabilities on the issuer side, much as Salomon Brothers had done in the past. Prudential-Bache Securities was capitalizing on the AAA credit rating of its parent and its ability to act as a counterparty on swaps to improve its presence in investment-grade debt.

Group IV (Alex. Brown; Dillon, Read; Donaldson, Lufkin & Jenrette; L.F. Rothschild; and Lazard Frères) comprises what are often referred to as "niche firms." As suggested by this reference, they had a low degree of diversification (equal to or less than .10). Lazard Frères and Dillon, Read were especially strong in M&A and served both very large and middle-market customers. Alex. Brown, Donaldson, Lufkin & Jenrette, and L.F. Rothschild concentrated more on middle-market companies and were especially strong in IPOs and other common stock offerings.

According to members of the niche firms, their strategies emphasized high-margin, value-added products while ignoring the low-margin commodity ones. Implicit in these strategies was the belief that the value-added services could be sold to customers without also having to meet their needs in the commodity products. Individuals in these firms spoke of the need to have the courage to say no to particular types of deals and to take the risk of another firm using a low-margin deal as an entrée to a broader relationship. In contrast, implicit in the strategies of the special bracket firms was the belief in the necessity of being in low-margin businesses in order to get the high-margin deals. This belief was explained in terms of the need to protect the relationship with the customer and the advantages of having as much contact as possible in order to get information about potential, and more lucrative, deals.

For the firms in Group III, an obvious alternative to breaking into one of the two strategic groups of special bracket firms (Groups I and II) would be to decrease their level of diversification and become a niche player. At the time of our interviews, however, none of these firms was seriously contemplating this. Some of the people in the firms expressed the opinion that they were in an awkward strategic position, between being big and diversified, and small and focused. Those who felt this way apparently perceived the very high barriers to breaking into the strategic groups of diversified firms who served large and active customers to be less threatening than the organizational and political barriers to getting out of certain businesses, or at least reducing their commitments to some of them. And at least implicitly, they also shared the belief of the special bracket firms that doing high-margin business was inseparable from doing low-margin business.

We are not in a position to evaluate the wisdom of those attempting to move northeast in the map, but it is apparent that there is room for only so many firms in this portion of the plane. Any firm successful in breaking through the mobility barriers would probably have to do so at the expense of one or more of the special bracket firms.

One area of the map is conspicuously empty: the top left or "northwest" corner of the plane. This suggests one of two things. The first is that there are no viable strategies to enable a less diversified firm to concentrate on heavy investment banking users. But it may also suggest that this is precisely where strategic opportunities exist. This would be the case if industry arguments about product interdependencies and the need for a full product line were overstated. Determining which of these alternative explanations is most valid would require a complex and sophisticated strategic analysis.

Although it is beyond our study, this analysis is no doubt being conducted, if somewhat informally, by firms that are finding it increasingly expensive to compete effectively on all product fronts. We would not be surprised to see some firms occupy a position in the currently empty northwest part of the map in the future. Even the largest firms such as Salomon Brothers are being confronted with the necessity to make choices. Its decision to exit the money-market business and municipal securities is a repudiation of the loose linkage argument and effectively moves the firm to the left. Other candidates for positions in this area are advisory boutiques such as The Blackstone Group, James D. Wolfensohn & Co., and William Sword & Co. which eschew underwriting business altogether and market it as a conflict of interest to providing high-quality professional financial and strategic advice to the CEO.[18] For their services they are paid an annual retainer, which they supplement with fees earned on M&A deals.

Being on retainer is similar to how consulting firms, law firms, and accounting firms are compensated. This reduces the pressure to generate deals in order to get revenues to cover the costs of services provided. Earning fees on M&A deals, however, still represents a potential conflict of interest because it creates an incentive for seeing that M&A deals get done, particularly since these fees can be much larger compared to the retainer, which is generally $250,000 to $1,000,000 per year. Some might argue that conflict of interest with respect to M&A is even greater than with respect to underwriting, since the necessity and value of M&A deals is harder to define than raising capital. A true advisory role may be best conducted when there is no deal-based compensation. It is unlikely that investment bankers with sufficient reputation to establish a boutique would be satisfied with the much more modest compensation entailed in not getting paid for deals. At least for now the pricing structure of M&A deals, though controversial, is accepted. Charging equivalent fees based on time or availability would be difficult if not impossible given how much larger such fees would be compared to payments for other high-priced professional services such as general management consulting and legal advice.

An interesting role that has emerged for these boutique firms in an age of multiple relationships is to help the customer manage purchasing services from a number of large investment banks, as Wolfensohn did for Burroughs (see chapter 4). This role is similar to the close financial advisor in the one-bank model, now adapted to more complex market conditions that require doing deals with more than one firm. The extent to which companies will end up using such boutiques partially depends upon the number of individuals with sufficient credibility to play this role. There are obvious limits on the number of clients any boutique can have, since the relationship fundamentally depends upon the CEO having ready access to one of the few key senior bankers in the boutique. In selling this high-priced advisory service, conflicts of time are as serious as conflicts of interest.

Differentiation through Reputation

Reputation is an important mobility barrier separating the strategic groups in the industry, and is reinforced by tombstone advertisements. It can, for example, inhibit the ability of firms in Groups III and IV to hire the people they need in order to diversify and get business with large customers. This reinforces any misgivings customers might have about doing business with these firms out of concern for their investment banking or distribution capabilities.

Reputation is also an important issue within each strategic group. By definition, firms within the same group have similar strategies, and thus to a certain extent compete for business in similar ways. They also compete for people, which is especially important in a professional services business. This puts pressure on firms within a group to differentiate themselves from one another.[19] For particular products, many of which are commodity items or quickly become so because of the speed with which innovations can be copied, this is done through brand names such as LYONS, TIGRS, and CATS mentioned in chapter 3. This is similar to the attempts in consumer goods to differentiate essentially identical products through shaping perceptions that they are different.

Efforts are also made to differentiate the firm as a whole. One way of doing so is along dimensions of strategy not used in defining strategic groups, such as the use of the firm's own capital in facilitating deals. Another way is through establishing a particular image or reputation with positive connotations for one's own firm and with negative connotations for one's competitors, in a way similar to what is done with particular products.

The production process of investment banking makes differentiation through reputation, within and between strategic groups, especially important. Because every deal is different and is customized to at least some extent, it is difficult for an investment bank to distinguish itself in terms of enduring product characteristics once it has overcome the mobility barriers to establishing a strong position in a business, such as technology in mortgage-backed securities and experience with big and complicated deals in M&A. Thus there is nothing enduringly distinctive about a mortgage-backed security deal done by Salomon Brothers or First Boston or Merrill Lynch, or an M&A deal done by First Boston, Goldman, Sachs, Morgan Stanley, or Shearson Lehman Brothers in terms of how the deal is structured, although there may be differences in style in terms of how it is executed.

Furthermore, since a deal is performed in real-time interaction with the client, characteristics of the customer organization have an important influence on the characteristics of the deal. This also makes it difficult for an investment bank to differentiate itself from its competitors through enduring product characteristics. To the extent that a firm can establish product characteristics that are invariant from deal to deal, such as the dutch auction process in money-market preferred stock, competitors can easily copy them.

In a service business of unique deals, the customer does not buy a finished product that can be inventoried. In selecting an investment bank, the customer must base expectations about future performance on past experience, the experiences of others, and impressions gained from marketing presentations. Reputation has a strong influence on these expectations and impressions. And because reputation extends to particular people, customers will sometimes select an investment bank if they are guaranteed that certain people will work on the deal.

The production process makes reputation important to both investment banks and customers. For investment banks it is a way of differentiating themselves from each other in a business in which product differentiation is difficult. This differentiation helps customers make purchasing decisions among firms within an acceptable price range, which is particularly important in deals where the stakes are high. The most common example of this is large M&A deals, which can be the subject of shareholder suits. A CEO and his board of directors can protect themselves should the deal run into trouble, or should questions arise about the fairness of the price, by using an investment bank with the reputation of being one of the best in the business. The old saying "Nobody ever got fired for buying IBM" comes to mind.

The dimensions along which firms seek to differentiate themselves by establishing a particular reputation are often general and difficult to measure, such as "quality people," "commitment to relationships," and "teamwork and communication." This is inevitable, since the differentiating feature must be relevant across many product lines, each of which includes unique deals performed as a service for customers. The utility of a differentiating feature diminishes, however, if others claim the same quality, making it difficult to evaluate the reality behind the rhetoric of the different firms. When this is the case, the differentiating feature becomes a common rhetorical device and loses its usefulness as a way of establishing a positive reputation.

Commitment to relationships and teamwork and communications are features that firms in our study claimed differentiated them from their competitors. Thus, while noting that the investment banking business had become more transactional, everybody heartily professed the importance of and a commitment to relationships. For example, Joe Low, recently hired as a managing director by Donaldson, Lufkin & Jenrette after spending twenty-one years at Merrill Lynch, said, "I'm very much against transaction banking. The rise of traders to dominance at some firms is not what investment banking is all about. I see DLJ as a return to what investment banks are supposed to be." But the claim that a firm is different from its competitors because of its commitment to relationships will be taken with a grain of salt by customers when all of the other firms are making similar claims.

Firms also claimed that they were different from their competitors in that they encouraged teamwork and communication, as a way of building relationships, through the use of bonus pools based on the aggregate results of a number of departments. Their competitors, in contrast, were said to base bonuses on individual profit center results, which encouraged self-interest at the expense of what was best for the customer and for the firm as a whole. Yet all of the firms in our study based bonuses on aggregate pools. Although it was also true that some had not in the past and were in the process of changing, no firm was moving in the direction of discrete bonus pools.

Another, and less common example, was how firms strong in M&A described their relationship with the corporate finance department. Firms represented themselves as working very hard at maintaining the balance between these two functions for the sake of customer relationships and internal cohesion. Their competitors were characterized as having let M&A dominate corporate finance, to the detriment of customer relationships and to cross-selling from M&A to other product lines.

The phenomenon of a common practice presented by each firm as a quality that distinguishes it from its competitors is the opposite of the "mimetic processes" described by Paul DiMaggio and Walter Powell, whereby "organizations model themselves on other organizations" that are perceived as having found solutions to common problems.[20] The investment banking industry would seem to be fertile ground for mimetic processes, given the similar challenges facing firms and the ability to rapidly transmit information about one another through working on deals together and interfirm mobility. At Prudential-Bache Securities, for example, the thirty managing directors and thirty vice presidents hired as part of its Project 89, who came from the six special bracket firms and a number of others, no doubt provided a wealth of information on the strategies and management practices of their former employers.[21]

These opportunities for obtaining reasonably accurate information about the practices of one's competitors suggest the possibility that even when firms consciously engage in a mimetic process, for strategic purposes they represent borrowed practices as a unique and distinguishing feature of their firm. It is also quite possible that in responding to similar challenges, firms have independently developed similar practices and really do believe that these differentiate them from their competitors. In either case, the ability of any feature to differentiate the firm is diminished if all of its competitors make similar claims, and if customers do not perceive any differences in firms along this dimension.

Examples also exist of efforts by firms to distinguish themselves in more specific ways as they compete for customers and employees. A common way is through descriptions about the culture of the firm. For example, Bruce Wasserstein, co-head of Investment Banking and M&A at First Boston, said, "We like difficult people. We pride ourselves on managing difficult people." Such a statement made to a person who perceived himself as an iconoclast would have an obvious appeal over a firm that emphasized the importance of being part of the team.

A distinguishing feature may not necessarily be a competitive advantage. Philip Purcell, CEO of Dean Witter, described the culture of his firm: "Our biggest competitive disadvantage is that we have people with good values, but the alternative is unacceptable. You have to make a choice. Do you bring in killers without values, or do you stick with a culture that is less money-driven and more client-driven?" Of course, it is possible that a firm perceived by customers as having a less aggressive culture with "good values" could actually have a competitive advantage. To the extent that customers do not trust investment bankers, an opportunity exists for an investment bank to differentiate itself by values that engender trust. The boutique firms described in chapter 4 were attempting to do this by emphasizing the role of the financial advisor who did not engage in underwriting or distributing securities.

Image and Self-Concept

The reputation a firm does have, or what will be called its *image*, can be quite different from the reputation it would like to have, its *self-concept*.

Firms are not always successful in establishing their preferred reputations with customers, potential hires, and, for that matter, competitors. Although determining a firm's image, or external reputation, and comparing this with its self-concept, or internal reputation, was not a major topic for our research project, we naturally ended up with data on this topic through discussions with firms about their strategy and organization and how these compared to those of competitors. These data, supplemented and supported by data from the industry and business press, revealed two clear patterns of perceptions by members of the industry.

The first is that each firm, especially those in Groups I and II (the special bracket firms) and selected others such as Drexel Burnham Lambert and Lazard Frères, had a well-defined image. For example, Goldman, Sachs was often described as a firm with great client relationships that encouraged teamwork through avoiding a star system but as less innovative than some of its major competitors.[22] Morgan Stanley was described as an arrogant firm with an enviable history of blue-chip client relationships that had slipped for a period in the late 1970s and early 1980s but was rapidly on the rebound. Merrill Lynch was described as a large bureaucratic firm with lower-quality people that was managed by former retail brokers. First Boston was described as an M&A powerhouse with internal tensions because of the dominance of M&A and the large proportion of total revenues it was believed to represent. Shearson Lehman Brothers was believed to be still struggling with the integration of Lehman Brothers Kuhn Loeb with its acquirer, Shearson/American Express, which was made more difficult by the political nature of the "old" Lehman Brothers.[23]

The second pattern of perceptions is that a firm's image often differed from its self-concept, and in some cases dramatically so. Salomon Brothers was described to us by its competitors as a very transaction-oriented and aggressive trading firm with a rugged internal culture that emphasized individual initiative and performance at the expense of cooperation and teamwork. This firm's image was described in an article entitled "Salomon's Power Culture," which appeared while we were conducting our interviews at the firm. The article described "Salomon's transactional approach to the business" and claimed that "Salomon staffers cannot be accurately said to 'squabble' over anything—chiefly because this is far too mild a term for what routinely goes on inside."[24]

Executives at Salomon Brothers took exception to the way they were portrayed by their competitors and the business press, since their self-concept was quite different from this image. Harold Tanner, co-head of Corporate Finance, said, "We think relationships are very important." His fellow co-head, Jay Higgins, also said, "It is not true that relationships are not important to us." Bob Scully, head of the Capital Markets Desk, observed, "If we were a transaction-oriented house, we would not have the market share we have today. You have to think about relationships."

Higgins further explained that, unlike the issuer-oriented investment banks, Salomon had not inherited relationships and had had to develop them through its transaction expertise. Terry Connelly, a managing director in Corporate Finance, said, "We try to use our transactional capability to get in the door to establish a relationship," and "we've had some liberty to stress relationships, since we have transaction expertise." He actually saw advantages in the efforts of others to characterize his firm as only interested in transactions: "There's an old toast, 'Confusion to the enemy.' I think it's marvelous that people think that all we do is transactions and that we are not good at relationships."

Other executives at Salomon Brothers felt less positively about the image of the firm as portrayed by others. Bill Voute, a vice chairman who was the head of trading and a member of the firm's Executive Committee, remarked: "That's such a lot of B.S. It's unbelievable what people say about us. But it makes good stories for our customers."

Fellow Executive Committee member Jim Massey, who was head of sales, also felt that the "false image" had not hurt them with customers, but "it has made recruiting more difficult. We have to combat stories that this is not a nice place to work." He rhetorically asked, "How do we deal with the perpetuation of an inaccurate image of the firm when it is in our competitors' interests to do so?" He noted that "this has been the subject of several Executive Committee meetings." Whereas he felt that this was an important concern, he also realized that "although we try to spend time to change our image, once it's in place, it takes a long time to change." In the meantime, "it is very frustrating to hear what others say about us that isn't true."

Tom Strauss, the firm's president, felt that correcting a false image was important in recruiting, and that the firm had not done as good a job correcting its public image as it could with potential hires: "We haven't merchandised our image properly. At the end of the day's worth of interviewing, people see the firm is not like the stereotype that people have of it. Competitors have latched onto it. People here are sensitized to the image issue and bury it pretty quickly."

The reactions of top-level Salomon Brothers executives to the image of their firm illustrate the competitive aspects of a firm's image and self-concept. Because a firm's self-concept is shaped by the firm itself, often by comparisons with the image it has of its competitors, it is bound to be more favorable than its image, which is heavily influenced by its competitors. Another reason for differences between image and self-concept is that the former largely depends on what the firm has done in the past, whereas the latter contains a strong element of what the firm hopes to do.

What each firm desires is for its own reputation to match its self-concept, and for its competitors' reputations to be based on their image of the firm, particularly its negative aspects. In the case of firms acknowledged to be strong, such as those in Groups I and II, this often takes the form of turning a strength into a weakness. For example, the transaction expertise of Salomon Brothers was often described to us as their lack of interest in relationships. In the case of firms that have weaker competitive positions, such as those in Group III, their competitors often deny that they have any particular strengths at all and denounce the overall quality and expertise of their professionals. Along with this, people who move to these firms from higher-status ones are described as "mediocre" or "has-beens" for whom their new employer is paying an extravagant amount of money. This was said, for example, about the people hired by Prudential-Bache as part of its program to significantly strengthen its investment banking business. Jim Crowley, co-head of Investment Banking at this firm, was aware of this and said, "What's fun about the snipes is that some of them are really nasty."

There are three audiences for negative remarks made about one's competitors. The first is a firm's own employees. Negative remarks about competitors are used to create a positive self-concept by emphasizing how one's own firm differs from its competitors. Casting aspersions on one's competitors is also a way of building internal cohesion. Crowley noted, "As a general policy, we don't bad-mouth other investment banks to customers. We say, 'They're a fine firm with good people.' But internally we vilify them as the enemy, since we don't want to fight internally."

The second audience is customers. The more favorable a firm appears to customers vis-à-vis its competitors, the better its chances are of getting business. Nevertheless, the general policy Crowley described for Prudential-Bache Securities about not "bad-mouthing" competitors is a strong industry norm. In spite of this norm, investment bankers do make negative comments about competitors to the business press, often without attribution.

Perhaps the most striking example of this was the treatment of Drexel Burnham Lambert. During our project the firm was described to us by its competitors in the most unflattering ways; an article in *Investment Dealers' Digest* reported some of these descriptions by quoting people who referred to the firm as "a bunch of schmucks," "a bunch of crooks," and "a bunch of sleazes."[25] These descriptions were accompanied by rumors about how many people from this firm were soon to be indicted for violations of securities laws (up to sixty at one point) and the size of the settlement the firm was about to reach with the U.S. attorney general of New York (up to $1 billion at one point). Competitors sought to take advantage of the firm's negative image in order to attack its dominant position in the high-yield bond business (42.2 percent in 1986, compared to 9.7 percent for Morgan

Stanley, which was ranked number two, and 9.3 percent for Merrill Lynch, which was ranked number three).

Executives at Drexel were well aware of the epithets cast about them and attributed these remarks to jealousy for their success in such a short period of time.[26] They, and their competitors for that matter, noted that other firms such as Merrill Lynch, Salomon Brothers, and Goldman, Sachs had experienced something similar when they had risen to prominence, although not to the same degree perhaps because their success had not been so sudden and so dramatic. David Kay, co-head of Mergers and Acquisitions at Drexel, noted another reason for the hard feelings of their competitors—the ability of Drexel to raise funds for so-called corporate raiders: "We work for companies that are on the move and that are often hostile to entrenched management. Through our abilities to represent them we represent a clear and present danger to companies that have been doing the same thing today as twenty years ago."

Although the business press was used to shape this firm's image, the press was aware of the competitive struggle in which it was involved. A number of articles noted that although the firm was involved in a major investigation by the SEC and the attorney general's office, no one had yet been indicted for activities conducted as an employee at Drexel, and concluded that "one cannot hear such [negative] comments made over and over again, by the most senior executives on Wall Street, without coming to one inescapable conclusion: Wall Street has declared war on Drexel."[27] James Balog, head of Retail Sales at Drexel, acknowledged the opportunities the firm's difficulties had created for its competitors: "If one of our competitors was a wounded animal in the jungle, I don't know that we wouldn't do the same."[28] Whether or not employees at Drexel and the firm itself end up being indicted or convicted, it is likely that investigations of it, and the opportunities the investigations created for competitors to reinforce a negative image of the firm, at least temporarily attenuated its competitive effectiveness.

The third audience for negative perceptions of competitors is potential recruits, particularly M.B.A.'s. At the time of our study, most firms were growing rapidly and were competing fiercely with each other for new employees from the top business schools. If potential hires think a firm is in the "second tier" or "unethical," they will be concerned about the firm's future and their own personal reputation and will be less likely to join it if they have other opportunities.

We do not have any direct evidence of the extent to which negative aspects of a firm's image hurt its competitive capabilities. Newly minted M.B.A.'s are more impressionable than customers, especially sophisticated customers that make extensive use of investment banking services. For this reason Salomon Brothers was more concerned about its image for recruiting purposes although it did not find this an insurmountable problem; as far as customers were concerned, Voute simply noted that the gossip "makes good stories for our customers." The data in chapter 4 suggest that this image had not prevented Salomon Brothers from building relationships. Its relationships with the customers for which it was the primary bank appeared comparable to those of Goldman, Sachs, which had an image as having the best relationship management. Reinforcing the conclusion that image has a limited effect on a firm's competitive capabilities, at least for firms within the same strategic group, is that the customers we interviewed made no distinction between Merrill Lynch and the other special bracket firms, even though this firm was often described by its competitors as having lower-quality people.

As professors at the Harvard Business School conducting a research project on the investment banking industry that would be reported in a book, we were a potential fourth audience. We have no way of knowing the extent to which firms told us things about themselves and their competitors that they knew were not true in an attempt to shape our perceptions. This must at least be considered a possibility, given the opportunities for accurate information about firms to be transmitted through the substantial interfirm mobility in the industry, through working on deals together, and through personal ties formed in business schools and in communities within and outside New York City. We found it curious, for example, that firms described their competitors as transaction-oriented and paying bonuses on individual profit center results, although no firm described itself in these terms. And while Robert Schoenthal, CEO of L.F. Rothschild, said, "Our bet is that other guys will get so big that they can't coordinate as well," Barry Friedberg, head of Investment Banking at Merrill Lynch, felt, "I don't see us as cumbersome and bureaucratic. This is wishful thinking by the boutiques."

We do not have sufficient data to take a position on how what a firm is really like compares to its self-concept and to its image as described by its competitors and the press. There is even a question about the extent to which a reality exists beyond self-concept and image, but we do not intend to address this philosophical issue here. What is important to note is that firms risk hurting their own competitive positions if they believe things about their competitors that are not true and as a result overestimate or underestimate them. Terry Connelly, a managing director at Salomon Brothers, identified this possibility in recalling the old toast about confusion to one's enemy.

It is our impression that firms in the investment banking industry do not spend much time thinking about the strategies and organizations of their competitors. Whatever vulnerabilities this creates are compounded by confusing the descriptions of their competitors intended for the consumption of their own employees, customers, and recruits (and perhaps Harvard

Business School professors) with an understanding of the actual capabilities and intentions of the competitors. One of the characteristics of the industry is that major firms have diminished or disappeared completely, often through acquisition, and minor firms have risen to prominence.[29] If anything, this phenomenon should accelerate, given the forces operating on the investment banking industry today. Firms that fail to perceive their competitors accurately do so at their own peril.

6

THE SELF-DESIGNING ORGANIZATION

Despite the similarities among firms in each strategic group, and to a certain extent even between strategic groups, investment banks differ in their strategies and how these strategies are implemented. A firm's strategy is reflected in the external ties it has with issuers and investors and the products it uses to link them together. The external ties require a corresponding set of internal ties for the strategy to be implemented.

Because of the complexity of the investment banking business and the speed with which market opportunities open and close, strategic decisions regarding which businesses the firm will compete in, the way in which the firm will compete, and the resources that will be allocated to the businesses are made throughout the firm. Within the broad guidelines of corporate strategy established by top management, people throughout the organization, including those at fairly junior levels, contribute to the business strategies that in turn shape future corporate strategy. Through this *grass-roots strategy formulation process* top management is able to take advantage of the knowledge held by those in the firm who are closest to the markets.

Those who develop strategies are also in the best position to determine what resources are needed and what organizational structure makes the best use of the resources. From top management's perspective, although it is responsible for setting the broad organizational design for implementing the corporate strategy, the high degree of autonomy throughout the organization for people to determine how to organize their unit and relationships with other units means that the firm is a *self-designing organization*.

The building block of design is specialization. Decisions about which businesses to compete in and how to compete in them require decisions about what kinds of specialized units are needed and how these units are structurally related to each other. Specialization results in a differentiation in attitudes and behaviors of people in different units that complicates the integration necessary to coordinate their efforts. Especially in the largest firms, the high degree of specialization and the very real pressures to integrate along all dimensions results in a massive problem of integration. Achieving integration requires a complex network of internal ties that is flexible, flat, and rife with conflict.

The pattern of these ties, in terms of their number and strength, depends upon the firm's strategic intentions. To accomplish these intentions, a variety of structural devices are used to shape the internal network of ties and achieve the appropriate degree of integration of units. These devices include customer-focused units, multiple and shared responsibilities and reporting relationships, special integrating roles and units, lateral processes, personnel flows, and physical location.

Changes in market conditions require changes in strategy, and these are reflected in changes in external ties that require concomitant changes in the internal network of ties. Thus to varying degrees investment banks are constantly reorganizing. One important reason for doing so is that a structure designed to implement a given strategy constrains the development of future strategies. By changing structure, the range of future strategies is increased.

Much of the reorganizing is done at lower levels in the firm through the firm's self-designing capabilities. This reorganizing is supplemented by changes in corporate strategy and overall reorganizations initiated by top management, which occur from time to time. The interventions by top management act as an annealing process, which heats up the organization. As it cools down, grass-roots strategy formulation and self-design become prominent once again. As long as top management is satisfied with the firm's performance, it tends to leave strategy and its implementation to others in the firm. When this is no longer the case, it heats up the organization once again and the annealing process continues.

Grass-Roots Strategy Formulation

The strategy of an investment bank can be described in terms of its external ties with issuers and investors and the types of assets or products that constitute these ties. The overall corporate strategy, defined in terms of the relative emphasis on broad market segments, such as large, frequent financers versus middle-market companies, and on broad product categories, such as equity, investment- and noninvestment-grade debt, mortgage-backed securities, and M&A, is determined by top management. (Kenneth Andrews defines *corporate strategy* as "the pattern of decisions in a company that determines and reveals its objectives, purposes, or goals, produces the principal policies and plans for achieving those goals, and defines the range of business the company is to pursue, the kind of economic and human organization it is or intends to be, and the nature of the economic and non-economic contribution it intends to make to its shareholders, employees, customers, and communities.")[1]

Salomon Brothers provides a good example of a corporate strategy in which top management decided to leverage the firm's trading capabilities to build up its primary business. After doing this, it leveraged its strength in debt underwriting to improve its position in equities. From here it was making an effort to build up its M&A business by building on the fact that the CEO bought both equity and M&A deals. Top management had also made the decision to invest considerable resources in the mortgage business and in London and Tokyo.

Within the broad parameters of corporate strategy, business strategies for particular products and markets are developed, largely by people below the top management level and down to fairly low levels in the organization.[2] Business strategies that are especially successful, such as noninvestment-grade debt at Drexel Burnham Lambert or M&A at First Boston, end up having a substantial influence on the firm's corporate strategy. Because of the large extent to which business strategies and the linkages between them are determined by the lower levels of the firm, investment banks have what one investment banker described as a *grass-roots* strategy formulation process. Another investment banker called this process *bottom-driven*.[3]

Philip Purcell, CEO of Dean Witter, observed that "strategies are developed in the middle of the organization. Some of them result in businesses you get really good at and they start to define you." Mark Winkelman, head of the J. Aron Division (commodities and foreign exchange trading) at Goldman, Sachs, described a similar process: "What makes good strategy is good people on the front line. By osmosis you get the direction you go in." Formulating these strategies requires decisions on which new products to develop, which customers and markets to target, and what resources to devote to particular activities.

Executives at First Boston considered grass-roots strategy formulation an important part of the culture of their firm. Joe Perella, co-head of Investment Banking and M&A, pointed out that "First Boston has a breadth of culture that enables a lot of people to thrive. We get a lot of things percolating—the hothouse concept. Sometimes you get strange things growing. There are product areas that exploded from a junior person who was given lots of room. The secret is that senior management recognizes what it takes to be creative and does not suffocate people."

There is a certain irony to strategy formulation in investment banking. The changes in the capital markets that create opportunities make it difficult to establish strategies for taking advantage of these opportunities. The greater the rate of change, the more the opportunities and the more difficult and complex the strategy formulation process becomes. This is especially true for the largest firms, which are competing in a large number of often interrelated businesses. They face a myriad of possibilities for fulfilling their function of mediating the flow of assets between issuers and investors.

These conditions of complexity and uncertainty require a grass-roots strategy formulation process, since business strategies are best determined by the people who are closest to the markets and can identify opportunities and act on them in a timely fashion. Top management simply does not have the time and expertise to get deeply involved in all business strategies, especially in the largest firms. If it were to attempt to do so, the unavoidable delays this would introduce or the deterioration in the quality of the decisions would inhibit the firm's competitive effectiveness.

Although responsibility for strategy formulation is delegated throughout the organization, this is not to say that top management has no involvement at all. It has to strike the right balance between encouraging autonomy and innovation and exercising control over the decisions that are made. Tom Strauss, president of Salomon Brothers, described how the top management of his firm managed this balancing act: "We have a 'reverse funnel effect' in the flow of ideas. We let ideas percolate up and most get discarded. There also must be hundreds of ideas that we never hear about. But the great ideas continue to sift up and withstand the test of time. Things that get sifted out prematurely get started again." He described his firm as bottom-driven and noted that special efforts were taken to preserve this characteristic: "Sometimes ideas even start with senior management. We have to plant them in the middle of the firm, since we need the organization behind them. If people want something to happen it will happen."

Steve Friedman, a vice chairman and co-chief operating officer at Goldman, Sachs, also emphasized that top management at his firm sought to foster the generation of ideas throughout the organization: "The basic issue is whether you have established structures and systems so that gadflys can challenge you and get lateral thinking. Among the junior partners there is a reservoir of good ideas if you can force debate." Like Strauss, he saw the need to get these ideas to bubble up to the top of the firm: "You need a mechanism to push these ideas upstairs, since the best ones come from the trenches." One way he attempted to accomplish this was through the Investment Banking Strategy Committee, which was "composed of bright and iconoclastic people who argue a lot among themselves."

In addition to encouraging, accepting, and rejecting ideas, and introducing ideas of its own, top management also plays a role in clarifying, testing, and refining ideas from others in the firm. This is particularly important, since many ideas are from very junior people whose experience is limited and whose quality of judgment is unknown to both top management and themselves. But since they can be a source of creative ideas, they must be encouraged to pursue them without undue risk to the firm.

Michael Keehner, a group managing director at Kidder, Peabody, felt that this was his firm's experience as well, and he reinforced the role of top management in testing and shaping new ideas: "Typically we have found that it is the interested person who comes up with new ideas, so we need to create the right sounding board for him." He described the origins of the firm's takeover defense as an example of this. "Takeover defense was an idea which originated from M&A and a young corporate finance guy. They started exploring client-related ideas related to tender offers and were encouraged by senior management. It is an example of a grass-roots idea where senior management acted as an effective anvil."

Top management's role can also enhance grass-roots strategy formulation by helping create space for more junior people to try out new ideas that middle managers might be reluctant to pursue. Winkelman remembered the important role played by John Whitehead, former co-chairman of Goldman, Sachs, who supported him while he developed a strategy for Goldman's foreign exchange business: "Whitehead encouraged me and I felt protected sticking my neck out."

Even when strategy is formulated by those most intimately involved with a business, the speed with which market opportunities appear and grow, market share positions are consolidated, and profit margins decline constrain the utility of techniques for strategic analysis and planning. Philip Purcell, CEO of Dean Witter and a former partner at McKinsey & Co., the management consulting firm, emphasized that "McKinsey's techniques of strategy don't work. Things move too fast. We have had three different key products in four years, so what is strategy? You simply get great people and back them. And even they can't tell you what they'll be doing next year." Fred Joseph, the CEO of Drexel Burnham Lambert, also noted how quickly markets changed: "One of the paranoias you work with is knowing that everything is cyclical. Today's hot product won't be in three to four years." Francis Jenkins, one of the four members of the Executive Committee at First Boston and head of all sales, trading, research, and financing products, explained the implications of the rapid rate at which products came and went in his industry: "Anybody in investment banking that says they have a five-year strategy is mistaken. This is a reactive business. We don't control the minds of clients, Congress, or the whiz kids thinking up new ideas." Richard Menschel, head of Security Sales at Goldman, Sachs and a member of the Management Committee, also felt that it was difficult to plan too far into the future because of product diversification, globalization, and deregulation. "These don't help in formulating a strategy," he observed. Menschel felt that in investment banking "you're governed by the moment," which results in an emphasis on market share, and that "it is hard to be judged on strategy when you are ranked every six to twelve months."

Given the high level of uncertainty surrounding strategic decisions and their consequences, a certain element of luck is involved in the extent to which a firm's corporate strategy affects its financial performance. Unexpected changes in the capital markets can increase the importance of certain capabilities while decreasing the importance of others. For this reason, a number of senior bankers we talked to used gambling metaphors when discussing strategy.

The relative fortunes of Salomon Brothers and Smith Barney, Harris Upham are a good example of how luck affects the relationship between strategy and financial outcomes. Increased interest rate volatility and regulations allowing shelf registration improved opportunities for Salomon Brothers with its expertise in bonds, a historically moribund and low-status business. Terry Connelly, a managing director at Salomon, mused, "A priori we did not know how much we would be advantaged by 415. We didn't focus on debt in the mid-1970s because we decided it was going to become interesting and profitable. Our business was accelerated by things we didn't have anything to do with."

In contrast, the changed environmental conditions that benefited Salomon Brothers severely hurt Smith Barney. Perry Ruddick, vice chairman of Smith Barney, explained that "the major changes in the 1970s favored those firms who had developed a significant position in fixed income. The equity market was effectively dead for ten years and the debt business became the driving force in investment banking due to interest rates and oil shocks."

Perhaps the most dramatic example of how market changes can turn a firm's capabilities into a major competitive advantage was Drexel Burnham Lambert. Under the already legendary and somewhat reclusive Michael Milken, the firm had developed a preeminent expertise in high-yield bonds, working for issuers who had been ignored by other firms. By building strong relationships with people and institutions interested in investing in high-yield bonds, the firm was in a good position to take advantage of market changes, some of which it had a substantial hand in developing, which increased the demand for junk-bond financing.

Although other firms, such as Bear, Stearns, had done early junk-bond deals, Drexel was the only one to emphasize the business. When junk bonds were invented some ten years ago, Drexel was a small and relatively insignificant firm, ranking nineteenth in the 1975 league tables.[4] This had changed dramatically with the growth of this market, partially fueled by the use of junk bonds in hostile takeovers, LBOs, and other transactions that fell under the general label of "restructuring."

G. Chris Andersen, a managing director at the firm, described this experience: "Fred Joseph and I had conversations for five years about whether we had a business with continuity yet. I said, 'No, we have the longest run of luck in history.' We had a phenomenon until we took control of our own destiny and fleshed out transactions with clients. As long as business kept coming in over the transom and was directed from the outside, we had a phenomenon, not a business. It was like following an elephant through the jungle. The elephant was bigger than we were and we were trying to hang on for dear life. We didn't have anything else, so we couldn't get distracted." Philip Purcell pointed to Drexel as an example of a firm that was not a member of the special bracket group but developed a strategy that vaulted it past the special bracket group in revenues and profits: "Surely over time other firms will develop strategies that will give them growth into 'special bracket' status."

Of course, luck is not the only ingredient of success; there is the old saying about people making their own luck by working hard. Success also depends upon how effectively people throughout the organization identify and capitalize on unexpected opportunities, which happened at Drexel, for example. Because of the complexity of the capital markets this must be done by the people who are on the line doing deals. There are simply too many businesses that change too rapidly for top management to have either the capacity or the time to make the necessary decisions. This creates opportunities for a number of people to contribute to the strategy of the firm. Carl Eifler, a managing director at First Boston, remarked, "By the time a once-obscure idea has developed enough to merit senior management focus, it could very well be over a year old." His CEO, Peter Buchanan, noted: "It is hard to make all important decisions at the most senior level. Important decisions are made at all levels."

Structural Design

The external ties created by the firm's strategy, at both the corporate and business levels, require a corresponding set of internal ties for implementing the strategy. Just as top management specifies the broad outlines of a corporate strategy, which comprises and is changed by business strategies developed through a grass-roots strategy formulation process, so does it specify the general organizational design in terms of specialized departments and their relationships to each other. Thus the organization chart that depicts this broad design is a summary of the corporate strategy of the firm.

Within this broad organizational design, more detailed design takes place by the people who are responsible for formulating business strategies. In order to implement these strategies, they need substantial autonomy to organize the units for which they are responsible and to establish relationships with other units that have resources they need through various structural and systems devices. From top management's perspective, the large amount of organizational design done by people throughout the firm means that it is a *self-designing organization*.[5] Such self-designing capabilities are necessary to implement grass-roots strategies, since people need to be as directly involved in implementation as they are in formulation. The complexity and time pressures of implementation require the quick response capabilities of the self-designing organization. A distinctive characteristic of the firms in our study was the extent to which people throughout the organization could affect organizational design.

Organizational design by top management and by others throughout the firm involves the creation of specialized units to perform specific tasks and the coordination within and between these units. Strategy determines which specialized units exist and the patterns of coordination within and between them. This coordination takes place through internal ties between individuals; the stronger the necessary degree of coordination, the stronger the tie. In a self-designing organization, individuals bear most of the responsibility for establishing ties of the appropriate strengths with those they need help from or should give help to.

Specialization results in differentiation, which Paul Lawrence and Jay Lorsch defined as "the difference in cognitive and emotional orientation among managers in different functional departments."[6] Investment bankers and traders, for example, have very different orientations. Such differentiation is necessary, but it makes it difficult to coordinate or integrate the efforts of different departments. This integration, defined by Lawrence and Lorsch as "the quality of the state of collaboration that exists among departments that are required to achieve unity of effort by the demands of the environment," is necessary as well.[7] The more highly differentiated the organization, the more difficult it is to achieve the required level of integration. Management in investment banking, particularly in the largest firms, can be described as a massive differentiation and integration problem because of the large number of specialists and the many interdependencies that exist among them.

Although extensive specialization creates substantial coordination or integration problems, the solution is not to limit the degree of specialization, given the many advantages that accrue from it. The advantages include more efficient processing of deals, greater knowledge of the markets (which improves pricing accuracy and reduces risk) and a larger number of external network ties for matching issuers and investors. As Peter Buchanan explained: "You have to specialize. If you don't you won't get focus. Specialization is expensive but effective." Specialization also facilitates the formation of small units with a group identity. This helps to counter the feeling of being part of a large bureaucracy, which is a growing problem in the largest firms in an industry that mythologizes the "good old days of small private partnerships." Finally, specialization creates an external perception by customers that the firm has special expertise in doing certain types of deals or serving particular market segments. In a professional service business, a reputation for being particularly good at certain deals or serving particular market segments is an important competitive advantage.

Although some specialization is clearly desirable, there are risks in going too far. Rapidly changing markets reduce or even make obsolete the need for certain specialists and increase or create the need for others. The advantages of specialization must be balanced against the advantages of keeping people fungible, as investment bankers like to say, so that the firm's human resources do not become so specialized that they cannot adapt to changing market circumstances. The way Goldman, Sachs dealt with this problem was to insist that investment bankers be generalists while also having a specialty. Geoff Boisi, co-head of Investment Banking, described this in terms of "concentration rather than specialization."

The extent to which specialization is desirable depends upon a firm's volume of activity and its strategy. Clearly a sufficient volume in some activity is needed to justify allocating one or more full-time people to specialize in it. In addition, firms serving a broad variety of sophisticated issuers and investors make much greater use of specialists than do those serving middle-market customers or niche firms that emphasize a narrow range of products for large customers. Because large and sophisticated customers are themselves more specialized according to the products they buy, they create pressures on their investment banks to specialize as well.

Thus we found the greatest degree of specialization in the largest firms, such as First Boston, Merrill Lynch, Salomon Brothers, and Goldman, Sachs.[8] A dramatic example of how size makes substantial specialization possible is provided by the 110-person M&A department at First Boston, which was divided into industry, geographical, and product subspecialties. Joe Perella, the co-head of Investment Banking and M&A, had emphasized the importance of specialization even when the department was small. "You can't run a professional services organization without individuals having a focus on what they do with their time," he commented, and referred to this as "containerized responsibility."

Industry specialties, the first type of specialization in M&A, included financial services, health care, media, natural resources, retailing, technology, and utilities/communications. Industry specialization had begun with insurance, where someone who knew this industry was trained to do M&A. It had been followed by natural resources, where petroleum engineers had been hired to do valuations of oil and gas companies. M&A personnel were also assigned to domestic and North American (Atlanta, Boston, Chicago, Dallas, Houston, Los Angeles, San Francisco, and Canada) and international (Asia [non-Japan], Australia/New Zealand, Continental Europe, Japan, Latin America and Spain, and the United Kingdom) regions. Bill Lambert, with the title of creative director for the department, claimed that First Boston was the first firm to locate M&A people in the regional offices. "Having somebody there full time to call makes a dramatic difference," he noted. M&A product subspecialties included defense and divestitures.

In contrast to this extensive specialization of the M&A product at First Boston was the rudimentary specialization at the smaller firms in our study such as Dillon, Read; Lazard Frères; Bear, Stearns; Donaldson, Lufkin & Jenrette; and L.F. Rothschild. Although the niche firms Dillon, Read and Lazard Frères emphasized the M&A product, in both firms the M&A department was only roughly and amorphously separated from corporate finance, which itself contributed substantially to M&A deals. The same was true for Kidder, Peabody, Bear, Stearns, and Smith Barney. Mike Keehner, a group managing director at Kidder, Peabody, explained that M&A was "conspicuously understaffed in order to make them pull from the general staff to get their work done."

There are three key dimensions along which specialization can occur. As illustrated by the First Boston example, the three dimensions are functions, products, and market segments. Within the investment banking function at First Boston was the M&A product specialty, which was further subdivided into different market segments and product subspecialties. Market segments can be defined in a variety of ways, including industry groups and geographical areas. They are sometimes also defined by customer size and level of investment banking activity. Some firms, for example, have groups that concentrate on larger frequent financers, noninvestment-grade issuers, or emerging growth companies.

Functions—investment banking, sales, trading, and research—are the most basic form of specialization. It is rare for an individual to engage in more than one of these functions. People in investment banking are involved in the issuer interface, people in sales and trading are involved in the investor interface, and people involved in research form a separate department created to provide objective information on issuers to investors.

Mediating the flow of assets between issuers and investors requires coordination of the investment banking and sales and trading functions. Given the differences in cognitive and emotional orientations between those serving issuers and those serving investors, referred to as cultural differences by members of the industry, the integration problem between these functions is especially pronounced. In the past this was exacerbated by differences in social class and educational background. So-called white shoe investment bankers came from upper-class backgrounds and attended Ivy League schools. Sales and trading personnel were "street smart kids" from lower classes who attended public schools in New York City. These social and educational differences were reflected in differences in speech and dress.

Although cultural differences still exist, the general perception of the people we interviewed is that they have diminished. To the extent these differences exist, they result more from differences in skills and task requirements than from education or social class. The increased importance of the sales and trading functions—especially fixed income—to the revenues of firms has been accompanied by a leveling in status between them and investment banking. Traders in particular have risen to prominence as senior executives in a number of firms, such as John Gutfreund, CEO at Salomon Brothers, and Peter Buchanan, CEO at First Boston.[9] The reduction in status differences between investment banking and sales and trading has been reflected in similarities between them in terms of where their new employees come from—all functions recruit extensively for analysts and new associates at prestigious universities and business schools.

How broad or narrow an individual's responsibilities within a functional assignment depends upon the extent to which the function is further specialized along the other dimensions. Units defined along one dimension may be further specialized according to another dimension. A common example is the sales function. It is typically divided into product specialties (debt and equity), each of which is divided into geographical areas (various U.S. and foreign locations), and within the largest geographic subdivisions is further specialization according to product (e.g., for fixed-income instruments there are short-term corporate, long-term corporate, and government specialists).

Strategy influences the dimensions along which a function is specialized. A firm that emphasizes product expertise will specialize according to products, and each product specialist will serve customers in a variety of industries and geographical areas. In contrast, some strategies are defined in terms of external market segments, and emphasize serving all of the product needs of a customer in a particular industry or geographical area.

A firm has a variety of choices in how it organizes its resources. The specific choices reflect the extent to which units are integrated. The choices are determined by strategy, and correspond to the three dimensions of specialization: functions, products, and markets.

The first is to organize in terms of functions. When this is done, integration within a function is emphasized over ties between functions. The advantage of this organizational design is that people performing similar tasks are tightly integrated and functional career paths can be established. This facilitates the coordination of different investment banking specialists on deals, the sharing of information between traders about related markets, and the assistance sales personnel can give each other. Historically, most investment banks were organized in this fashion, with divisions for investment banking, sales, trading, and research. Sometimes there was an overall head of sales, trading, and research at the same level as the head of investment banking. The smaller and less diversified firms in our study, such as Lazard Frères, Dillon, Read, L.F. Rothschild, Donaldson, Lufkin & Jenrette, and Bear, Stearns were still largely organized on this basis.

As is true in all industries, the functional structure comes under a strain when the number of products is large.[10] Integrating the efforts of people serving both sides of the market interface becomes extremely difficult when there are a large number of products linking issuers and investors. When this occurs all of the functional resources needed for a particular product connecting issuers and investors are gathered into one unit for at least some products. The integration between the functional resources devoted to a particular product is greater than the integration of each functional resource with other specialists in the same function. This is especially appropriate when the interfunctional ties are more important than the intrafunctional ones. Perhaps the classic example of a product-based organization is the municipal business. In many of the firms engaged in this business, municipal finance, sales, trading, and research formed one department, which was quite separate from the rest of the firm. To varying degrees, the mortgage-backed securities business at such firms as Salomon Brothers, First Boston, Merrill Lynch, and Goldman, Sachs also approximated this product structure although not nearly as completely.

Similarly, the functional structure comes under strains from market diversification. Distinct market segments can best be served by a single department that contains all functional resources needed to serve that market, as in the municipal business, which has a distinct issuer market segment (public organizations) and a relatively distinct investor market (tax-paying institutions and individuals). In contrast, when markets are defined geographically, choices have to be made about which functional resources to locate in the region, thereby reducing their ability to integrate with similar functional resources at headquarters. This problem was especially vexing to the firms in our study, such as Goldman, Sachs, Merrill Lynch, and Salomon Brothers, which were emphasizing international diversification in London, Tokyo, and other financial centers. In attempting to manage their firms on a global basis, they faced pressures to emphasize both intrafunctional integration across locations and interfunctional integration at each location.[11]

The problem with making structural choices to implement a strategy is that emphasizing one structural dimension at the expense of others can create vulnerabilities for the firm. An investment bank that emphasizes products over market segments is vulnerable to firms that emphasize market segments and get to know the customers' needs especially well. But in organizing around a market segment, such as a geographical area, a firm may be vulnerable to competitors who go after customers with product specialists, who have greater expertise than a generalist covering a market.

The product-versus-market trade-off is particularly vexing for the sales function, such as whether to organize the fixed-income sales function by product or by market. If organized by product, specialists call on customers in all market segments. If organized by market, salespeople specialize according to market segments, selling all products to the customers in their segment. The difficulty firms have in making this choice is revealed by their tendency to oscillate between the two choices. Richard Davis, head of Fixed Income Sales and Trading at First Boston, pointed this out when he mused, "The generalist versus [product] specialist debate is held at the firm every year."

The trade-offs in organizational choices can be illustrated through the issues confronting the investment banks involved in mortgage-backed securities and serving the thrift industry. By creating a specialized unit that focuses on serving all of the needs of the thrift industry including mortgage securities, equity, and M&A, the potential is created for maximizing the firm's penetration of these accounts. The price for this will be a failure to fully exploit mortgage opportunities in nonthrift institutions, such as commercial banks and insurance companies, since the mortgage specialists will be concentrating on thrifts. At the same time, investment bankers who call on commercial banks and insurance companies will probably be too unfamiliar with this product specialty to be comfortable pushing it in a big way.

Of course, mechanisms can be devised to mitigate this as much as possible, such as assigning thrift specialists to support the sales efforts of nonthrift and nonmortgage specialists, but these mechanisms cannot completely eliminate this problem. The best way to do so is through a product-focused organization comprising people whose mission is to maximize the firm's efforts in mortgage securities across all market segments. This risks opportunities for nonmortgage business in thrifts, such as equity and M&A, if the specialists for these products do not find it an attractive industry. If they do, however, there is the benefit of serving it through product specialists, who have greater expertise than thrift specialists, who are in fact generalists.

The complexity of the structural design problem is compounded by the fact that the market and product dimensions, though conceptually independent in theory, are not so in practice. Certain products are used more by some market segments than others. Organizing by product inevitably results in some market specialization. Conversely, organizing by industry or geography has a degree of product specialization.

The importance of all dimensions for strategy and the difficulty firms have in choosing among them is illustrated by the attempt in the largest firms, and most of the medium-sized ones, to organize functions along each of the other dimensions. For example, Smith Barney had originally subdivided its investment banking function into geographical specialties through what it termed a "regionalization program." As the firm grew in the early 1980s it added product specialties (M&A, Private Placement, Leasing, and Project Finance). Soon after, it added industry specialties (Financial Institutions, Energy, Health Care, and Utilities). In the larger firms there is even more specialization along each of these dimensions.

Despite the pressures to treat all dimensions as equally important, and the overlapping of dimensions, choices have to be made. In the complex network of ties within and between specialized units, some ties are stronger than others. The stronger ties reflect a higher degree of integration. Certainly at some level all ties are important, but failure to distinguish among them will result in some that are too strong and others that are too weak, creating a competitive disadvantage. Both too much and too little integration need to be avoided.

In the presence of strong ties, weak ties take on a special importance. Mark Granovetter has shown that people who share strong ties can become isolated from other sources of information unless they also have weak ties to others outside their group.[12] This isolation can be detrimental, since those within the group tend to have the same information. Weak ties are an important way of connecting groups with strong ties while avoiding merging them into a larger group of strong ties.

The importance of making choices about which ties to emphasize can be illustrated by comparing the different ways in which First Boston and Salomon Brothers went about building their asset-backed securities business. First Boston placed a greater emphasis on the distinct product and market characteristics of receivables compared to mortgages than did Salomon Brothers, which attempted to leverage more off existing resources in its mortgage business. At First Boston, Anthony Dub was made head of the Asset Backed Securities Unit. He explained that creating a separate unit was "a conscious bet that we can get technologically ahead of the marketplace by putting six to eight people on this." Dub considered this specialization one of the reasons why his firm had a 90 percent market share of the business in 1986, which included the $4 billion auto receivables deal the firm did for GMAC.

Salomon Brothers, in contrast, had not created a separate unit and regarded this business as part of the mortgage business. Its strategy was to use less specialization around the product and maintain a very strong tie with the mortgage business. The reason for this was the importance of technological expertise in the form of analytical tools and software that had been developed for mortgages and could be used for asset-backed securities.

In an article comparing the strategies of the two firms, competitors attributed part of First Boston's initial success to its difference in organization.

"Officials at several major Street firms contend that because asset-backed deals require so much time, unless an investment banker is told to devote himself entirely to asset-backed securities, he is more likely to ignore them and focus on the most lucrative part of the business."[13] The way to get this focus is to create a distinct specialty with a weak internal tie to the mortgage business and a strong tie to a customer, which can supply the raw material for the receivables product.

Characteristics of the Network Structures

The network structures of investment banks are flexible, flat, complex, and rife with conflict. Lawrence and Lorsch pointed out that "recurring conflict is inevitable" in differentiated organizations.[14] The high degree of differentiation resulting from high degrees of specialization and the effort to integrate across all dimensions of specialization means that this conflict is extensive.

Flexibility and a flat organization structure enhance the self-designing capabilities of the organization. Flexibility provides the opportunity for people to adapt the organization as they see necessary. Flatness improves the flow of information that should be considered in making these adaptations. Even though complexity and conflict are inevitable consequences of self-design, a self-designing organization provides the capabilities for resolving conflict.

Flexibility is required because of the production process. It is impossible to anticipate the deals a firm will do and what combination of resources will be needed. Because of the time pressures under which deals are done, flatness is required so that people at many levels can communicate directly with each other. Many deals are in process at any given time, the resources needed on each one change over time, and individuals are typically involved in a number of deals to varying degrees over time, resulting in a structure that is complex.

In fulfilling its function of mediating the flow of assets between issuers and investors, flexibility is also required to enable the firm to adapt to changing market circumstances. Herb Bachelor, head of Investment Banking at Drexel Burnham Lambert, spoke of the need to "maintain a nonrigidly organized organization," in describing the need for flexibility. Enhancing self-designing capabilities is the most important way to create the necessary flexibility, since it enables those closest to particular markets to make the structural adjustments necessary in order to respond to them in an effective and timely fashion.

Flatness is important because communications that must go up and down many hierarchical levels do so too slowly for the firm to respond in the

short time that characterizes the market in investment banking. Jim Freeman, a managing director at First Boston in charge of research, explained
that "investment banks work well and are creative when they have the most
horizontal structure possible. This is very difficult, since it means there are
a tremendous number of people to work with. To get creative input you
don't want to block the flow of information. And while it is important to
keep the structure as flat and horizontal as possible, doing so is a real pain."

Because of the interdependencies in the markets linking issuers and investors, to some degree there is a need for everybody to talk to everybody else.
Even ignoring the weakest ties, the strong ones constitute a web of ties that
go in all directions. Charles McVeigh, a managing director and co-head of
Salomon Brothers' London office, expressed it well when he said, "Our
web of management reporting relationships would be a business school
nightmare with our dotted, straight, curved, and crossed lines." Barry
Friedberg, head of Investment Banking at Merrill Lynch, explained the
firm's web of reporting relationships: "In the investment banking business,
everybody is accountable to everybody else." This sentiment was echoed by
Peter Solomon, head of Investment Banking at Shearson Lehman Brothers,
who said, "We had to build a structure where everybody reported to everybody else."

Having "everybody report to everybody else" serves to flatten the hierarchy, since it disperses authority throughout the organization. Rather than
having a person's authority be strictly related to his or her position in the
formal hierarchy, it is also related to whoever has the relevant information
for making a decision. The complex web of reporting relationships also
contributes to flexibility. Because many ties already exist, responding to
changing circumstances requires simply strengthening some ties while
weakening others, rather than creating completely new ties while dissolv-
ing others.

Complexity also results from the need to adapt structures to their members. When each position involves a large number of internal ties, changing
an incumbent means changing the configuration of ties between this and
other positions. People are not interchangeable within a fixed structure,
since the structure is largely defined by the people themselves, particularly
in a self-designing organization in which individuals adjust their ties according to their own strengths and weaknesses. Steve Friedman at Goldman, Sachs recognized the importance of adapting structure to the people
who define it: "I try not to develop too many dogmatic rules, but one iron-
clad rule is that structure should follow the person."

The flexible, flat, and complex network structures found in investment
banking fit Tom Burns and G. M. Stalker's description of the "organic" organization.[15] It is a "network structure of control, authority, and communication"
with "a lateral rather than a vertical direction of communication," which

"consists of information and advice rather than instructions and decisions." The organic organization is also characterized by "the adjustment and continual redefinition of individual tasks through interaction with others" and "the spread of commitment to the concern beyond any technical definition."[16]

The continual redefinition of tasks and the high levels of interaction among people in the firm result in some ambiguity about an individual's responsibilities. This encourages a sense of commitment to the firm as a whole. As Burns and Stalker noted, clarity about what one is responsible for also provides clarity about what one is *not* responsible for. Without this clarity, a person is compelled to take broader responsibility and in doing so increases the number and strength of ties he has with others.

Complex network structures create a system of debits and credits that facilitates conflict resolution. As people work together on deals for clients, obligations and favors are created. Unique deals that require unanticipated combinations of resources help to multiply the number of debits and credits created. Conflict can be resolved by paying off debits or obtaining credits. Evidence of the importance of these debits and credits for resolving conflict is the emphasis investment bankers put on "personality" over "structure" in describing how their organizations work.[17]

This is not to say that structure is unimportant. Creating the appropriate ties is essential for implementing strategy and creating opportunities for future strategies. But when the structure is complex, amorphous, and in constant flux, interpersonal skills are taxed to a much greater extent than they are in simple, clear, and stable structures. In the latter (described as "mechanistic" by Burns and Stalker), which are rigid, tall hierarchical networks, job descriptions, reporting relationships, rules, and procedures play a more important role than they do in organic network structures, which depend on individuals with the interpersonal skills to confront and resolve conflict in a constructive way.

Shaping Organic Network Structures

The general characteristics of flexibility, flatness, complexity, and conflict were found in the network structures of the firms we studied.[18] Although there were substantial variations among firms in the specifics of their configuration, a number of similar structural devices were used to shape network structures for implementing strategy and resolving the conflict this entails. The structural devices produce ties of varying strengths in order to obtain the required degree of integration. The higher the level of integration, the larger the number and the stronger the ties.

Ties are created by top management and, as would be expected in a self-designing organization, by many others throughout the firm. We found six categories of structural integrating devices for creating ties: (1) customer-focused units, (2) multiple and shared responsibilities and reporting relationships, (3) special integrating roles and units, (4) lateral processes, (5) personnel flows, and (6) physical location. The number and complexity of devices in a firm was directly related to its degree of specialization and concomitant need for integration. Thus, the large firms in Groups I and II made more extensive use of these devices than did the firms in the other two strategic groups. The niche firms in the fourth group actually went out of their way to avoid formal use of the devices in order to avoid increasing structural complexity.

Customer-focused units facilitate the formation of ties between individuals who share responsibilities for a particular issuing or investing client. One way of doing so is to create client teams of the various specialists who call on the customer. At Shearson Lehman Brothers, for example, a computer printout listed which investment bankers were assigned to each issuing client. This was a common practice in the other large firms and a number of the medium-sized and even smaller ones. The membership of these teams signals the desired communication ties. These ties can be enhanced through relationship managers, who are responsible for coordinating the activities of the specialists. The number of ties created by this structural device can be quite extensive when the composition of a team changes from account to account. A person assigned to a number of accounts, each of which has at least a slightly different team, has the opportunity to create ties with a large number of people.

Although relationship managers are most commonly used with issuing clients, similar integrating roles are used on the investor side as well. An interesting example was the Resource Units created at Salomon Brothers in the first half of 1987. These units contained salesmen "who don't write day-to-day tickets, but who have macroconceptual ideas," explained James Massey, head of Sales. Each unit acted as a kind of relationship manager to the units it was assigned to by making recommendations on the customer's overall portfolio mix in terms of types and currencies of assets.

Multiple and shared responsibilities and reporting relationships are the principal mechanisms for creating a situation "where everybody reports to everybody else." A common form of multiple responsibility, which can also be considered a customer-focused integrating device, is what Jay Lorsch and Peter Mathias call the "producing manager," also referred to as the "player/coach" at First Boston.[19] Anthony Dub, who was in charge of Asset Backed Securities at First Boston and who also had relationship management responsibility for IBM, General Motors, and Philip Morris, is an example. When a person has both external client management and internal firm management responsibilities, he is well positioned to influence the formation of internal ties to serve his customers. Another advantage of this role is that it distributes management responsibility throughout the firm—which is essential in a self-designing organization—while maintaining important senior-level contact with customers. If knowledge about customers is divorced from those who are responsible for managing the firm, there is a risk that decisions about organization will inhibit rather than enhance service to customers.

In addition to maintaining contact with customers, an individual can be responsible for two or even more units of the organization. When someone is put in charge of two units, he appears twice on the organization chart. A common example is a person responsible for both a geographical specialty and an industry specialty in investment banking. This often occurs when there is substantial overlap between a geographical area and an industry, such as oil and gas in the southwest or high technology in the San Francisco Bay area, which was the case at several firms. A person with this dual responsibility can facilitate the formation of ties between units. This is further enhanced when nonmanager bankers have dual membership in the two units. These ties facilitate the flow of ideas between the two units.

The converse of having one person responsible for two units is to have two people responsible for one unit. For example, First Boston, Salomon Brothers, Shearson Lehman Brothers, and Goldman, Sachs had co-heads for investment banking. Since each co-head has his own set of ties outside the unit, the capacity for building ties between the unit and others in the firm is increased. This is especially true when either or both co-heads have management responsibility for another unit as well.

The use of co-heads creates dual, and even multiple, reporting relationships, which increases the number of ties and therefore the amount and accuracy of information transmitted. An interesting variation on dual reporting relationships is when an individual reports to managers who are at different levels in the organizational hierarchy, such as his boss and his boss's boss. At Shearson Lehman Brothers the reporting relationships of the heads of investment banking in foreign locations included one to Peter Solomon, the co-head of Investment Banking, who was three levels above them, or their boss's boss's boss. (In between were the head of the foreign location and France de St. Phalle, the head of International Investment Banking and Capital Markets.) These nested reporting relationships have the further advantage of flattening the organizational hierarchy. When a manager has direct access to information through his subordinate's subordinates, he avoids the distortions, particularly when the news is bad, that are inevitable when information is communicated through hierarchical channels.

Another mechanism for flattening the hierarchy is by inverting management responsibilities between levels. This often occurs when the manager of a department is heavily involved in customer relationships. In order to preserve his time for this important activity, lower-level managers take on responsibility for both planning and day-to-day operating management. At First Boston, units within Investment Banking defined in terms of industry and geography were assigned a chief operating officer (COO), who was typically a vice president with four to six years of post–business-school experience. The COO was responsible for developing a strategic plan for the unit and more senior bankers helped to implement it. More senior bankers can actually end up being more involved in the implementation of these plans than they are in their formulation.

Special integrating roles and units comprise the third category of structural devices. Product managers, who were common in a number of firms, perform an integrating role that coordinates the efforts of bankers, salespeople, and traders involved in a particular product. Product managers and product sales specialists are especially useful to generalist salespeople who need assistance in representing a broad line of products. Another integrating role is the liaison between two departments. Liaison roles are often useful when one department, such as mortgage securities, needs product expertise from another, such as M&A, but does not want to develop this expertise within the department itself.

Entire units can play integrating roles, and in doing so they foster the development of ties throughout the firm. New product development groups are integrating units that consolidate information from specialists dealing with issuers and investors for the purpose of developing new types of securities. In doing so they form ties with a large number of people throughout the firm.

Three of the most common integrating units are the syndicate function, research, and the capital markets desk. All three units are especially important for facilitating the integration necessary to mediate the flow of assets between issuers and investors.

The classic example is the syndicate desk, which, in addition to integrating the firm's efforts with other members of the syndicate, integrates investment banking with sales and trading by balancing the needs of the issuer with the needs of investors. When the firm has both retail and institutional distribution, the syndicate function integrates their efforts as well by managing the conflict over allocations. Although the importance of syndicates has diminished as the proportion of the deal taken by the lead manager and co-managers has increased, the syndicate desk still plays a useful integrating role. This unit also keeps track of the firm's experiences with its competitors, to construct a more or less formal system of debits and credits from underwriting deals.

The research function is another integrating unit between investment banking and sales and trading. Research analysts provide information on issuers and their industries, which in turn helps salespeople represent the equity product to investors. In some firms, research analysts are an important contact with issuing customers and help to bring in deals.

One of the newer integrating units is the capital markets desk found in all of the larger firms in the first two strategic groups, and an increasing number of the medium-sized ones in the third strategic group. This unit maintains close contact with both issuers and investors in order to execute debt underwritings in the very short time required by market volatility and made possible by shelf registration. Members of this unit are assigned to issuing client teams, but are located on the trading desk in order to have up-to-the-second information on the markets. The head of the unit typically reports to both the investment banking and the sales and trading functions. Even more recently, some firms have developed an equity capital markets desk as well, for performing a similar function on the equity side.

The capital markets desk is a dramatic example of a reduction in the cultural differences between investment banking and trading, at least for debt products. People on the capital markets desk are expected to think like investment bankers by understanding issuer needs and by being an effective member of the client team. They are also expected to think like traders by understanding investor needs and by being sensitive to market opportunities. Individuals in this function often receive training in both investment banking and trading.

Another common integrating unit is joint ventures, which were especially prevalent in the larger firms, such as between M&A and high-yield debt, or M&A and private placement, and which link product capabilities often combined in deals. The emergence of joint ventures reflects the growing importance of providing financing for M&A deals. Like external joint ventures, internal ones are funded by two departments, which also supply people. Joint ventures multiply the number of ties between the departments involved.

Central resource pools also serve an integrating function through tie formation. The primary reason for forming these units is to have a group of professionals, most typically corporate finance generalists, which other departments can draw on as needed. This is useful when the needs of other departments are unpredictable taken one at a time, but are reasonably stable in the aggregate. For example, although it is uneconomical to assign enough investment bankers to meet peak load demand from every industry and geographical specialty, the needs of these units for processing capacity to execute the deals they bring in can be at least partially met by a centralized pool of more junior bankers. In working on these deals, the bankers in the central pool form ties with a large number of other bankers in the firm. They can also contribute to ties between them when they find themselves working on a deal similar to another they have worked on before and suggest that those who brought in those deals talk directly to one another.

Lateral processes, the fourth category of structural devices for tie formation, include meetings, both planned and ad hoc, committees, and task forces. Certain types of periodic and short meetings were especially prevalent in all of the investment banks we studied, such as weekly (often on Monday) meetings of investment banking personnel to discuss products and deals and daily meetings of the salespeople and traders to discuss expectations about the market for the day. Lateral processes place as much emphasis on interdepartmental communication as on intradepartmental communication. Telecommunications technology plays a supporting role to lateral processes, as well as being important in its own right for maintaining ties. Through "squawk boxes," people in different locations can conduct their meetings, as is done in the daily meetings before the market opens.

Personnel flows, the fifth category of integrating devices, include recruiting, training, and career paths.[20] Because the recruiting process makes extensive use of bankers at all levels throughout the firm, prospective employees meet a large number of people, which provides a foundation for future ties. During our research project, investment banks were a major presence on leading business school campuses.[21] For new employees training programs provide the opportunity to form ties with members of their cohort, some of which will endure. Training programs typically involve a rotation process through various departments, both for building up the new employee's knowledge about the business and for matching new recruits with departments, a process that contributes to the formation of ties between new and old employees. The largest firms had formal and extensive training programs for analysts and new associates that typically started in late summer or early fall.

Finally, during the course of a career, investment bankers add to their own network of ties. Over time they are able to meet more and more people in the course of doing deals. If their career paths involve changes in departments, they both extend their network of ties and contribute to the formation of ties between the departments in which they have worked. When they are reviewed for promotion to vice president and managing director, senior bankers who have not had the opportunity to work with them find out something about them and this information can be the basis for future ties.

Physical location, the sixth and final category, is something that receives a great deal of attention, particularly in determining the positions of salespeople and traders and the members of the capital markets desk on the trading floor. Since the intensity of a person's communications with others is directly related to how close they are, physical location is an important determinant of the strength of ties. As the size of the trading floor has grown, and as firms have reached the point where more than one trading floor is necessary, decisions about physical location have become even more difficult and important.

The network structures created by the six categories of structural devices are fertile ground for innovation. In her studies, Rosabeth Kanter has found that innovation "is most likely to flourish where conditions allow flexibility, quick action and intensive care, coalition formation, and connectedness," which occur "in organizations that have integrative structures and cultures emphasizing diversity, multiple structural linkages both inside and outside the organization, intersecting territories, collective pride and faith in people's talents, collaboration, and teamwork." [22] Since investment banks fit this description almost perfectly, it is no surprise that they are able to innovate at the rate and to the extent that they do.

Reorganizing and Annealing

The flexibility, flatness, and complexity of network structures make it easy to reorganize them on an ongoing basis. Because of the large number of ties created by the structural devices, almost any particular structure is already latent in the organization. It is a matter of strengthening some ties and weakening others. For example, in describing how bankers at Goldman, Sachs had membership in units defined by clients, regions, products, and industries, Geoff Boisi, co-head of Investment Banking, noted, "This structure gives us flexibility we haven't had before. With multiple group membership it is easier to move people out of departments."

Investment banks take advantage of the ease with which their organizations can be changed by changing them often, which reinforces this capability. Another benefit of reorganizing, whatever the reason for doing so, is that the number of ties is increased. Reorganizing strengthens some ties and creates new ones. These are added to past ties, whose strength is not immediately diminished, but instead decays over time. Until this decay becomes significant, the new ties fostered by the new structure are added to the old ones, a legacy of the old structure.

Constant change exists, not simply because it is easy, but because it is necessary. Continuing changes in the market necessitate changes in strategy, which result in changes in the external ties investment banks have with their customers. These, in turn, require changes in the internal ties in order to coordinate the external ties. The porous boundaries of investment banks mean that changes in external ties rapidly translate into changes in the internal ties.

The effect of market changes on external and internal ties is most visible when a number of firms make similar organizational changes. One example, already mentioned in the discussion of integrating units, is the capital markets desk. Interest rate volatility increased the desire of frequent financers to quickly take advantage of low-cost financing opportunities. This was facilitated by shelf registration. The large investment banks were the first to respond by creating a new investment banking product specialty with a tie to assistant treasurers in issuers that had especially strong ties with

the trading function, as well as ties with other investment banking specialties.

Another example is the increased importance in the M&A product in an
environment of rising stock prices, restructuring, and a laissez-faire administration in Washington. Firms strong in M&A found that the M&A specialists had stronger ties with the CEO and CFO than did the traditional
corporate finance generalist. In some of these firms, such as First Boston,
Morgan Stanley, Salomon Brothers, and Goldman, Sachs, M&A specialists
ended up running the entire investment banking function. Their responsibilities included facilitating their firm's ability to leverage high-level customers into other products, while at the same time improving the internal
ties between M&A and other investment bankers. As the importance and
amount of M&A business increased, M&A specialists often lagged in their
attention to how their efforts contributed to the firm's overall relationship
with the client.

A more recent and especially revealing example is the changes that had
taken place in the organization of the municipal business at a number of
firms. Changes in the tax laws in 1986 eliminated tax exemptions on interest payments on nongovernment-purpose municipal bonds and restricted
their use on others. Because the investor base for new taxable municipal
bonds was expected to be the same as that for other taxable instruments,
and the products they purchased were expected to resemble the taxable
products of corporate issuers, a number of firms had made various moves
to more closely integrate municipal and corporate functions. Many years
ago municipal and corporate finance were not separate departments, but
changes in the markets resulted in the fairly complete separation described
above.[23]

This recombination was especially common for markets that had had
both taxable and tax-exempt segments, such as housing and health care.
Thus Merrill Lynch combined its municipal and taxable housing finance
departments, as did Kidder, Peabody, and Dean Witter and Salomon Brothers did the same with health care.[24] Other firms combining municipal and
corporate finance were Shearson Lehman Brothers, Prudential-Bache Securities, and Bear, Stearns.[25] For similar reasons, some firms were also combining sales and trading functions. Smith Barney, for example, combined
short-term taxable and tax-exempt sales and trading because the buyer of
these securities was the same.[26]

Even when strategy is relatively constant, changes in structure are also
necessary. Within a given strategy, structures are used to solve particular
problems. In solving a problem, others that also require structural changes
for their solution are created and ignored. For example, in reorganzing a
sales force based on products to one based on markets in order to improve
account penetration across product lines, the change can mean that a gen-

eralist salesperson has to sell a complex product to a specialist buyer, and this may result in lost business in the product line. Making these changes is possible, since although structure must be adapted to strategy, there is always a range of structural possibilities for any given strategy.[27]

However flexible these network structures are and even though they foster innovation within the firm, the current structure does act as a constraint on future strategies.[28] New structures broaden the range of possible strategies. A firm's structure influences the information it collects from its environment and how it combines and processes this information to generate future strategies. Changes in structure result in changes in information flow, which in turn result in changes in the strategic opportunities that are considered and pursued. Changes also help to dissolve power bases that can interfere with necessary changes in strategy in an attempt to protect vested interests.

In the self-designing organization, much of the reorganizing concerns parts of the firm rather than the firm as a whole. This can lead to constraints, when reorganizing in one part should be, but is not, accompanied by reorganizing in another part. Another constraint is the understandable reluctance to make changes that sever ties between particular customers and particular employees. Conceivable but uncertain future benefits may prove to be an insufficient motivation to risk a possible decrease in fees from these customers.

Finally, in the self-designing organization it is ideal if people are indifferent to adding to or subtracting from their management responsibilities. Organizational changes frequently involve an increase in the management responsibilities of some people and a decrease in those of others. Self-designing capabilities are reduced when more senior managers have to get involved in order to persuade others or even insist that certain changes take place. Even though the common perception that managers arc reluctant to have their responsibilities reduced does occur in investment banking, more notable is that people in the industry resist *increases* in management responsibility because this will take them even further away from what is generally regarded as the fun part of the business—doing deals.

These constraints make it necessary for top management to institute major reorganizations every now and then that involve changes in both strategy and structure and affect the entire firm or large portions of it. When viewed over a long period of time, reorganizations initiated by top management resemble the annealing process used in crystal formation. Eric Leifer and Harrison White described this process as one in which "a system of particles at high temperature can be cooled very slowly, allowing equilibrium configurations to form at each temperature change. At the temperature zone where crystals begin to form, the cooling process can be repeatedly *reversed* until a satisfactory initial configuration is obtained (which shapes the progressive refinements formed through further cooling). Reversal is key to the annealing process, as it allows one to avoid 'bad' local optimums."[29] They argue that a similar process occurs in organizations "where no global situation is known, and where the incremental improvement techniques stand the risk of getting stuck in a local optimum"—a precise description of the problem of formulating strategy and designing structures to implement it in investment banking.[30]

In the self-designing organization, top management's unique responsibility is this annealing process, which changes the parameters within which the self-design takes place. It "heats up" the organization and then waits to see what the resulting configuration of strategies and ties is once the organization "cools down." If it is satisfied, top management cedes strategy formulation and structural design to others throughout the firm. But when top management is no longer satisfied with the direction in which the firm is going and the way in which it is getting there, it heats up the organization again and the process continues.

Annealing can be done in a variety of ways including changes in corporate strategy, rapid restructuring of the firm, and changes among high-level personnel.[31] Changes in corporate strategy occur when the firm makes substantial shifts in the people and capital allocated to particular businesses, including entering completely new ones and completely exiting existing ones. Rapid organizational restructuring has the greatest impact when it comes as a surprise and the reasons for the new structure are incompletely and ambiguously explained. Such restructuring is often accompanied by changes in high-level personnel. Senior managers can be given new and comparable responsibilities, they can have their responsibilities substantially diminished, or they can be fired. The changes can be accompanied by the sudden rise to prominence of middle-level managers.

The dramatic decision in 1987 at Salomon Brothers to exit the municipal business, in which it had the largest market share, and the money-market business, with a total reduction of eight hundred people, or 12 percent of its work force, may be an example of the annealing process at work. The move was both criticized and lauded by Salomon's competitors.[32] Critics questioned why the firm would exit the municipal business, which it had worked so hard to build, and the money-market business, which is an important way to maintain contact with customers despite its low margins. Supporters of the moves pointed to the declining profitability of the municipal business, to the shift of this business away from institutional buyers with whom Salomon had strong ties, and to the poor prospects for ever making much money in money markets.

The concept of annealing suggests an alternative to the economic argument, or at least an additional explanation. Top management may have decided to get out of these businesses partly to do something dramatic to heat up the organization. That persuasive arguments could be made for both exiting from and staying in the businesses made them especially good candidates for the annealing process. So did the fact that they were businesses in which Salomon Brothers had a strong position. Throughout the firm people may have thought, "If we're willing to get out of these businesses, how secure is the one I'm in?" In retrospect, the prior departure of vice chairman Lewis Ranieri, who built the firm's strong and profitable mortgage-backed securities business, looks like the beginning of the heating-up phase in the annealing process at Salomon Brothers.[33]

Exiting the municipal and money-market businesses was accompanied by statements about an increased emphasis on merchant banking, M&A, and international equities, areas in which Salomon Brothers was not a traditionally strong competitor. And despite its progress in these businesses, the firm has had a difficult time shaking its image as a "bond house run by traders." Completely exiting two traditionally strong businesses may have been a way of shifting the internal allocation of resources and power structure while at the same time changing external perceptions of the firm. Exiting these businesses may also have been intended to affect recruiting and career paths in a way that would reinforce the new organizational formation long after the event.

Although we do not have any direct evidence from Salomon executives about the reasons for these strategic decisions, it is certainly plausible that they could have the consequences described here, whether intended or unintended. Top management in investment banks may or may not consciously engage in an annealing process, and if it does, it most likely thinks of it in different terms. All that is required for annealing to occur is for periods of major change instituted by top management to be followed by periods dominated by grass-roots strategy formulation and organizational self-design.

The periods themselves create the need for annealing because of the phenomenon of *creeping diversification,* which results from grass-roots strategy formulation in the self-designing organization. Aggressive individuals charged with the responsibility, or who seize the opportunity, for developing a business will naturally look for ways to make it grow. One way is a form of mitosis: as the business grows it is broken up into smaller businesses, whether defined by product or by market, each of which is assigned to a group of individuals. Innovation naturally leads to this by creating product extensions and finding applications in new markets for existing products.

Creeping diversification also occurs when the base business is used to enter related businesses, which in turn become a base for businesses related to them, and so on. Because of the highly interrelated nature of products and markets in investment banking, top management may ultimately find that the firm has become active in a number of businesses that are beyond the broad parameters it has attempted to lay down.[34] This form of creeping diversification is especially difficult to manage properly, since the interrelatedness of businesses, both in the present and in the future, is difficult to assess in a rigorous way. This interrelatedness, worsened by loose linkage, also makes it difficult to perform economic analyses for evaluating the returns on the costs of diversification.

Because of creeping diversification, top management must decide whether or not to prune the company's portfolio of businesses on some periodic or episodic basis. Although exiting a business is something that investment banks are loathe to do, because of the decrease in revenues and the vulnerability of its client base to approaches by competitors, the decision to do so must be top management's. It is unlikely that those responsible for a diversification move will advocate getting out of the business at the risk of their jobs. The annealing process is an excellent way to pare down the number of businesses a firm enters through creeping diversification.

A final reason for annealing is that in organizations engaged in a constant process of change, change itself becomes a steady state. People get as used to this condition as others do to no change. When change is constant, its benefits are attenuated.

Although top management is limited in its ability to determine in detail how the firm should adapt to major discontinuities in the markets, it can improve the firm's chances of doing so by introducing discontinuities within the organization so that the people who make the more specific and detailed adjustments do so from a perspective in which many of their traditional assumptions have been challenged. However ironic, the best way for top management to ensure the organization's survival is to periodically put it at risk. A little fear goes a long way toward sharpening the firm's competitive edge.

— 7

SYSTEMS FOR CONTROL

Despite its many virtues, the self-designing organization has its flaws. The flat, flexible, and complex organization structure makes it possible for people and units in the firm to respond to market opportunities. But the same characteristics also make it possible for people to pursue customers and activities that are not in the long-term interests of the firm. As a result, senior management in investment banks imposes tight control systems that measure activities and outcomes. This is in contrast to the looser systems needed in an organizational structure that give management more control.[1]

These management control systems complement the self-designing structure and act as an integrating device. The organizational structure is an endoskeleton that provides the means for accomplishing objectives. The management control systems are the exoskeleton that encourages employees to engage in activities that are measured or affect measured outcomes. Variables measured by systems, and the objectives set for these variables, define the ends toward which structural means are directed.

These systems are tight in the sense of being precisely defined and difficult to change. In addition, they are also largely imposed by top management; this is another way in which systems complement structure. Although many people are involved in structural design, very few are involved in systems design. This gives the senior managers involved an important form of control, particularly since the system measures are an important tool for evaluating an individual's performance and determining bonuses. The self-designing features of the organization, the control systems imposed by management, and the process used to determine bonuses (discussed in the next chapter) complement one another.

There are four basic categories of systems: (1) reports related to *calling activity,* (2) *evaluations from customers,* (3) internal *cross-evaluations* within and between departments, and (4) measures of *financial outcomes.* The design and use of the systems result directly from the mediation function, economic characteristics, and production process of investment banking discussed in chapter 2. In their mediation role, investment bankers must develop and maintain external ties with issuing and investing customers, and internal ties of appropriate strength to process deals. The quantity and quality of contact with customers is measured through reports on calling activity and evaluations from customers. Correspondingly, internal cross-evaluations monitor the network of ties needed within the firm to process deals. Specific outcome measures are also used that take into account the economic characteristics of the business, such as the loose linkage between services provided and revenues received.

Calling Activity

Call reports—which generally include the name of the company and the person contacted, issues and products discussed, and short- and long-term opportunities for deals—are a source of control for senior management. They are also an important source of information for all members of the client team and others in the firm. In fact, the distribution list for call reports helps reinforce the network of ties between people in the firm.

"When a large number of people are involved in serving an account, it is important for them to share information with each other. Face-to-face conversations and telephone calls on a timely basis are the best way of accomplishing this. As Jay Higgins, head of Corporate Finance at Salomon Brothers, put it: "There is no substitute for picking up the telephone." But as the firm grows larger in the number of accounts, the number of people involved with each account, and the total number of people included on a client team, a more systematic approach is needed to supplement personal interaction. In larger firms, for example, a client team can include several product specialists. Thus, we found calling report systems more prevalent and more extensive in the largest firms.

Information in the reports keeps everybody on the client team well informed, which helps to prevent embarrassing situations in which someone in the customer organization assumes that the banker he is talking to is aware of other discussions being held with the investment bank. Reports also convey information about opportunities for others. Even if the marketing efforts of a banker do not result in a deal in his specialty, they are worthwhile if they result in a deal for another specialty in the firm. This is especially important given the loose linkage between value contributed to the customer and revenues earned.

We found that senior managers took an active interest in call reports. For example, Herb Bachelor, head of Investment Banking at Drexel Burnham Lambert, received copies of all call reports daily. He believed that his review of the reports provided an incentive for bankers to fill them out and enabled him to keep informed about the firm's contacts of current and potential customers. When reports are aggregated, information can be generated on the time being spent with particular clients, market segments, products, and products by market segment. From this information, management can tell if bankers' efforts are consistent with its general strategic intentions and if corrective actions are needed.

In order to facilitate the analysis of information from call reports, a number of firms had computerized, or were in the process of doing so, the accumulation and analysis of the data. Bill Benedetto, head of Corporate Finance at Dean Witter, got computerized reports on a weekly basis. In early 1986, Barry Friedberg and Peter Solomon, heads of investment banking at Merrill Lynch and Shearson Lehman Brothers, respectively, were in the process of developing computer-generated reports of calling activity.

The utility of the information generated from a call report is a function of its accuracy, completeness, and timeliness. Since filling one out takes time, and is seen by many investment bankers as a bureaucratic annoyance, to say the least, various incentives are used to encourage employees to take the activity seriously. One firm withheld expense checks until call reports were submitted. Another firm reminded bankers that business would not always be good and a day would come when they would want to be paid for their calling efforts.

Call reports are especially important for encouraging bankers to call on clients with whom the firm has only a transactional or a conversational tie. The level of disappointment, rejection, and frustration is greater with these accounts than with customers with whom the firm has a stronger relationship. By emphasizing the importance of new business development with transactional or conversational accounts, senior management controls the natural tendency for bankers to concentrate on customers who are more receptive to their entreaties for business. Because large and growing firms face constant pressure to expand their client base, call reports are especially important for creating incentives to engage in this activity. Several firms, including PaineWebber and Merrill Lynch, set up explicit criteria for the frequency of calls on different categories of customers. At PaineWebber specific quantitative standards were established, covering the number of hours devoted to the account, the frequency of personal visits and telephone conversations, and the frequency of written communications and presentations for customers classified as, in order of importance, focus, secondary, or monitor accounts. Smaller firms, such as Dillon, Read and Lazard Frères, which can rely more on referrals and other informal means for developing new accounts, are under less pressure to establish a formalized call reporting system to aid in new business development.

Similarly, one of the reasons Shearson Lehman Brothers was developing a more formal call reporting system was to encourage bankers to spend more time calling on potential accounts. Peter Dawkins, a managing director who was heavily involved in the development of the system, acknowledged the difficulty in using systems for this purpose: "We are asking people to do things that are counterintuitive. They think their purpose is to generate fee income for this year. They pay lip service or threshold attention to recruiting, development, and prospecting. We are asking people to take some time at the margins and work on prospecting, which is almost sure not to produce anything in the short term." He further noted the importance of rewards in buttressing the system: "You have to convince people that they will be compensated for work that does not produce revenues this year. Maybe you even have to penalize people if they bring in lots of revenue without building a business foundation."

More generally, Shearson Lehman Brothers' efforts to develop a formal call reporting system is an example of the tension created when tight systems are combined with loose structures, a tension this firm was explicitly trying to maintain. Managers there spoke of becoming systematic in an unsystematized way. Thus, on the one hand Peter Solomon, co-head of Investment Banking, claimed, "We have changed drastically from haphazard to systematic." He also admitted, "I don't know if it [the new system] will be successful, but if it's half as successful as Dawkins expects, it will be successful." Dawkins himself had great hopes for the system because of the need "to establish teams with clear responsibilities, to establish a system of monitoring, and to hold people accountable."

At the same time, Dawkins recognized that the system might not be viewed with favor by senior bankers, who did not "want to be part of a commercial bank." Nevertheless, he felt that at least "some realize that there is a threshold of discipline which is needed in order to bring the capabilities of the firm together." In order to be sensitive to both, "You have to run a system that is not systematized." His fellow managing director, France de St. Phalle, who was in charge of International Investment Banking and Capital Markets, echoed this view: "We ask for feedback from people. If they feel that they are being overly systematized or corporatized, they should let us know. We work hard to keep it as unsystematic as possible, but the reality is that the most successful firms are more organized and systematized." He felt that these firms resolved the tension inherent in attempting to be systematic in an unsystematic way by denying the control intended by the systems. "They simply dress it up and pretend that's not what it is."

Another system used by most of the firms was a report of deals lost to competitors, commonly termed "deals done away." These were, in effect, "noncall reports," or reports of the consequences of insufficient calling effort. Attention to deals done away obviously provides an incentive to stay in close touch with customers. Barry Friedberg, head of Investment Banking at Merrill Lynch, said, "I think that what we didn't do is as important as what we did," when explaining how his firm kept track of deals done away. Friedberg got a report of lost deals every two weeks and expected at least a note concerning what had happened from each banker affected. The other firms we talked to generally required investment bankers to explain in writing or verbally why their customer did the deal with another firm, and several spoke of the pressure of having others know that a deal had been lost.

The least acceptable reason for a deal done away is not knowing that the deal was under consideration. In describing the consequences of losing a deal, Allan Brumberger, a managing director at Drexel Burnham Lambert, noted, "Ignorance of the situation is the worst sin in this business." Almost as bad is knowing about the deal but losing it through ineptitude. Losing a deal is acceptable when a conscious decision is made not to pursue it, or if the firm that won the deal is perceived as having submitted a "suicidal" bid "below the market" in the hopes of being taken out by improving market conditions or to gain entrée to the customer. (Since firms accuse their competitors of bidding below the market more often than they admit doing so themselves, some of the accusations may be self-serving.)

Keeping track of deals done away reinforces the importance not only of the external ties but also of ties internal to the firm. Externally, the bankers involved with a customer are responsible for developing the tie and for protecting the firm's relationship from competitors. Doing so, however, requires information sharing and coordination among those assigned to the account.

At first glance it might seem odd that investment bankers, who pride themselves on their professionalism, customer service, and willingness to work hard—and who can be amply rewarded for it—need the same kind of control exercised over door-to-door encyclopedia salespeople. Given the loose linkage between value provided and revenue received, however, it is not so surprising. The long lag that often exists between calling activity and getting mandates for deals attenuates the link between effort and reward. Call reports are a stick to supplement the carrot of getting deals. Carl Eifler, a managing director at First Boston in charge of Mortgage Finance, explained the utility of call reports in these terms: "People do not perform at optimal levels based on internal motivation alone. You need cattle prods at the right time."

Customer Evaluations

Although call reports are a good measure of the *quantity* of calling activity, they do not measure the *quality* of the activity or the customers' perception of its value, which are obviously important for a service business such as investment banking. This information is obtained by asking customers to evaluate investment banks, and even the individuals within them. This is done predominantly through surveys conducted by third parties and, to a much lesser extent, through surveys conducted by the firms themselves.

A major source of information is the customer surveys conducted by Greenwich Associates. The firm conducts annual interviews of issuing and investing customers. Because of the extensive coverage of customers provided, their surveys function as a kind of public industry report card. Each investment bank that subscribes to the service obtains data on its own performance, as well as comparative data on its competitors. Managers can therefore evaluate their own firm's performance over time and confirm or revise their views about competing firms.

With regard to issuing customers, representatives of Greenwich Associates interview members of the financial staff at fifteen hundred companies about their contact with and use of investment banks. The resulting reports provide extensive information about the quality of each firm's calling effort. Each investment bank, for example, can compare its intensity of solicitation in a particular product area to that of its competitors. Measures are also generated on the quality of this effort, including the effectiveness of investment bank presentations. Such information is an important part of the control systems used by firm managers. It is helpful for managers to know when the solicitation effort and calling effectiveness of a unit within a firm, or even a particular person, is slipping vis-à-vis its competitors.

Respondents are also asked to indicate which firms they did business with in the past year and which firms they consider themselves to have important relationships with. Although the interview data on the allocation of investment banking business is not as useful for competitive analysis as data on actual deals done and revenues earned, the Greenwich surveys cover some products for which data are not normally available. Furthermore, as discussed in chapter 4, the existence of a relationship is based on the perception of the customer, not just the amount of business done. Thus, the Greenwich data are an important source of information about the existence and strength of a firm's relationships.

Data are reported for the total sample and by market segments defined in terms of size, industry, geographical location, and fees paid. In addition, special studies will be run for market segments specified by the firm. These reports can be used to measure how well a unit of the firm, or even an individual banker, is doing with a customer set. When the data are considered in the bonus determination process, they can be a powerful control.

Similar data are available for evaluating the firm's sales, trading, and research functions. Interviews are conducted with over five hundred institutional equity investors, eighteen hundred institutional buyers of fixed-income securities, and twelve hundred security analysts. An overall rating of the firm's equity sales force is provided and they are evaluated in fifteen different areas regarding quality and quantity of contact, such as the timeliness of information and suggestions, and their understanding of the customers' needs. Similar evaluations are provided for fixed-income salespeople, including data on how well the salesperson is perceived to work with the firm's traders. The surveys of equity and fixed-income investors are also used to evaluate firms' traders, by measuring such areas as market making and execution capabilities and quality of contact with customers. Finally, analysts are evaluated in such areas as knowledge of industries, quality of reports, and quality and quantity of customer contact.

In addition to the Greenwich survey of equity research analysts, *Institutional Investor* also conducts interviews to determine its "All America Research Team," which is reported annually in its October issue. Institutional investors are asked to rank all of the analysts in each industry according to four criteria: stock selection, earnings estimates, written reports, and overall service. The analyst with the highest rating in an industry is named to the first team, the one with the next highest to the second team, then the third team, and finally a runner-up group is picked.

The Greenwich and *Institutional Investor* surveys have been institutionalized and are an important part of the social fabric of the investment banking industry. Issuing and investing customers are sufficiently curious about the perceptions of their peers and trends in the industry that they are willing to respond to surveys—at least those conducted currently—in return for the results. In addition to its control uses, the data provide a very public statement about each firm's role as perceived and described by customers. Greenwich Associates, in particular, furnishes data that provide a description of the industry's structure and shape the perceptions of its members about the strengths and weaknesses of themselves and their competitors. When a firm's reputation as described by its competitors differs from that suggested by the Greenwich data, at least some of the variation is probably from the competitive use of reputation shaping discussed in chapter 5.

Some investment banks even find it useful to go beyond the institutionalized third-party survey data. They obtain information from customers on a more ad hoc basis, either directly or through outside market research firms. The data are used for both competitive analysis and as part of the system for controlling who has contact with the customers. Finally, many firms have annual account reviews, particularly with important issuing and investing customers, to discuss the state of the relationship, future opportunities, and areas needing improvement.

Cross-Evaluations

While call reports and customer evaluations monitor the external ties with customers, the quality and quantity of internal ties are monitored by asking people within the firm to evaluate one another. Although there was substantial variation among firms in their use of such cross-evaluation surveys, all of the larger firms interviewed asked people in one part of the firm to evaluate colleagues in another. On the investment banking side of the firm, for example, investment bankers with account responsibility are asked to evaluate product specialists with whom they work, and vice versa. Similarly, on the sales and trading side of the firm, cross-evaluations are conducted between salespeople, between salespeople and traders, and between equity salespeople and research analysts. The evaluations are used to monitor the linkages among people who should be working together within the firm and to signal the importance of internal ties.

Merrill Lynch had developed an especially comprehensive cross-evaluation system in investment banking. Relationship managers were asked to rate product specialists in eleven areas, including their understanding of the technical aspects of their product, the effectiveness of their presentations to clients, the extent to which they identified opportunities for product applications, the effectiveness of their execution, and their level of cooperation. Product specialists, in turn, evaluated relationship managers on complementary criteria. These included the extent to which the relationship managers had a strategy for each account, their understanding of the product, the level of communication with client team members, and their level of cooperation. Barry Friedberg, head of Investment Banking, found these cross-evaluations to be very helpful. He noted that he used them to identify problem areas, such as linkages between product specialists and bankers that needed to be more frequent or more effective.

An example of a cross-evaluation used for people who worked with the investor side of the market interface was the one between equity salespeople and research analysts used at Donaldson, Lufkin & Jenrette. Research analysts were asked to rate the overall quality of each salesperson on a scale from zero (0) ("no value whatsoever") to ten (10) ("perfect"). They were also asked to rate each salesperson on items such as product knowledge and contribution to helping analysts build relationships. Salespeople were asked to evaluate analysts in areas in which they particularly stood out, including quality of analysis, writing, marketing, communications with sales, and future potential.

The very act of filling out such surveys reinforces internal ties. In addition, managers use data from the cross-evaluation surveys to analyze how well the network structure is integrating the efforts of the various specialists. By looking at absolute and relative ratings, management can identify individuals who are perceived as particularly effective or ineffective by those with whom they work and identify those who have particularly positive or negative ties with others in the firm. Ties working well can be encouraged and less effective ties can be identified for correction. In some firms, the results of cross-evaluation surveys affect the size of bonuses, strengthening their role in the control system of the firm.

Financial Outcomes

Call reports, customer evaluations, and cross-evaluation surveys are important measures of the quality and to some extent the quantity of service provided to customers. They are an incomplete measure, however, of the performance of an investment bank. Measures of results are provided by data on deals won, revenues earned, and, to the extent possible, the profitability of deals and specific activities within the investment bank. The loose linkage between value provided and revenue received and the need to encourage internal cooperation have a major impact on the measures used by investment banks.

In their measurement of results, the investment banks we studied placed considerable emphasis on revenues generated. Many bankers described investment banking as a "revenue-driven business." During a period of increasing business, which it was at the time of our study, revenue generation is of more concern than controlling costs. In fact, the problem was sometimes one of increasing costs fast enough by getting the necessary personnel to process the available business. In addition, bonuses, which are a large share of compensation (itself one of the largest components of total costs), are considered to be at least partially variable and linked to revenues.

Some investment banks define their businesses partly by the way revenues are measured.[2] Measuring revenues by product group, for example, encourages members of the product group to consider their products as a business. Similarly, if revenues are reported by function, the various functions are considered to be businesses. Thus, senior managers can design the revenue measurement system to help shape the strategy of the firm.

Great care is taken, however, not to place too much emphasis on narrowly defined revenue measures. An emphasis on product revenues, for example, can discourage product specialists from helping out with customers to whom they are not assigned and who do not purchase much of their particular product. Bruce Koepfgen, head of Sales in Salomon Brothers' London office, solved this problem by emphasizing total product revenues for the office as a whole as well as total customer revenues: "Because people here have a product bent, we define their job for them to be maximizing the total amount of business done in their product area in the entire office, as well as their own accounts."

Attempts to measure revenues by departments or other units in a firm are complicated because many deals involve a number of departments. Nevertheless, none of the investment banks in our study went to any extraordinary effort to carefully allocate deal revenues to departments in proportion to their contribution. Peter Aranow, a managing director at Bear, Stearns, expressed the common attitude about revenue measurement when he said, "It isn't that formal in the counting of revenues." To attempt to do otherwise would ultimately be futile, given the high levels of interdependence created by the economic characteristics and production process of the industry.

The most common way of measuring each department's contribution to a deal was simply to let each one involved book the total revenues of the deal, what one investment banker referred to as "the magic of internal accounting," as was done at First Boston for the Union Carbide deals. Doing so sends a very clear signal about the importance of departments working together for the firm as a whole. Such double or even multiple counting vastly overstates the total revenues of the firm if departmental revenues are added up. The great virtue of the sum of the parts being greater than the whole is that it makes it more difficult for a single department to assess its relative contribution to the total performance of the firm as a percentage of total firm revenues. The only "real" revenue measure is the actual total for the firm as a whole.

If multiple counting is not used, then the revenues earned on a deal have to be split and allocated to the departments involved. This has obvious potential for conflict, since departments will be inclined to argue that they were not given a "fair" proportion of the deal's revenues. The greater the effort management and its bookkeepers exert to devise precise and pseudo-scientific fee-splitting algorithms, the more likely and the more vigorous the conflict will be. When a great deal of effort is expended in measurement, it is natural for the people affected to assume that it is taken seriously in deciding bonuses for individuals, resources for the business, and even its future existence. In fee splitting, as in transfer pricing and cost allocations, there are no right answers.[3]

Firms that practice fee splitting have recognized the futility of doing this with any scientific precision. Simple and arbitrary rules, such as evenly dividing the total revenues among the departments involved, instead of complicated fee-splitting algorithms, are generally used. For example, at First Boston fees on M&A deals done in the thrift industry were split fifty-fifty between the M&A Department and the Mortgage Finance Department. Consistency is more important than accuracy in evaluating trends in closely related businesses. Jay Higgins, head of Corporate Finance at Salomon Brothers accepted this, explaining, "I don't care about the revenue allocation system as long as it's consistent so you can see trends." If two businesses are not closely related, it may be worthwhile to try to split revenues more carefully to evaluate the businesses independently of each other. Thus more effort is typically made to obtain precision in splitting revenues and allocating costs between the institutional and retail sides of the firm than is done within the investment banking division.

Even when fee splitting is purposefully made arbitrary and inaccurate as a way of signaling the greater importance of collective over individual outcomes, it can affect behavior in negative ways. An M&A department that only gets half of the fees on the small deals typical in the thrift industry has little incentive to devote energy to this business when it faces other opportunities that yield a better return on the resources expended. In extreme cases a department will not help another department get a deal even when it is lucrative for everybody out of fear that contributing to strong performance in another department will redound in negative ways. For this reason, some firms, such as Merrill Lynch, that had formerly practiced fee splitting shifted to multiple counting of revenues.

Ray Minella, a managing director and head of High Yield Finance at Merrill Lynch, explained why Barry Friedberg, the head of Investment Banking, had made this switch: "Historically, different areas were antagonistic to each other, rather than cooperative. Friedberg abolished the idea that departments were profit centers. In the past, departments didn't want to split fees. Because there is now full credit to everybody, this removes disincentives for cooperation." Salomon Brothers practiced multiple counting for the same reasons. When asked about fee splitting Harold Tanner, cohead of Corporate Finance, stated, "I dread the day we go to allocations."

Ultimately it is the profitability of deals and businesses that count, not revenues. The economic characteristics of the investment banking business, however, make it difficult to measure the profitability of deals. The loose linkage between value contributed and revenues earned is one problem. There is little relationship between hours spent on marketing and production and revenues earned from these activities. An investment banker may spend a great deal of time calling on a customer and doing various things for the company before getting a deal of modest size. A true measure of the profitability of this deal would have to include these marketing expenses, some of which might have been incurred two or more years earlier. Even if an estimate from earlier call reports or time sheets were available, the fact that more than one deal is often discussed severely limits the accuracy of such data.

For the same reasons, limitations exist on the accuracy of measuring the production expenses of the many people who spend time working on a deal. Measuring these costs is further complicated because bonuses would have to be factored back in at the end of the year across all of an individual's marketing and production efforts on the many deals on which he worked. Finally, administrative and operations functions necessary for getting deals done would have to be allocated in order to achieve measures closer to net profits. The growing importance of these costs, and the notorious difficulty in allocating them in a way that is both economically sensible and perceived as fair, further constrains measures of deal profitability. Because of these difficulties, none of the firms in our study used call reports and time sheets to calculate labor costs, although a few were toying with the idea.

Interdependencies between deals also complicate efforts to measure a deal's profitability. Deals done at a low margin, or even a loss, in an effort to establish a relationship with a customer in order to get more lucrative business can be regarded as marketing expenses in the same way that calling activity is. Similarly, origination business in investment banking may be undertaken at least partly to generate securities on which trading profits can be earned.

The difficulties that appear in measuring marketing, production, administrative, and operations costs also appear in measuring customer profitability. Aggregating deal data for a customer, particularly if the customer does a number of deals, helps solve the loose linkage between value and reward that exists for individual deals. There are still substantial cost allocation problems, however, and the problem of interdependencies between primary and secondary market activity. In theory, customer profitability should include profits earned on the secondary trading of its debt and equity paper. Although investment banks had some sense of which types of customers were profitable, or at least desirable, only a small number made a serious attempt to measure customer profitability, and this was usually to put customers in profit categories.

More firms attempted to measure product profitability, and we noticed an increased interest toward the end of our study in measuring the profitability of broad product groups, such as debt, equity, junk bonds, mortgages, and municipals. When the product area has dedicated specialists located in investment banking, sales, trading, administration, and even operations, as some of these products often do, it is easier to measure costs. The greater the extent to which a product depends on shared resources, the more cost allocations are involved, and these, despite the heroic efforts of accountants, will always remain somewhat arbitrary.[4]

Product proliferation and the increasing capital and costs required to be in the various investment banking businesses have stimulated interest in profitability measures in order to make resource allocation and entry and exit decisions. In the fall of 1987, for example, Salomon Brothers, Shearson Lehman Brothers, Kidder, Peabody, and others announced decisions to exit or scale down their municipal finance business. Of course, since product profitability measures still do not take precise account of product inter-dependencies, care must be taken when making these decisions to minimize ripple effects on other product lines. Critics of Salomon Brothers' decision to get out of the money-market business cited this as one of the reasons for their concern.

Like revenue measures, measures of product profitability across primary and secondary activities point to the businesses the firm considers itself to be in. The very act of measuring the profitability of a set of activities indicates that the activities constitute a business. This is as true for measures of market segment profitability, such as business done out of regional or foreign offices, as it is for product profitability. Such business definitions are reinforced when these activities form a relatively distinct unit in the network structure; that is, ties within the unit are stronger than ties connecting it with other units.

Because of the difficulty of measuring profitability, firms place a great deal of emphasis on measuring market share. The greater a firm's market share in debt underwriting, for example, the more extensive its contacts with issuers and investors and the more information it has on the market. This improves the firm's ability to price deals and lowers the risk of loss. Thus, since market share and profitability are believed to be highly correlated for a number of products, market share is used as a proxy for profitability. Market share measures for investment banking activities are based on data collected by Securities Data Company and IDD Information Services.[5] Market share measures for equity trading by investors are made available by McLagan Partners.[6]

Since profitability measures are difficult to generate, the relationship between market share and profitability is not well understood and no doubt varies according to product. Thus it is not surprising that the relative emphasis firms placed on market share was highly correlated with the share they had. The largest firms regarded it as extremely important, but did not always feel that more was better. For example, Jay Higgins at Salomon Brothers said, "After you're number one, how much ahead of number two you are comes at some cost to the P&L." Second-tier firms opined that although it was not always necessary to be in the top five, there were advantages to being in the top ten. Niche firms, with highly focused strategies, tended to regard market share as unimportant. John Birkelund, the president of Dillon, Read, said that his firm consciously did not worry about market share: "You will never hear the word *market share* in this firm.

The term is nonoperative." Similar sentiments were expressed at Lazard Frères, although they also spoke with pride about their dominant market share in certain niche businesses.

Despite the uncertainty about the relationship between market share and profitability, the former is a useful way for measuring performance, since it takes market conditions into account. Given the difficulty of forecasting a firm's volume of activity, measures of market share are more useful than comparisons of actual volume to planned performance. A firm that experiences an increase in revenues beyond its expectations will still lose market share if the industry grew at an even faster rate.

The Gaming of Systems

There is always the risk that systems designed to direct people to achieve specified ends will become ends in themselves.[7] People can become more concerned about affecting the measures reported than about accomplishing the ends that the systems attempt to measure. During our study, ways of manipulating the measures produced by call reports, customer evaluations, cross–evaluation surveys, and financial data were described to us. We have no way of knowing how much gaming behavior takes place, but there must be some because of the imperfections inherent in all systems.

Information on call reports may be inaccurate or exaggerated; call reports can even be fabricated. Some of the investment bankers we interviewed admitted indulging in the practice. Controlling this can be difficult if the manager who receives the report does not have much contact with the person in the customer organization listed in the report. Cross–evaluation surveys are also vulnerable to manipulation. Product specialists, for example, may pay particular attention to investment bankers thought to be influential.

Similarly, customer surveys used to obtain evaluations of investment banks can be influenced. Surveys conducted by Greenwich Associates take place on an annual basis so that a banker who knows the approximate timing of the survey can make a special effort to intensify his client interaction right before this period. In addition, bankers believed that the *Institutional Investor* research analyst rankings were easily managed. Jim Freeman, head of Equity Sales, Trading, and Research at First Boston, believed that he had developed a system that, if followed properly, would enable an analyst to get on one of the teams within three years. "We know exactly what to do from day one to day one thousand," he asserted. John Hoffman, manager of Equity Research at Smith Barney, Harris Upham, also felt that this poll was conducted in a fashion that made it subject to "game playing" by participants and that results "should be taken with a grain of salt." Of course, senior managers may be aware of these difficulties with customer surveys and not be particularly concerned. After all, the gaming methods require customer contact, which is one of the objectives of using these measures.

Finally, measures of financial outcomes are also subject to manipulation. Since any internal accounting system requires discretion in how and when revenues are booked, how costs are allocated, how transfer prices are set, and how fees are split, there are obvious opportunities to influence measures in the desired direction, particularly by those who have the most power to do so. Even the data in the SDC and IDD databases, which become the basis for league table rankings, are subject to the influence of investment banks. Because vendors rely on these firms to help ensure the accuracy and completeness of their databases, opportunities exist to improve one's standing in the battle for a high league table ranking through the timing and classification of reported deals.

Because systems are designed and imposed by top management in order to help give them control over the self-designing organization, people subject to the systems may wish to lessen this control by manipulating them. Senior managers we interviewed responded to this phenomenon in three different ways. In some cases they ignored it because the manipulation was minimal. Another response was to create redundancies in the measurement of certain performance indicators. When more than one system is used, such as call reports combined with customer and cross-evaluation surveys, gaming can often be identified through discrepancies. Finally, senior managers were ambiguous about the ways in which system measures were used and the relative importance placed on them in evaluating an individual's performance when bonuses were determined. Thus the bonus determination process compensates for some of the problems inherent in the management control systems.

8

THE BONUS DETERMINATION PROCESS

The process used to determine bonuses is directly related to the self-designing organizational structure and management control systems used by investment banks. The systems compensate for some of the weaknesses of self-designing organizations; for example, cross-evaluations encourage internal cooperation that might otherwise be ignored as people pursue their own self-interest. Yet even with the complementary role systems play with respect to structure, problems remain. People may ignore activities and outcomes that are *not* measured by systems. Even when outcomes are measured, as revenues are, people may pay too much attention to them. Because revenues measure current performance, there is a natural temptation to sacrifice activities that contribute to the long-term profit-generating potential of the firm if they are not likely to lead to revenues in the near term. This is exacerbated by the very short-term orientation of investment bankers that results from the brief windows of market opportunity in which they operate and the large uncertainty about future market conditions. Thus concentration on revenue generation may discourage other activities that contribute to the good of the firm, such as recruiting, training, internal management, and calling on customers with whom the firm has only the weakest of ties.

Just as systems are used to compensate for problems created by self-designing organizations, investment banks have established methods for determining bonuses that deal with problems created by systems. (We focus here on bonuses rather than salary, since bonuses are often quite large and typically more variable and therefore more important in terms of signals sent to the organization.) Top management addresses the problem of too much concentration on individual performance by basing bonuses on aggregate performance measures rather than on the performance of individual units in the firm. In larger firms, for example, the bonus pool for the investment banking division is based partly on the performance of this large segment of the firm and partly on the firm's overall performance.

To address the short-term orientation problem, senior managers use subjective judgment in determining how funds from aggregate bonus pools should be allocated to individuals. Furthermore, they take into consideration a great deal of quantitative and qualitative information beyond revenue measures. This is obtained from other systems (e.g., call reports, customer evaluations, and cross-evaluation surveys) and from conversations with people throughout the firm.

Once a person's overall performance has been evaluated, two factors are taken into account in deciding upon the actual figure of his or her bonus. The first is the level of bonuses being paid by other firms—what would this individual be paid by competitors? To pay below someone's market value is to risk losing the employee to another firm. The second is internal equity or fairness—are bonuses fair relative to one another? Although employees may or may not know one another's bonuses, relative rewards are as important to people as their absolute value and top management must be prepared to explain differences.[1] Responding to both external and internal pressures is a balancing act that is made even more difficult by the fact that overall compensation levels vary across the different specialties within the firm.

The bonus determination process acts as an integrating device that reinforces the industry's emphasis on flat, flexible, and complex network structures, since it encourages people to take a total organization perspective by forming ties with others in the organization as needed. Since bonus pools are established for a group of units, individuals have an incentive to make this aggregate pool as great as possible rather than focusing strictly on their own unit's performance. Utilizing a wide array of measures along with substantial subjective judgment is another incentive for individuals to focus on the total needs of the organization. In addition, investment banks exercise substantial subjectivity in determining the size of the bonus pool in the first place, which also encourages people to broaden their focus beyond measures of financial outcomes. This is in direct contrast to formula-determined bonus pools, which are based on various quantitative measures. The power of bonuses to act as integrating devices is especially great when their average size and variability are large, as was true at the time of our study.

This power also gives the bonus determination process an important role in defining the strategy of the firm. By grouping a set of activities into its own bonus pool, top management uses the bonus process to help define the businesses of the firm. For example, if all fixed-income trading is a bonus pool, then fixed-income trading is a business. If separate bonus pools are established for governments, corporates, municipals, and so on, then fixed-income trading comprises a number of businesses. Similarly, high-yield bond trading can be made part of the high-yield business when it is part of a bonus pool that includes the high-yield finance, sales, and research functions. Alternatively, it can be part of the corporate bond business if a bonus pool is established for all investment- and noninvestment-grade corporate bonds.

When bonus pools are set up to cover the same organizational units that the revenue and other systems measure, strong ties are reinforced and it is clear how businesses are defined. Greater flexibility and, necessarily, greater ambiguity about business definition exist when the system measures encourage a pattern of structural ties that is not isomorphic to the pattern encouraged by the bonus pools. The greatest flexibility exists when there is one giant bonus pool for the entire firm, so that investment banking and sales and trading are all paid out of the same pool. Several investment bankers we talked to called this the ideal situation given the interdependencies among businesses, but they also felt that it was impractical given the large numbers of people involved, especially in the big firms, and what were described as "cultural differences" between investment banking and sales and trading.

Investment Banking

All of the firms in our study paid bonuses in the investment banking division out of a bonus pool calculated for the division as a whole, rather than for individual departments within it, or were rapidly moving in this direction. This was even true for firms such as Salomon Brothers, Shearson Lehman Brothers, Merrill Lynch, and, in a more complicated fashion, First Boston and Credit Suisse First Boston, which established a global investment banking pool. Nevertheless, a number of them, as noted in chapter 5, mentioned that they were distinctive in this practice and that their competitors paid bonuses out of departmental pools. Whether mentioned out of a true misconception or not, these comments indicated to us the competitive importance of aggregate bonus pools.

The importance of an aggregate bonus pool was felt keenly by those firms that had used departmental pools in the past. Barry Friedberg, head of Investment Banking at Merrill Lynch, explained why he had implemented this practice upon becoming head of the division: "The central thing that binds people together or blows them apart is the compensation structure. In years prior to Kenney's management of Investment Banking, we had separate bonus pools in the division. Now we have one."

Bear, Stearns, Donaldson, Lufkin & Jenrette, Dean Witter, L.F. Rothschild, and Prudential-Bache Securities had also moved from multiple bonus pools within investment banking to one. Bill Benedetto of Dean Witter recalled that when he first came to the firm there were sixty people in Corporate Finance and "each banker was like his own profit center. It was a disaster." He changed this by creating a common bonus pool and eliminating fee splitting. Similarly, Donaldson, Lufkin & Jenrette had switched from separate bonus pools to a combined one because, according to a managing director, "there wasn't enough teamwork."

At the time of our interviews, Prudential-Bache Securities, which had retained an emphasis on allocating fees to relevant departments, had partially moved toward a common bonus pool, with 50 percent of the pool based on combined results and the other 50 percent based on individual "pot" or departmental results. This was viewed as a transitional step to a combined bonus pool, but was already having the desired effect. According to Leland Paton, managing director and head of Capital Markets, "We are in the middle of the compensation procedure now and none of my managers has mentioned individual pots. In effect, pots are gone from the mentality. This is terrific."

No simple formulas are used in determining the size of the investment banking bonus pool. In making this decision top management looks at total earnings, makes an estimate about what other firms will be paying out (adjusted for size), and considers how much of earnings should be retained for the capital base of the firm. In some firms a first cut at this pool was taken by having the departments submit estimates of how much they thought they would need to pay out in bonuses. Other firms did not ask for estimates, including some that used to but found that they always vastly exceeded top management's expectations and were therefore not a good starting point.

Procedures used to determine an individual's bonus were similar among firms. The typical procedure begins with a memorandum submitted by the person describing his or her contributions to the firm over the past year. This was called a "puff sheet" at Merrill Lynch and a "brag sheet" at several other firms. Consistent with multiple counting, people tend to include revenues from deals in which they were only tangentially involved or where the work for the client was done in the past and its connection to current deals is tenuous at best. Bill Mayer, a member of the four-man Executive Committee at First Boston, referred to this as "touch revenue," since anyone who "touches" a deal takes revenue credit for it. This memorandum also includes other contributions such as recruiting, training, and marketing efforts to new clients.

Data from the reports are combined with data from call reports, customer evaluations, cross-evaluation surveys, and various financial measures. In evaluating contributions to revenues, adjustments are made for how much a banker had actually "touched" a deal and for the fact that earning revenues from "house accounts" is less difficult than from new accounts. The senior managers involved in the bonus determination process also have direct discussions with a number of people in order to better ascertain who contributed what to various deals. This information is gathered throughout the year, particularly on the big deals, as was the case at First Boston for the Union Carbide deal, in which Mayer had substantial oversight.

Based on all this information, top management differentiates performance in some way, such as by rank ordering bankers at various levels (associate, vice president, managing director) or by putting them in performance categories such as superior, very good, good, and fair. It then estimates what competitors will be paying for specialists at different levels according to performance.

There are two ways in which these market prices are obtained. One is conversations between people at different firms to get a feel for what each other is expecting to pay. Recruiting discussions are an especially useful way of getting such information. Bill Mayer of First Boston explained, "Over the year you get a good feel for what other firms are doing. It's still the kind of business where there aren't that many secrets."

The second major source of information is salary survey data from McLagan Partners. This vendor supplies data on salaries and bonuses by level and function to all firms that contribute their own compensation data to the survey. Although these data are for the past year, they are a useful starting point in enabling firms to see how they stand vis-à-vis their competitors. These data also serve as a baseline for the current year and are supplemented by discussions with McLagan employees, who indicate the ranges competitors are thinking of paying. Thus, McLagan is used by investment banks as a mechanism for signaling to each other the appropriate compensation levels in an effort to keep any one firm from gaining competitive advantage at the expense of others.

The central role played by McLagan was the source of some controversy. Since no firm wants to be known as paying below the median for comparable people, a number of investment bankers we interviewed felt that the McLagan data were an important factor in the rapid escalation in compensation the industry had experienced over the past three or four years. Peter Buchanan, the CEO at First Boston, said, "McLagan is a real problem and is causing us to ratchet up salaries. It is particularly bad in the lower ranks. Nobody wants to be rated number one in pay, but nobody wants to be below the market either." His colleague Alvin Shoemaker, who was chairman, agreed: "What this has done is drive firms way beyond what they should have done. Our mistakes become the baseline for someone else. Excesses all around become the median." But fellow Executive Committee member Mayer noted that there was also a tendency to "shoot the messenger." He commented, "We are all our own worst enemies. Nobody is willing to bite the bullet and say 'enough.'" Shoemaker thought this might come: "When the crunch comes a lot of the survey stuff goes down the tubes."

Despite the controversy, the McLagan data are an important source of information on market prices. Armed with these and other data, top management then decides on individual bonuses. This is a complex and time-consuming process, which was described by many senior managers as one of the most important things they did. For example, when asked to describe it, Buchanan asked, "Have you got a couple of months?" He went on to say that "it is an agonizing process that takes a huge amount of management time." His counterpart at Drexel, Fred Joseph, described it as "a major pain in the neck," although he recognized its central importance.

There are four reasons why the bonus determination process is so important and why it deserves a great deal of time and energy. One obvious reason is the potential size of the bonuses. The years of our study, 1985 and 1986, were very good years indeed for the investment banking industry. In 1986, entry-level associates were being paid $70,000 and more with guaranteed bonuses of $20,000 to $50,000. Thirty-year-old fourth and fifth year associates had the potential to earn bonuses of several hundred thousand dollars. Vice presidents could earn middle six-figure bonuses, and a number of managing directors, who in most firms had salaries between $100,000 and $150,000 per year, were receiving over $1,000,000 in bonus compensation. When this kind of money is involved, determining bonuses deserves a substantial amount of top management time and attention.

The potentially large size of these bonuses provides a strong incentive for people to identify new business opportunities. This reinforces a grass-roots strategy formulation process. Investment bankers who are willing to take the personal career and financial risks involved in pursuing a new business are amply rewarded if they are successful. In economists' terms, these people share substantially in the rents (high profits) earned in the new business before competition drives margins down.

The second reason is the substantial variation that exists in large bonuses. For individuals at the same level in the same specialty, the highest performers can earn five to ten times the bonus paid to the lower performers who still rate a bonus. High performers at one level can also receive substantially larger bonuses than even medium performers at more senior levels. Thus hierarchical position does not determine compensation. At some firms the link was actually reversed somewhat in that a high bonus for someone might trigger a review for a vice president title.

The high degree of variation makes internal equity considerations particularly important. In a professional service firm where outstanding contributors can make a big difference, it is important to reward them accordingly. These people not only want to receive large amounts but also want their greater relative contribution to be recognized in proportionately larger bonuses. Several top managers described to us conversations they had with employees, especially with managing directors, who wanted to know how their bonuses compared to those of others. And given that network structures are extremely efficient information-processing devices, it is reasonable to assume that they do a relatively efficient job of communicating information on bonuses throughout the firm. Even when such conversations are not expected to take place, great care needs to be taken when differences in performance evaluation result in big differences in bonuses.

Maintaining a sense of internal equity is particularly difficult when the firm employs a large number of specialists who have different market compensation levels. In order to maintain a sense of fairness, which is essential to cooperation across departments, an effort needs to be made to ensure that comparable individuals in different departments are paid comparable amounts. This approach can lead to underpaying one specialist, at the risk of losing him or her, or overpaying another, which exacerbates the problem of escalating compensation levels in the industry. But if the firm responds only to market prices, the quality of internal teamwork suffers and management risks an imbalance in the internal supply and demand for specialists. For example, at the time of our study, the M&A department and capital markets desk paid especially well. But other departments have to be staffed as well to meet current needs and be ready for shifts in the key specialties of the future. Getting the right balance between internal and external definitions of equity takes a substantial amount of time.

The third, and a more subtle, reason for spending a substantial amount of time on the bonus determination process, and for making sure that people know what a large commitment top management has to it, is to shape the perceptions people being evaluated have of this process. Because the stakes are so high, the reputation of the process will be enhanced if it is judged to be carefully done. One way of accomplishing this is to allocate a great deal of the precious resource of top management time to it. Barry Friedberg, head of Investment Banking at Merrill Lynch, felt that the firm's bankers "derived some comfort over my involvement in the details given that it's a very subjective process that affects compensation a lot."

When the time and data included in this process are known by those being evaluated, the importance of contributions to the firm beyond revenues narrowly defined can be reinforced. It does not take much time to determine bonuses calculated through a straightforward formula based on a few simple measures of financial performance. It takes a great deal of time when substantial judgment must be exercised in weighing all of the qualitative and quantitative indicators of performance. Although top management can never eliminate the suspicion that individual revenues are the dominating factor in determining bonuses, a time-consuming process involving many different kinds of data at least creates some ambiguities about their relative importance. Furthermore, some ambiguity in just how bonuses are determined reduces the possibilities for gaming behavior.

The fourth reason for spending a substantial amount of time on deciding bonuses is that this is a good opportunity for top management to learn about the people in the firm and how well they are working together. Particularly in the largest firms, it is difficult for top management to keep abreast of all employees, especially the more junior ones on whom the firm depends for its future, and to keep in touch with what is going on in the self-designing organization.

Trading and Sales

Given the ease with which the profitability of an individual trader can be measured each day, it is especially significant that all the firms we studied paid traders subjectively determined bonuses based on an aggregate bonus pool, such as all government securities or corporate bonds. Although the bonus determination process is not quite as elaborate as that in investment banking, data from customer evaluations, cross-evaluation surveys, and financial measures of performance are used in evaluating each trader's contribution to the firm for the past year. Both internal equity considerations and market prices from McLagan and informal conversations with competitors are taken into account when translating performance evaluations into bonus figures.

The reasons for using aggregate bonus pools and subjectively determined bonuses are similar to those in investment banking. In addition, because the markets in which traders trade are so interdependent, and because a number of traders are involved in executing trades for each investing customer, cooperation among them is important. They must be willing to share information with one another so that traders in one market can respond to the changes in other markets. Furthermore, a trader who optimizes his or her own profits by taking advantage of a customer can interfere with the ability of other traders to do business with it.

Deemphasizing individual trader profitability is also important for control purposes. Because the opportunities to make and lose a lot of money in trading are significant, it is important to achieve the right amount of risk taking. Bonuses based solely on profitability might well encourage a trader to take excessive risks in order to have a "good year." Trading limits and other risk control measures are also used to contain this possibility, but with sufficient profit incentive there will be attempts to game the system, which may have happened at Merrill Lynch where one trader was responsible for losses of at least $150 million.[2]

In contrast to the trading function, compensation practices in the sales function were more varied among firms. There are two basic approaches. The first, and traditionally most common, is to pay individual salespeople on a strict commission basis, which creates a direct relationship between the revenues they bring in and how much they make. The second approach is the salary-plus-bonus practice found in investment banking and trading. At the time of our study a number of firms were moving to the second approach. The movement was taking place for the same reasons that subjectively determined bonuses based on aggregate pools were used in the other two functions.

Firms that use the commission approach to compensation cited its incentive benefits; it is supposed to motivate individuals to work hard, since the harder they work the more they earn. Robert Dewey, head of Institutional Equity at Donaldson, Lufkin & Jenrette, expressed this view when he said, "I'm a firm believer that the closer the carrot is to the guy's nose, the faster he runs." This method of compensation is also simple, easy to apply, takes less top management time, and is usually perceived as fair. Although some complain about the quality of the accounts to which they have been assigned, this compensation practice is consistent with the common ideology found in the sales function: compensation is limited only by a person's ability and willingness to work hard, since he or she depends neither on the efforts of others nor on subjective evaluations made by higher-level managers.[3]

Commissions vary by product, which is common in fixed-income sales, and by account, which is common in equity sales. Higher commissions are associated with products that are harder to sell or that top management wants to emphasize. On the equity side, commission pay-outs are lower for capital-intensive accounts, which involve greater risk to the firm and where the relationship is primarily an institutional rather than an individual one, than for less capital-intensive accounts, where an individual salesperson can make a bigger difference in the amount of business the customer does with the firm. At Smith Barney, for example, accounts were classified according to capital intensity. Commission pay-outs were then adjusted to reflect this commitment and service requirements from other areas of the firm, such as research.

There are some obvious limitations in the strict commission approach to compensation. Because it is explicit about what is rewarded, it is also explicit about what is not rewarded. Activities that contribute to the revenues of others, or are important to the long-term competitiveness of the firm, such as recruiting and training, are likely to be ignored, since they do not contribute to an individual's own revenues.

A salary-plus-bonus approach to compensation encourages an emphasis on firmwide performance over the long term rather than individual performance over the short term. Jim Massey, head of Sales at Salomon Brothers, cited this reason in explaining why his firm used this approach: "We do not pay any salesman on a commission basis. Instead, we use a subjective and fluid management evaluation process. This is based on a philosophy of evaluating someone's contribution to the whole. If you pay on commission, you can't pay for management, recruiting, training, and ideas used by others." As with investment banking and trading, performance is evaluated using a variety of data, and bonuses take into account the need to balance internal equity with prices in external labor markets.

As the number of product specialists calling on an account increases, the complexity of a strict commission system increases. In order to encourage cooperative behavior and a willingness to make product sacrifices for the good of the overall relationship, complicated commission splitting and sharing arrangements need to be developed. This eliminates one of the virtues of the commission approach—its simplicity. It can also lead to disputes about the accuracy and fairness of the conventions, which occurs with attempts to be overly precise about transfer prices, cost allocations, or fee splits. These problems are eliminated by shifting to a salary-plus-bonus approach.

Another weakness of paying on commission is that salespeople may reduce the amount of contact they have with customers when there is little business to be obtained. This inhibits the development of a relationship. For this reason Carol Einiger, head of Capital Markets at First Boston, paid the Corporate Coverage sales force (which called on issuers that invest excess cash in short-term instruments) on a salary-plus-bonus basis "in order to provide an incentive to develop a relationship and provide continuity." She worried that if she paid commissions, since "cash positions come and go," salespeople would go to where they could earn a commission even though this sacrificed existing relationships. This would negatively affect the other members of the client team who represented the liability side of the balance sheet, since this source of information would no longer be available.

Finally, a strict commission approach, although seemingly precise, can be a cumbersome way to control the relative emphasis salespeople place on various products and customers. Differences in commissions are a clear signal about what top management regards as desirable differences in emphasis. But if the desired differences change over time, making the corresponding changes in commissions can become a complex exercise, particularly if there are a large number of product or customer categories. Making these changes takes time and energy, and uses up time and energy of the sales force, which is already prone to spending time calculating bonuses and looking for ways to manipulate measures in a way favorable to compensation.

The limitations of the commission approach were the cause of what appeared to be a fairly general trend to move to a salary plus bonus.[4] One example was Kidder, Peabody, which had used a strict commission system until three years ago. According to Max Chapman, then head of Fixed-Income Sales and Trading, his firm was in the process of "trying to change to a more subjective basis." During 1987, 60 percent of scheduled commissions were paid out directly to the fixed-income salespeople, with the other 40 percent of commissions going into a pool, which was later divided up into bonuses for salespeople as determined by a number of subjective criteria. Chapman felt that this approach had an additional benefit. He expressed the concern that, under a strict commission approach, a salesperson's efforts might diminish once he or she had achieved the desired level of income. Chapman explained, "Financial incentives alone are not enough, since a guy can have a good month and then relax. We need other ways to 'incent' them." Under the salary-plus-bonus approach, salespeople would be less able to gauge their effort to income, which would reduce any tendency to slack off.

For similar reasons Goldman, Sachs was also moving in the direction of a salary-plus-bonus approach for its fixed-income sales force. The vice chairman and chief operating officer, Steve Friedman, noted that in the past "we used to have close to a commission system, which almost gave everybody their own franchise based on the accounts to which they were assigned." When he took over the division, he found that it was "in the middle of a revolution" to encourage more teamwork and contributions that "are not quantitatively measurable." In late 1987, 50 percent of compensation for fixed-income sales was subjectively determined.

Research

Research analysts receive a salary plus bonus that is determined by a subjective evaluation of their overall contribution, similar to the approach used in investment banking and other parts of the firm receiving a salary plus bonus. (Historically, the term *research* meant equity research. Fixed-income research was relatively insignificant. Its importance has grown tremendously, although in most firms expenditures are still much greater for equity research.)[5] One difference with the research function, however, is that unlike other functions, it is not considered a revenue generator. In all of the firms we studied, research was regarded as a cost that contributed to the ability of sales and trading to generate revenues from investing customers. Money for its bonus pool was contributed by the revenue-generating functions it supported. At Dean Witter, for example, the costs of research were allocated as follows: 45 percent to institutional equity sales and trading, 40 percent to retail distribution, 8 percent to international, and 7 percent to corporate finance.

The funding of the research bonus pool by other functions is an important integrating device that reinforces the service nature of the research function. Analysts want to be responsive to the needs of the functions that pay for their bonuses. This facilitates the formation of ties.

As with all integrating roles, a certain amount of tension and conflict is involved. In the case of research this is because it has two sets of internal clients, investment banking and sales and trading, which represent the two sides of the market interface. The primary role of research is to furnish information on companies, industries, and the overall economy to investors. This information is given to investing customers and is intended to lead to revenues from transactions with them. The loose linkage between value provided and revenues earned makes it difficult to assess the contribution of each analyst, although customers do indicate what percentage of their soft dollar payments are allocated for research-versus-trading capabilities.

The primary performance measure of research is the investing customer evaluations. In a good evaluation, the customer must perceive the analyst as providing objective advice. In a poor evaluation, the customer might feel that the analyst was unduly positive or negative about an issuing customer. Pressures to be unduly positive can come from investment banking if it feels that a "hold" or "sell" recommendation by the analyst will hurt the firm's relationship with the customer, for example, if the company is considering an issue of equity. (Once a debt or equity issue is announced, however, research reports are suspended to prevent any conflict of interest.)

Conflicting pressures on research analysts also arise out of their access to issuers when they try to serve both the investment banking and sales and trading sides of their firm. In acting as a distribution channel for information on issuers to investors, analysts build relationships with issuing customers and often develop access to high-level executives. Information resulting from these relationships, plus their general knowledge of the industry, can lead to suggested deals for the analyst's investment bank. A number of firms encouraged this by paying transaction-based bonuses to analysts for bringing in deals. The amount of money involved can be large; in 1985, one research analyst at Donaldson, Lufkin & Jenrette earned more than $500,000 in incentive fees. Other firms reported bonuses in the five- to six-figure range.

An analyst who has the opportunity to earn a substantial amount of money by helping his firm get an equity underwriting or an M&A deal with a customer may be less inclined to make "hold" or "sell" recommendations on this company's stock.[6] A more subtle form of conflict emerges when an analyst spends so much time pursuing deals that he or she is not following other assigned companies and providing information to investors to the extent expected. This is exacerbated by the clear relationship between bringing in a deal and receiving a bonus calculated as a percentage of the fees earned on the deal, which is the common practice, and the unclear relationship between serving sales and trading through good research and customer support and the year-end bonus earned for this activity.

The practice of paying analysts deal-based bonuses was more prevalent in the medium-sized firms, which did not have the same strong client relationships, than it was in the larger firms. Thus, Dean Witter, Donaldson, Lufkin & Jenrette, and Smith Barney, Harris Upham paid them, but First Boston and Merrill Lynch did not. John Hoffman, head of Equity Research at Smith Barney, noted that "Research has been an important historical strength of Smith Barney," and since the early 1960s the department has made a special effort to "coordinate tightly with Corporate Finance." He reported, "We tell our senior analysts to keep their ears open and alert to new business opportunities."

Similarly, John Chalsty, who became CEO of Donaldson, Lufkin & Jenrette, explained, "I've always thought that the analyst should be the best source of transactions. He knows the industry, its direction, and who can benefit." He also acknowledged the need to avoid conflicts of interest, as did the head of Research, Frank LeCates. LeCates also noted that not all analysts were interested in being involved in deals even when there was no conflict of interest: "There's something oddly conservative about some research analysts. They're worried that deals might affect their research franchises; but, in some cases, that is just a rationalization for avoiding the inherent risk of making rapid decisions under uncertainty."

For those analysts who do like being involved in deals, a variety of structural devices are used to reinforce the incentive created by deal-based bonuses. The most common one is to define industry specialties in investment banking that match up with identically defined specialties in research. This was done at Donaldson, Lufkin & Jenrette, for example, where Sabin Streeter, a retailing specialist in investment banking, emphasized the importance of the retailing research analyst, Stu Robbins (on the *Institutional Investor's* second team in 1986), in bringing in deals. "We pay people a lot of dollars for generating and participating in deals," Streeter said.

The matching of investment banking and research industry specialists was felt to have improved the ability of research to generate M&A ideas. Some years ago a liaison person from research had been assigned the responsibility of sifting the good ideas from the bad ones submitted by research analysts, since according to Tony James, the head of M&A, "90 percent of the ideas were crummy." Replacing the liaison role with direct contact between bankers and analysts had improved things, so that James estimated that research was now involved in some fashion in 30 percent of the M&A deals. LeCates explained why this change had been successful: "The real way to get research and banking together is to align them to be strong in the same areas, to choose people who are interested in banking, and to be sure analysts have financial incentives to help bankers. We don't want people communicating through a bureaucracy. If every analyst has only one or two bankers to talk to, communication will take place."

Shaping Strategy through Bonuses

Bonus pools are a way of shaping the firm's strategy because they define the businesses in which the firm competes. When research is subdivided into industry specialists that match the industry specialization in investment banking, and analysts earn deal-based bonuses for bringing in issuer deals, the research function evolves from a common support function to closer to a revenue-generating function. The most complete definition of a separate business, whether defined by product or by market, exists when the sales and trading functions are added as well, and all functions together form one bonus pool.

One of the most common examples among the firms studied was the municipal business. A group of activities that share a bonus pool constitute the functional resources for competing in a business. This can occur when the activities are structurally self-contained, with strong ties among themselves and weak ties with other parts of the firm, as is common with municipals. It can also occur when the various functional activities retain strong ties with functional counterparts, which is often the case with mortgage-backed securities where the traders and salespeople are part of the overall fixed-income trading and sales functions.

Bonus pools are an important integrating device, as in the case when the origination and secondary-market activities for a particular product or market segment are combined. Those who deal with one side of the market interface will be willing to make sacrifices that increase overall profitability because of benefits obtained from the other side. This may require a greater emphasis on interfunctional as opposed to intrafunctional coordination. Given the so-called cultural barriers between investment banking and sales and trading, intrafunctional coordination does not always happen as easily as required. Even though these cultural barriers have been coming down, placing functional specialists in a common bonus pool with different functional specialists is a clear signal about the importance of interfunctional coordination.

Placement in a particular bonus pool can have a negative effect, for example, when it inhibits coordination with others outside the common pool. The ties that facilitate this coordination always exist to some extent, and can dramatically increase in importance with a change in external markets or the introduction of new products. When people receive no financial rewards for maintaining these ties, there is always the danger that they will receive too little attention while ties known to contribute to bonuses will receive too much. One solution is to have businesses contribute to the bonus pools of one another based upon an assessment of the value of inter-business cooperation, and to allocate these contributions to the people making them. Although this solution is conceptually sound, in practice it is nearly impossible to implement because of the measurement difficulties of assessing the degree of cooperation and putting a dollar figure on its value.

The alternative is to simply have one giant bonus pool for the firm as a whole. Given what one person referred to as "the seamless web" of activities in the industry, this option was viewed as the ideal solution by a number of top managers we talked to for preventing local suboptimization. Salomon Brothers had recently taken a step in this direction by establishing a joint compensation committee for investment banking, sales, and trading. Prior to that, each side of the firm had been given a pool and had made allocation decisions without input from the other side.

The larger the firm, the more difficult it is for top management to be directly involved in determining the bonus for every single person. Even when the objective is to determine bonuses based on an assessment of a person's contribution to the firm as a whole, the collection of data for evaluation must be done by a less senior person. Top management can then review these and make the necessary adjustments.

In order for managers below the very top to come up with a first estimate of the bonuses they are responsible for, they must be given a pool of money to divide. This is a critical event in using bonuses to shape strategy. Unless bonus pools for each business are calculated at the same percentage of revenues earned, revenues from some businesses will be used to subsidize the bonus pools of others, in addition to the pools for non–revenue-generating functions such as research and operations. For example, strong existing businesses such as M&A may subsidize new businesses with great potential but little revenue, such as asset-backed securities. If this is not done, the firm will have difficulty attracting people to small or low-margin businesses that are important to the firm's future and its ability to serve its customers in the present.

This pattern of subsidies is one of the ways in which top management allocates resources to the firm's business portfolio.[7] In doing so top management shapes corporate strategy to a significant extent. For example, when people in a business that has generated few revenues receive large bonuses, this is a statement about both the perceived importance of their business to the future of the firm and their efforts in building this business. At the time of our study, M&A, equity underwriting, mortgages, and trading were all highly profitable businesses in the largest firms. Their profits helped to fund the bonus pools of other activities considered important but much less profitable, such as commercial paper, medium- and long-term investment-grade debt, and block trading. Perhaps the most dramatic example was Drexel Burnham Lambert, which was attempting to use the profits of its high-yield bond business to diversify into other businesses.

Shaping corporate strategy by starting with a common bonus pool that is then subdivided, and perhaps further subdivided, for the various units is most effective when individual bonuses reflect a person's contribution to overall corporate strategy. The value of this approach is mitigated when departmental breakdowns are based more on contributions to departmental results, since those contributing more broadly to the firm outside the department will be underrewarded. One way of controlling this, already noted, is for top management to review bonuses for everybody in the firm. In doing so, top management can ensure that individuals are rewarded for assisting others with whom they have weak ties, as well as those with whom they have strong ties stemming from the organizational structure and system measures.

The network structures of the self-designing organization, the management control systems, and the bonus determination process are linked together through three complementary relationships. First, systems compensate for structural weaknesses. Second, the bonus determination process compensates for system weaknesses. The great potential flaw of subjectively determined bonuses based on aggregate results is that such bonuses will not be perceived as fair. Network structures facilitate making the vast quantity of information available to top management that it needs in order to make an accurate assessment of an individual's contribution to collective outcomes. Thus, third, structure compensates for weaknesses in the bonus determination process.

However elegant these relationships among structure, systems, and the bonus determination process may be, there are limitations on the extent to which these organizational level variables can accomplish the implementation of strategy. In investment banking, strategy is ultimately implemented at the level of the individual customer. For this reason, it is necessary to have individuals who are concerned with what strategy means for specific issuers and investors. These relationship managers are an important integrating force at the customer interface.

— 9

RELATIONSHIP MANAGEMENT

Relationship managers are responsible for integrating the efforts of all specialists within the firm who share a common customer. In doing so they help the customer coordinate the activities of the various specialists. A recent survey found that 85 percent of the issuing customer companies responding reported that there was one person from the company's lead investment bank who normally coordinated all contacts between the firm and the company.[1]

Although relationship management was a common integrating device in the investment banks we studied, it was also a complex issue for which it was difficult to establish general principles. The reason relationship management is so vexing to practitioners and academics alike is the diffusion of these responsibilities throughout the firm. This makes the role difficult to describe in simple terms. We found descriptions of how firms managed relationship management as nebulous and fraught with exceptions as the descriptions of their organizational structures. Although all of the largest firms distinguished between relationship managers and product specialists, many of the so-called relationship managers had product responsibilities on at least some accounts, just as many of the product specialists had relationship management responsibilities.

Despite the acknowledged importance of building and maintaining relationships, questions existed about the role. To what extent should a relationship manager be involved in deals? Should a relationship manager have a product specialty? How much control should a relationship manager exercise over the customer interface? How should relationship managers be evaluated and rewarded?

The most striking empirical finding about these questions was the many different ways in which they were answered. Variation existed between firms, within firms at a certain time, and within firms over time. The ambiguity made it impossible to identify any common set of responsibilities attached to the relationship manager role. For example, although Goldman, Sachs was admired for its relationship management capabilities, many of its competitors had explicitly decided not to follow its practice of not involving relationship managers (in the Investment Banking Services Group) in the execution of deals.

A proper understanding of relationship management is based on variety and ambiguity. These characteristics are not evidence of a problem that has gone unsolved. Rather, they are the very essence of the solution. In order to be effective, relationship management must be in tension with the firm's efforts to simplify and clarify through organization. The purpose of relationship management is to provide the integration that is being incompletely accomplished by practices concerning organizational structure, management control systems, and the bonus determination process.

The Need for Relationship Management

It is important for both customers and the firm that there be some coordination among the many product specialists who execute transactions. Customers desire this for several reasons. Efforts by the CEO and the members of his financial staff to coordinate their activities are enhanced when the different individuals from an investment bank are coordinated as well. An important part of this coordination involves sharing information among the investment bankers within a given firm. This saves the customer from having to repeat the same things a number of times. It also increases the likelihood that the specialists will work with each other to the benefit of the customer, rather than against each other to the customer's detriment.

An example of the importance of coordinating specialists is the comment made by Union Carbide's CFO, Clayton Stephenson, about how well Bruce Jamerson and Bob Calhoun of First Boston coordinated the many specialists involved in his deal. "They brought all their key functional area people together in one room to be creative and work together. Any of the pieces free-standing made no sense. We had to work with the internal staff at First Boston, and they had to work together to make it all happen. Calhoun and Jamerson had access to the key people and could orchestrate the deal."

Coordinating product specialists is equally important to the firm itself. The reasons follow directly from the mediation function, economic characteristics, and production process of investment banking. Specialists who concentrate on one side of the market interface must share information with each other and with those who concentrate on the other side. This is necessary to take advantage of opportunities of direct interest to the specialist in which the help of other specialists may be needed, and to identify opportunities of interest to the other specialists.

The importance of sharing information among specialists is related to the economic characteristics of investment banking with its loose linkage between value added and revenues earned, both within and across products. However imperfectly, the investment bank attempts to achieve an equitable balance in resources consumed by customers and the return on these resources. This may require certain specialists to invest time and money in marketing and delivering deals for which they do not earn the same fees as they would if these resources had been invested otherwise. For the firm as a whole, suboptimizing one specialty may be the best way to optimize the combined efforts of all specialties. In doing so, the needs of the firm are balanced against the needs of the customer.

Finally, because the production process is one of performing unique deals in real-time interaction with customers, it is not possible to anticipate exactly which specialists will be required on any given deal, the extent to which they will be required, and when they will be required. Even the deals themselves cannot be predicted with any degree of certainty. This complicates the coordination problem.

The appropriate perspective for orchestrating the coordination required by the nature of investment banking is that of the CEO of the investment bank. If the CEO were omniscient, he or she would have all of the necessary information from issuers and investors to decide how the resources of the firm should be used to greatest advantage. But because no one can achieve omniscience, the CEO must develop mechanisms which at least approximate this perspective.

In the past, the role of CEO was divided among the senior partners of the firm. Each senior partner functioned, in effect, as the CEO of the firm with regard to a set of customers. He was responsible for understanding the total needs of each customer and for ensuring that the firm earned fees commensurate with the costs it incurred in serving a customer. Since this officer was directly involved in the execution of many of the deals, he directly experienced the opportunity costs associated with serving customers, which provided an additional incentive to monitor the balance between resources expended and revenues earned. Furthermore, he often had his own group of more junior bankers who worked largely on deals for his clients, and so had direct control over these resources as well. Through the syndicate desk, and directly with sales and trading, he exchanged information with those who managed the investor interface. Because there were fewer products, the needs of customers were less complex, and the markets were simpler, it was possible for the senior partner to do an effective job in solving the coordination problems.

In some of the smaller firms, which served middle-market clients with less complex financing needs (such as Bear, Stearns; Dean Witter; Donaldson, Lufkin & Jenrette; Kidder, Peabody; L.F. Rothschild; and Smith Barney) or firms that offered a narrow range of products to large customers (such as Dillon, Read and Lazard Frères), an approximation of this partner model still existed at the time of our interviews. Senior generalist bankers were assigned to particular customers and were directly involved in executing deals for them.

The need for product specialists is undermining this approach. It is no longer possible for even a superb investment banker to be proficient in the entire array of products available. This is especially true in the largest and most diversified firms. The emergence of product specialists raises the question of who will have responsibility for managing the overall customer relationship.

Thus the relationship manager bears a similarity to the senior partners in the past, who had "their" clients and took care of their needs. The personal relationship between the customer and his investment banker superseded the relationship between the customer and the banker's firm; if the banker changed firms, the customer went with him. Bob deVeer, a relationship manager at First Boston, described his role in a way reminiscent of this, using the metaphor of an itinerant farmer: "I'm a farmer. I can go to any number of firms. The firm that gives you the best plot of land is the place to be."

But although the relationship manager role looks similar to and developed out of the senior partner role, there is a crucial difference. Unlike the old partnership days when customers were definitely and strongly attached to individuals, who developed the customer relationships themselves or inherited them from a retiring senior partner after working on them for years, the relationship manager is often deeded accounts by top management. And although a loyalty may exist for particular investment bankers, in an era of multiple relationships the personal tie means much less. The tie with customers has shifted in large part from the individual to the firm.

Kim Fennebresque, another relationship manager at First Boston, explained his role in a way that illustrates both the independence of and constraints on a relationship manager: "I view myself as running a small business. I'm chairman and CEO of Kim Fennebresque Company, a wholly owned franchise of First Boston." In running this franchise, defined by a set of customers, the relationship manager is responsible for coordinating internal specialist resources—the farming tools, to extend deVeer's metaphor—in a way that effectively balances the needs of the customer and the needs of his firm.

The relationship management responsibilities described by deVeer and Fennebresque can be understood in terms of the concept of agency. In a provocative paper, Harrison White has identified a number of general theoretical points about the agency role in organizations that are applicable to relationship managers. First, he contrasts this role with that of specialists. "I wish to argue that operation of agency depends essentially on its *not* being specialized except on temporary ad hoc bases. . . . A central task of agents, and a major occasion of exerting influence and control, is responding to jurisdictional disputes, that is, to other orders' [particular departments'] problems of specialization."[2] In doing so, "agency is a mechanism of control to cut through and across specialization."[3] And by crosscutting specialists' roles, the agent remains outside the defined organization: "A role that is not specialized cannot be demarcated, and thus is not fungible."[4]

Second, although agency lies outside the rest of the organization, it is not removed from it. Indeed, in order for agency to operate it depends upon the energy generated by the various parts of the organization working with and against each other, since "agency is an endless ongoing process of end-running, of cutting into and around the sprawling congeries of bits and pieces that is what real organizations are, everywhere and whenever."[5] But the purpose of agency in doing this is not to order and clarify organizational roles; to do so would be to become enmeshed in the organization which would sacrifice the objective of integration or control from a CEO perspective. "Control presupposes and induces disorder, disorder with respect to the autochthonous, crescive corporative forms which are endlessly spinning and respinning themselves out in continuing fraternal strife. Agency does not fight that; it presupposes and operates on that, partly by exacerbating it."[6]

And third, agency is "unhistoricist." One of the barriers to a CEO exercising control in order to enforce his perspective through organization-level variables is that he must take into account the opportunities and constraints created by the organization's legacy. Through agency, the CEO "tries to neutralize, to some extent, for purposes of achieving some color of control, the overwhelmingly tangible historical concreteness of organization."[7]

Specialization, organization, and history can prevent the firm from taking a sufficiently broad view in how its resources are best used in providing services to and across customers. Agency—nonspecialized, removed from but depending on and working off the organization, and charged to ignore history—in the form of relationship management is the way top management seeks to introduce checks and balances into the firm by creating an individual role that mitigates the inevitable flaws in the evolving organizational design. Tension and ambiguity are intrinsic to this role, which is created to supply the necessary variety for dealing with unique and changing circumstances.

In an agency role, the relationship manager is responsible for seeing that the right things are done, even and especially if they go against the grain of the organization. It is through relationship managers that the investment bank's CEO exercises control over the firm, by having agents who, although part of the organization, are at the same time outside it. The authority of relationship managers comes more from their role in representing the CEO of the investment bank for a subset of the firm's customers than from any formally defined organizational position.

The Dilemmas of Relationship Management

There are two dilemmas of relationship management, a result of the fact that it is performed by individuals who are members of the organization but also outside it in their agency role. The first dilemma concerns whether or not the relationship manager should have a product specialty. The second concerns the degree to which the relationship manager should control the customer interface. Whether or not the relationship manager also has a product specialty, control over the customer interface can vary from high to low.

There are advantages and disadvantages to assigning product responsibility to relationship managers. Having a product specialty lends credibility in the eyes of the client and provides an opportunity for the relationship manager to do transactions. Because relationships are based on transactions, the person who is involved in them has a great deal of interaction with customers. Through interaction he gets to know the customer's needs and can suggest ideas that create opportunities not only for the product he delivers but also for products delivered by other specialists in his firm.

G. Chris Andersen, a managing director at Drexel Burnham Lambert, felt that his firm's relationships had developed out of transaction expertise: "I think it's almost ironic that when you look at Drexel, we were the one firm specifically not selling relationships. We went out selling a specific product and targeting very specifically on that product." In selling high-yield bonds, Drexel found that clients were "mistreated in the capital markets." Relationships developed naturally: "Once we showed them a better way to finance, they felt unfettered as entrepreneurs. Once you take the chains off the entrepreneurs they flex their imagination and start to think what to do. They came back to us to talk about it. Our relationships became very strong by accident, in an era when relationships were breaking down."

Product specialists are especially important in developing relationships with new customers. The only way to break into an account is to offer an idea for an appealing deal. This is usually best done by someone who has expertise in the deal being proposed. Cutting price by itself is typically insufficient, since customers accept bids from only a limited number of firms, which is usually a subset of those they have done business with in the recent past.

Firms are especially likely to break into accounts with products in which they have an established reputation, as illustrated by Drexel in junk bonds. Other examples of what are sometimes called "edge of the wedge" products include M&A at First Boston, debt underwriting at Salomon Brothers (Terry Connelly noted, "We try to use our transactional capability to get in the door to establish a relationship"), takeover defense at Kidder, Peabody, money-market paper at Merrill Lynch, and, in the more distant past, commercial paper at Goldman, Sachs. For example, Jerry Kenney, president of Merrill Lynch Capital Markets, noted that the major reason his firm had acquired A. G. Becker was to become number one in money-market products in order to "get a clear-cut area of leadership to talk about with clients." Bear, Stearns hoped to accomplish the same thing through its Special Investments Group (tax-advantaged investments to wealthy people that provide low-cost financing to issuers). Mark Sandler, the head of the group, remarked, "I tell my people to view themselves as having account management responsibility. They shouldn't let a single piece of business go by." Philip Purcell, CEO of Dean Witter, noted that, depending on what happened with tax laws, their strength in master limited partnerships could turn into a big advantage if this became a major financing vehicle for companies. The edge of the wedge does not even have to be an investment banking product. Firms concentrating on middle-market firms, such as Donaldson, Lufkin & Jenrette, L.F. Rothschild, and Smith Barney, spoke of using research analysts who followed a company as a way of generating business for fee-generating products, since the analyst often has ongoing communication with the companies he or she follows.

Further evidence of how transactions done by product specialists can be used to build relationships is revealed in the language used by different firms to describe certain products. All of the firms in our study distinguished between transaction products and relationship products, but differed in how they classified them. The classification of a product is not based on properties intrinsic to the product itself, but is instead based on the context, which it partially creates. Firms referred to their edge-of-the-wedge products, upon which they sought to build relationships, as transaction products. They referred to the other products they hoped to sell, once they got in, as relationship products even though these were not the basis of the relationship.

First Boston provides an interesting illustration of this classification. It viewed M&A as a transaction product while many firms referred to it as a relationship product. Those firms that did not have an established reputation in M&A rightly surmised that they would get this business only if they already had a reasonably good relationship with a customer. Similarly, most firms described takeover defense as a service that could only be sold to firms with which they had a relationship, whereas Kidder, Peabody viewed it as a service that could be used as the foundation for building a relationship.

The decision of whether to assign relationship management responsibility to product specialists of transaction products or to relationship products can affect a firm's competitive position. If a firm's transaction products are the ones in which it has a competitive advantage and its relationship products are the ones in which it does not, giving relationship management responsibility to a specialist in a weak product (or to someone who has no specialty at all) may limit the extent to which the firm benefits from its strongest products. The obvious solution to this problem is to assign relationship management responsibilities to transaction product specialists.

Despite the reasons for assigning relationship management responsibility to the appropriate product specialist, doing so also has disadvantages, two of which are especially important. The first is that the relationship manager may not devote enough time and attention to identifying opportunities for other specialists and for helping them develop ties with the customer. This may be a sin of omission or commission. The former occurs when the relationship manager is simply too busy taking care of his own business, defined in product terms, to worry about the businesses of others. This is most likely to be true when he has many lucrative deals and the payoffs on cross-selling are uncertain, long-term, and modest. But failure to involve others may also be done by intent if the specialist perceives other specialists as directly competitive, for example, a middle-market company can be sold (earning fees for M&A) or can issue equity (earning fees for corporate finance). It may also be done because the specialist doubts the professional capabilities of others and fears that their poor performance will sour the client on continuing to do deals with him.

The underlying cause of the temptation to take too narrow a perspective is that a product specialist generally has a restricted role in the organization. This is in contrast to the agency role of relationship management, which is designed to crosscut the organizational arrangements defining the network ties. Because the product specialist role is very much *in* the organization and the agency role lies more outside the organization, the product specialist who is a relationship manager faces a constant tension between his agency and specialist responsibilities. It is difficult to take a product perspective in some circumstances and a firmwide perspective in others, and it is especially difficult to do both at the same time.

The second disadvantage is that the product specialist will have an especially strong tie with only the subset of individuals in the company who purchase his or her product. Product-focused relationships should not be confused with a total overall customer relationship. M&A specialists have more contact with CEOs than with assistant treasurers and the reverse is true for individuals on the capital markets desk. Harold Tanner, co-head of Corporate Finance at Salomon Brothers, remarked, "The hardest thing this firm has had to do is move up the corporate ladder from calling on the AT [assistant treasurer] and treasurer to the president and chairman." Being restricted to calling on treasurers inhibits their ability to cross-sell other products, since there is no built-in opportunity for them to talk to people in the company who buy the products of other specialists. The fact that the specialist who is a relationship manager must make an extra effort to estab-lish contact with these people, both to gather information and to have a personal basis for making referrals to other specialists, heightens the pres-sures for sin by omission.

An obvious solution to these problems is to give relationship manage-ment responsibilities to someone who does not have product execution re-sponsibilities, a pure relationship manager. The best-known example of this is the Investment Banking Services Group at Goldman, Sachs, which some other firms were attempting to imitate, such as Prudential-Bache Securities. Professionals in the group were corporate finance generalists, who did not get involved in the execution of deals for any product specialty. Instead, the solicited business was executed by others in the firm.

Not assigning product execution responsibility to a relationship manager eliminates the problem of requiring an individual to be part of—yet out-side—the organization. A relationship manager without specific product responsibilities can concentrate totally on the agency role of balancing the global interests of the customer and the firm. Such a relationship manager is also more effective at new business development. He or she can better leverage customer satisfaction to other products than can a product special-ist. The lack of a specific product focus also eliminates any bias toward calling exclusively on a subset of the buyers in a customer.

Because of the problems inherent in giving relationship management re-sponsibilities to product specialists, Drexel Burnham Lambert, despite its noted success in building relationships through transaction expertise, cre-ated a separate group with exclusive responsibilities for relationship man-agement. G. Chris Andersen was put in charge of the Investment Banking Group (IBG) when it was created in 1984. As a sign of its commitment to upgrading the relationship management role, the firm started the depart-ment with twelve of its most senior and competent people, "more than we could spare," according to Herb Bachelor, head of Corporate Finance, to whom Andersen reported, at a time when the firm's business was at an all-time high. Fred Joseph, Drexel's CEO, emphasized, "We flat out have got to have it. It's a question of getting the right people and the right structure."

A major objective of the IBG was to protect Drexel's market share by solidifying relationships with existing customers and by expanding the firm's customer base. Andersen stated, "We took people in to worry about relationships for a very simple reason; loss of market share invites erosion of your margin." Joseph explained, "The main reason for developing the new business group is that in the next decade business won't just keep coming in. Twenty years from now Corporate Finance will just have processing power unless we have relationships."

Another reason for creating the IBG was that the firm's diversification effort would lead to a broader product line. When the major product was high-yield finance, it was easier for the person who processed the deals to fulfill the relationship management function as well. But the more successful the firm's diversification attempts, the more difficult it would be for high-yield specialists to manage the overall customer relationship.

Although pure relationship managers do not have to make decisions about how to allocate their time between new business development and doing deals, they do have to choose how to allocate time and energy across accounts. A relationship manager who has customers who are a source of a great deal of business (such as when his firm is the dominant bank with an active customer) and those who yield little if any business (such as when his firm has a transactional or conversational tie with a customer that uses the core group model) faces an obvious temptation to concentrate on the former. This temptation is analogous to the temptation faced by the product specialist to work on deals rather than to work on developing the relationship. One way of eliminating the problem is to give some relationship managers only potential customers. Although these relationship managers have nothing to distract them from attempting to break into these new customers, this can be a discouraging job unless they have strong egos and a great deal of persistence. Improving the quality of the banker's work life by giving him or her good customers so that the banker has the satisfaction of seeing business actually get done simply recreates the temptation to ignore new customers.

However accounts are allocated among relationship managers, there are three disadvantages when individuals play a purely agency role. The first is that without a product specialty, the relationship manager may have difficulty getting access to the customer and establishing credibility. Customers are much less interested in general and shallow conversations about what an investment bank can do for them than they are in specific ideas for financing or M&A deals. Relationship managers who call on specialists in the customer organization may have difficulty remaining sufficiently expert on the broad range of products in order to engage in value-added conversation.

The second problem is that pure relationship managers may also have difficulty establishing credibility with product specialists. When product specialists do not think the relationship manager contributes something of value, or when the relationship manager cannot influence product specialists however they view the relationship manager, it is difficult for the latter to coordinate the use of specialist resources in a way that is optimal for customers and the firm. A specialist who can ignore a relationship manager's pleas to invest time on a small or marginally profitable deal for the sake of future revenues in other products interferes with the effectiveness of the relationship manager.

The third problem, which is related to the first two, is that it is difficult to keep investment bankers from doing deals in their specialty. Since most pure relationship managers were former specialists, if only in general corporate finance debt and equity underwritings, there is always the temptation to get involved in deals. In doing so they can eliminate much of the credibility problem that might exist with customers and product specialists. This involvement in deals, however, interferes with their agency role in the same way that it does when product specialists have relationship management responsibilities.

Executives at Drexel were aware of this problem. Bachelor observed, "IBG bankers should spend most of their time cross-selling, but bankers like to see tickets punched to justify their existence. So the natural inclination for them is to call on new accounts, rather than to cross-sell products they cannot process themselves, in order to put darts on the board. They feel more pressures than they should to do deals. We've told them they have two years before we expect to see deals." The problem was exacerbated, in Andersen's view, by the fact that "the line banker doesn't want to sell so he is mistrustful of someone who's doing it." The problem of getting people off deals was one of the major reasons why the firm's five previous attempts in the past ten years to create an IBG function had failed. Joseph admitted, "We did not dedicate enough resources for long enough and we took guys off to do deals." Needless to say, these guys were more than happy with this.

Bear, Stearns faced a similar problem: its investment bankers were more interested in getting deals with new customers than in expanding the business to other specialists with customers for whom they had already done a deal. One idea being considered for improving the "conversion process" was to hire commercial bank calling officers who would concentrate on selling. This problem was particularly acute in large sophisticated accounts that the firm was attempting to penetrate, building on strengths it had developed serving middle-market clients. Whereas bankers could directly serve most of the needs of their middle-market clients, this was impossible for the large accounts, which required a broad range of product specialties.

Prudential–Bache Securities had experienced a similar problem in failing to take full advantage of inroads made by product specialists. The firm was attempting to correct this through what they referred to as the "Goldman model," in which nonspecialist relationship managers would be assigned to each account once a deal had been done. Their responsibility was to follow up and look for other business.

The relative advantages and disadvantages between product specialist relationship managers and pure relationship managers pose a dilemma. The disadvantages of the role of a pure relationship manager do not exist when product specialists are assigned relationship management responsibilities. But this creates other problems, which can be solved by stripping relationship management from product execution.

An interesting attempt to resolve the dilemma is the practice used by investment banks of defining relationship managers as industry or regional specialists rather than product specialists. The practice seeks to obtain the advantages of both options while avoiding the disadvantages. A relationship manager who is a specialist in a particular industry or geographical region may be able to use this to establish credibility for dealing with customers and product specialists. In chapter 6 we noted the high degree of specialization according to industry and geography that can exist, especially in the largest firms. But a market-defined specialty does not lend itself as easily to involvement in deals, with all the problems this creates. Furthermore, such a specialty leads to an expertise that should be relevant to all products, and to the extent that it is brought to bear on deals, there is no inherent product bias in it.

The extent to which market-defined specialties resolve the dilemma of relationship management depends on how much and how relevant the expertise is. Expertise in particular industries is especially useful for those that have complex and arcane tax, accounting, and regulatory issues (such as oil and gas and insurance) or are undergoing massive restructuring because of environmental pressures (such as thrifts). Geographical expertise is especially useful for countries and for regions of the United States with a high concentration of companies and the belief that they are somehow culturally distinct, such as California and the South. Otherwise, specialization by industry and geography is more of an organizing convenience that has little effect on the relationship management and product specialist dilemma.

Independent of whether the relationship manager has product specialist responsibilities, there is a second major dilemma concerning the extent to which he or she controls the customer interface. A high degree of control best enables the relationship manager to be effective in the agency role. When the manager has a high degree of control, contacts initiated by both the customer and others in the firm go through him, he decides whether or not to have meetings take place without his being there, and he is kept fully informed of exchanges that do not directly involve him. Exercising control requires authority that can be obtained by delegation (top management will sanction product specialists who violate the rules for customer contact), through influence based on competence, and through respect for seniority.

A high degree of control over the interface is an important source of influence over both the customer and others in the firm, since it puts the relationship manager at the nexus of information flow. He provides access to opportunities for product specialists, and makes resources available to the customer. Control also helps him fulfill his responsibility to use the firm's resources in a way which best balances the firm's and the customer's objectives. In particular, it enables him to build and sustain market shares with individual customers, thereby solving the loose linkage problem in an effective way.

There are potential costs to a high degree of control. Funneling communications through the relationship manager, and involving him in many of them, may slow communication down so much that deals are lost because of delays. It may also prove frustrating to customer and product specialist alike when the relationship manager's contribution is minor. There is also the risk that the relationship manager will avoid discussions about products he or she is less comfortable with, such as M&A or complex financings involving swaps and multiple currencies, and miss important opportunities. Opportunities may also be missed with potential customers because the relationship manager is concentrating so much on maintaining and building market share with existing customers. This inhibits the firm's ability to develop its customer base.

These problems are avoided when the relationship manager has a low degree of control over the customer interface, whether by senior management design or because relationship managers have insufficient competence or seniority. In this situation, product specialists are free to engage directly in conversations with both existing and potential clients, keeping the relationship manager as informed as possible. This can enhance sales effectiveness with the existing customers and facilitate building the customer base, since product specialists face fewer constraints to coordinate with others in developing their businesses.

The trade-off is that the advantages accruing to relationship managers with a high degree of control are lost. Both the customer and the firm may suffer from the unfettered entrepreneurship of product specialists. The low degree of control puts the relationship manager in a particularly vulnerable position, since it leaves him or her with no apparent source of influence to fulfill the agency role.

A Typology of Relationship Management

Each dilemma, whether or not the relationship manager should have a product specialty and how much control the manager should have over the customer interface, represents a choice independent of the other. By treating each choice as having two options, four types of relationship manager roles can be identified (see figure 9.1). Each type has its own strengths and weaknesses. Identifying four types, which admittedly oversimplifies reality by treating each choice as dichotomous rather than continuous, helps to explain why relationship management is such a vexing issue to practitioners and academics. The term *relationship manager* is used as a label for a role that can vary substantially in the responsibilities it comprises.

A relationship manager with a high degree of control and his own product specialty is a *penetrator,* since he is supposed to use his own product as a basis for penetrating the account and expanding the services it buys from the firm. This type has some obvious advantages. Having a product specialty facilitates interaction with customers, since the relationship manager can initiate discussions based on specific ideas. The contact can be with high-level (CEO and CFO) contacts (e.g., when the product is M&A) and fairly infrequent, or lower-level (treasurer and assistant treasurer) contacts (e.g., when the product is shelf-registered debt) and very frequent. Having a product specialty can also be an important source of authority for maintaining a high level of control, particularly when the product specialty involves high-level customer contact. The high level of control helps the relationship manager integrate the efforts of other specialists. But it can also inhibit useful interaction between the customer and other specialists. This is most detrimental when the relationship manager focuses more on product responsibilities than on managing the overall customer relationship.

The problem of product responsibilities displacing relationship manage-

FIGURE 9.1.   A Typology of the Relationship Manager Role

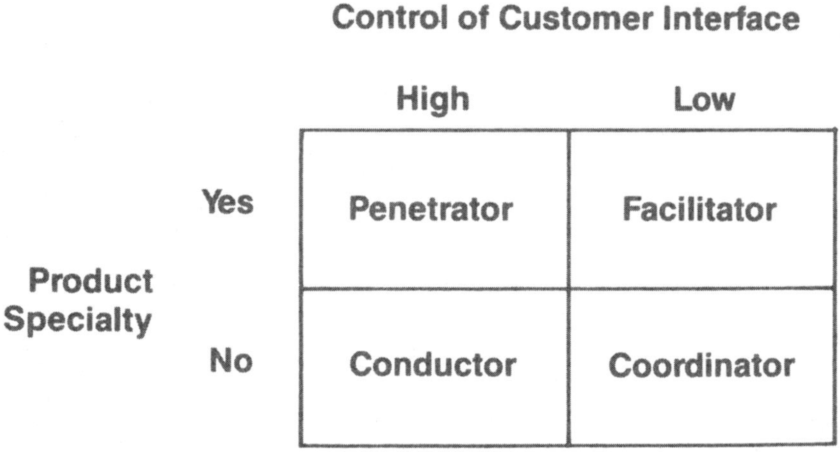

Control of Customer Interface

		High	Low
Product Specialty	Yes	Penetrator	Facilitator
	No	Conductor	Coordinator

ment responsibilities is eliminated when the relationship manager has no product specialty. When this is the case and the relationship manager maintains a high degree of control over the customer interface, he is a *conductor.* Like the conductor of an orchestra, he directs the instruments (specialists) so that they play together, but does not play an instrument himself. Because he does not have his own product specialty, he can concentrate on managing the overall relationship, and do this effectively if he uses a high degree of control in an appropriate fashion. He should not, for example, inhibit contact between product specialists and the customer when these contacts do not interfere with the efforts of other product specialists. He may inhibit contact in a mistaken attempt to demonstrate his authority, which does not come from a particular product expertise, especially when his authority is not derived, for example, from a close and long-term personal relationship with key customer executives.

The dangers of the conductor role can be avoided by simply reducing the amount of control the relationship manager has over the customer interface. When this is done the relationship manager becomes a *coordinator,* since he is only responsible for coordinating the activities of product specialists to the extent they find useful. Since he is not expected to exercise much control over contacts with the customer and his authority for doing so is correspondingly less, the temptation to reinforce one's authority by interfering with the product specialists is reduced. The obvious problem with this role is how the person in it gets enough authority to play even the coordinator role. This can come from a long-term customer relationship, seniority, or recognized competence. All of these sources of authority, however, can be used to increase the control the relationship manager has over the customer interface, despite the efforts of top management to limit control. And in any case, product specialists will be reluctant to go too often to top management with complaints about a relationship manager for fear that they will be perceived as poor team players.

The temptation for a relationship manager without a product specialty to increase his control over the customer interface exists partially because his sole responsibility is to manage the overall customer relationship. The temptation can be reduced by giving the relationship manager a product specialty of his own, which requires time and attention, and making him a *facilitator.* When the relationship manager has his own product responsibilities, he may be content with a low degree of control over the customer interface and satisfied with simply being responsible for facilitating the efforts of other specialists as much as he can. As is the case with the other three types of relationship manager role, this too has its disadvantages. The low degree of control may make it difficult for the facilitator to act as an effective integrator, especially when the other specialists make little effort to cooperate with each other.

The obvious way to get more integration is to increase the degree of control over the customer interface, which shifts the role from facilitator to penetrator. The solution, of course, has its own flaws. What this analysis demonstrates is that every form of relationship management has both strengths and weaknesses. One of the reasons this role is continually changing in firms is that in correcting for certain weaknesses, new ones are created and their resolution creates yet other ones, and so forth.

If this is true, over time a cycle will be observed in which relationship management responsibility shifts back and forth between product specialists (penetrators and facilitators) and corporate finance generalists (conductors and coordinators) who do not have a product specialty. Toward the end of our data collection phase, in late 1986 and early 1987, there were a few signs that such a shift was indeed taking place toward the conductor and coordinator types of the relationship manager.

First Boston provides an example of the various strengths and weaknesses in each of the four types of relationship manager and how one firm sought to manage the problem. The Investment Banking Group, under co-heads Joe Perella and Bruce Wasserstein, contained both M&A product specialists and advisory corporate finance generalists, referred to as "client coverage," for such products as equity, recapitalization, and LBOs. In the past, corporate finance generalists got involved in deals to varying degrees but they did not have a particular product specialty. Thus, to a large extent, the client coverage bankers acted as coordinators or conductors depending on the degree of control they had over the customer interface. Bruce Jamerson, for example, acted as a coordinator on the Union Carbide account. Bob Calhoun, although less involved than Jamerson, was in a better position to act as a conductor because of the authority he had as an extremely competent senior investment banker.

As its M&A product specialists became successful during the 1980s there was a certain irony to this development at First Boston. In the late 1970s people in the small M&A department had to sell its services themselves. The Corporate Finance Department was not especially interested in doing so, since at that time First Boston was a minor player in the business and it was a less important business overall. Bill Lambert, with the title of creative director of the department, recalled, "We started a new business development group in the late seventies. We tried to solicit new business by going to people with ideas, since some companies do business with the investment banker who generated the idea. It is surprising that other firms didn't do this earlier, but they didn't. They lost market share as a result, but have since followed suit." As part of this effort, First Boston was one of the first investment banks to locate M&A specialists in regional offices in order to call aggressively.

With the success of the M&A department came a set of relationships, based primarily with the CEO and CFO. The relationships had in some cases overshadowed the historical relationships maintained by corporate finance generalists, who varied in their level of contacts, in the extent of their product experience and involvement in deals. Some corporate finance generalists acted more as coordinators in accounts where the M&A specialist had strong high-level ties. And in a number of cases M&A was the basis of a new client relationship that created the opportunity for it to act as a penetrator, or at least a facilitator, if it was willing to take on relationship management responsibilities.

First Boston's response was to combine M&A and advisory corporate finance into a single Investment Banking Group, as mentioned. Because the M&A department was nearly equal in size to Corporate Finance (110 and 150, respectively), many accounts had two relationship managers. Not all M&A specialists had relationship management responsibility, however. For example, within M&A were certain product subspecialties such as divestitures and defense, performed by individuals who did not have relationship management responsibilities.

By sharing relationship management responsibilities between M&A and advisory corporate finance, First Boston hoped to take advantage of the relationship management opportunities created by M&A without undermining its product focus and without having relationship management suffer because of the pressures involved in executing M&A deals. At the same time, M&A specialists could supplement the efforts of client coverage people who did not have the access to customer CEOs and CFOs that the M&A specialist had. It sought to do this by keeping M&A and client coverage as separate departments, but combining them into a single group and organizing them into similar industry and geographical specialties to facilitate communication. Perella referred to this as "coordinated but not amalgamated," and explained, "We are trying to walk a fine line between using M&A as the edge of the wedge by being on the forefront of innovation while also having close coordination. If you are totally amalgamated, you lose the M&A edge. If you are totally separated there is no coordination. We are trying to achieve the first by having separate units and the second by physically locating these units close together and having them develop a common business plan." The result was that many accounts were covered by two types of relationship managers—a penetrator or facilitator from M&A and a conductor or coordinator from client coverage.

More broadly, the relationship management problem goes beyond the fact that for a given customer several different types of relationship managers are involved. Which role an individual plays is not intrinsic to the person, but varies according to the context. Any given individual can play two or more of the four roles, depending on the customer and the other people involved in the account. This further complicates the relationship management function, making it difficult to manage and understand in theoretical terms.

Because investment bankers are likely to be involved with customers with whom their firm has ties of different strengths, pressures exist for them to adapt the relationship manager role accordingly. An active dominant bank model customer is likely to have one person in the conductor or coordinator role (i.e., one without product responsibility) from the firm with which it has a very strong tie. Managing such a complex interface requires someone who is not distracted by his own product specialty. Firms that have weak ties with a dominant bank model customer are prone to use a penetrator or facilitator with product responsibilities to try to increase the amount of business they do with the company. Penetrators and facilitators are also more likely to be found when the firm has a strong tie with a core group model customer. Their greater sophistication and transactional orientation reduces the importance of the general financial advice that can be obtained from a conductor or coordinator.

Other causes for variations in the type of relationship manager played by an individual investment banker include relative seniority and competence and the relative importance of the manager's product specialty compared to other products, both in general and with respect to a particular customer. Investment bankers who have seniority or who are seen as especially competent, or both, are more able to exercise a high degree of control over the interface, whether or not they have product responsibility. A product specialist who does a lot of business with a customer is in a good position to play a penetrator or facilitator role. This is especially true if the specialty is an acknowledged strength of the firm, as illustrated by the First Boston example above.

Because investment bankers work with a large number of other bankers in serving customers, there is a bewildering complexity in the relationship management roles they play with respect to each other. Complexity turns out to be useful, since it establishes an informal system of debits and credits between bankers as discussed in chapter 6. (A similar system of debits and credits exists in the *sogo shosha*, or Japanese trading company. As intermediaries in the flow of assets, these firms have some characteristics similar to those of investment banks.)[8] For example, a product specialist who in his role as a relationship manager helps another specialist get a piece of business creates an obligation for the specialist to reciprocate if possible in his role as relationship manager on another account. The debits and credits created by the diffusion of relationship management responsibility are integral to the effective functioning of the network of ties within the firm. They provide a currency of exchange between virtually everybody in the firm. Directly or indirectly, everybody is linked to everybody else through a balance sheet of receivables and payables.

First Boston also provides examples of how the same person can fulfill several types of relationship manager roles, as well as serving as a product specialist on some accounts and as a relationship manager on others. Rela-

tionship management responsibilities at First Boston were further complicated by the existence of a new Corporate Finance Department, quite separate from Investment Banking, which reported to the head of Sales and
Trading. (Needless to say, the existence of a new Corporate Finance Department that was quite different from the old Corporate Finance Department made conversations about the organization difficult at first.) Corporate Finance contained the more transactional financing products including
asset finance, high-yield finance, private finance, project finance, leasing,
reorganizations, capital markets (originally debt and more recently equity,
which clouded the role of client coverage in equity deals), short-term finance, currency swaps, underwriting, corporate coverage, syndicate, and
product development. Perella explained, "We put the market-driven businesses together and the advisory-related businesses under people who have
the relationship." It is interesting to note that although First Boston considered M&A to be a transaction product, it was included in the Investment
Banking Group, which had the relationship, and not in Corporate Finance,
which had the "market-driven" transaction products. This is just further
evidence that whether a product is a transaction or a relationship product
depends upon the context in which it is being discussed.

The distinction was not clear-cut, however, since variation existed in the
extent of customer contact maintained by the financing specialists. In some
cases, such as leasing, the client coverage account officers identified opportunities and the leasing bankers primarily concentrated on executing deals.
Thus the role of client coverage with respect to leasing was that of a conductor. In other cases, such as the reorganization group, the bankers did
their own marketing to bankrupt companies that were of limited interest to
the client coverage officers. In these companies, the reorganization group
acted as a penetrator or facilitator, and corporate coverage was at best a
coordinator. High-yield bankers acted both as product specialists to conductor account officers and as penetrators or facilitators to accounts, such
as thrifts, that primarily required high-yield financing services. Other specialists with relationship management responsibilities that varied by account were debt-financing specialists in Capital Markets (which itself was
split into marketing specialists and product-based execution specialists) and
Corporate Coverage specialists, who sold short-term instruments to companies with excess cash to invest.

As the practices at First Boston make clear, relationship management is a
complex activity. It involves a number of people with different relationship
management roles, which in turn structure the relationships among the
people themselves. Alvin Shoemaker, First Boston's chairman, was well
aware of this complexity: "As you have more and more specialist sales
forces, you meet yourself coming around the barn." But he held out hope
of someday having one person responsible for the overall relationship. "My

great fantasy is to have a person who contacts the CEO," he mused, "and who can pull up every transaction [on a computer screen] and measure the trade-off."

Developing the technology for doing this is easy. The problem is being able to assign one person the overall responsibility for making the trade-off decisions and enforcing them. Given the dilemmas inherent in the relationship manager role, which result in at least four types, and the forces that lead to a single person fulfilling this role in two or more of these types, it seems unlikely that total relationship management responsibility can be consolidated in one person for accounts that involve a number of product specialists.

Managing Relationship Management

Despite the complexity in how relationship management is performed and the concomitant difficulty of describing it in simple terms, three practical implications can be identified. The first is the need for continuing change, both in practice and in rhetoric, in who has relationship management responsibility. The second is the importance of the relationship between the relationship manager and the CEO or another senior executive in the firm who has a CEO perspective. Third, even the most senior executives must be involved in relationship management.

Changing relationship management responsibilities is important for many of the same reasons more general changes in structure are important, including tie formation and fostering different perspectives. Such changes enable people to pay off debts to some while incurring debts to others, thereby facilitating the creation of network ties. A product specialist who is assigned management responsibilities for a customer has an incentive to develop a broader view by learning more about the customer and about other products. Giving product responsibilities to someone who has been a conductor or a coordinator contributes to one's professional development and helps to keep the person on the cutting edge of investment banking. And although changing the relationship manager(s) is generally not desirable for accounts with which the relationship is a good one, it can be a good way of making progress with customers who do little business with the firm. Even on accounts where the relationship is strong, if more than one person is making a substantial contribution to this relationship, at least one of them can sometimes be replaced in order to bring a new perspective and to broaden the perspective of the individuals assigned to other accounts.

In addition to structural changes, changes in rhetoric are also useful. Although the actual practice of relationship management is spread throughout the organization, many firms speak in terms of relationship managers *versus* product specialists in order to emphasize the dual importance of relationships and transactions. Although this rhetorical device oversimplifies an admittedly complex reality, it provides a useful mechanism for building relationships out of transactions. Changes in organizational structure are often accompanied by changes in rhetoric that reinforce the new structure. Rhetoric can also be used to signal impending structural change. Most subtly, rhetoric can fine tune the relative emphasis on transactions over relationships without relying on actual structural changes, which are ultimately more powerful but more difficult to use for implementing slight shifts in emphasis.

When top management wants to place greater emphasis in the firm on transactions, it can proclaim the declining role of the pure relationship manager, saying that the conductor or coordinator type is rapidly being replaced by product specialists taking management responsibility as penetrators or facilitators. In doing so, bankers with primarily a product focus get the message to start thinking about relationships, whereas those with primarily a relationship focus start thinking about upgrading their skills in a product specialty, changing their place of employment, or even finding another line of work. All of these responses by relationship bankers are desirable to meet the constant need to upgrade the human resources in the firm.

Conversely, top management may want to emphasize the importance of relationship management apart from product-based transaction expertise. Again, rhetoric can play a useful role when top management proclaims the renewed importance of relationships because of the recognition of their value by customers who have finally become aware of the perils of pure transaction banking. Along with rhetoric comes an increase in the general stature of bankers who in practice already have more of a relationship emphasis, thereby enabling them to exert more control over those with a product focus.

The second practical implication is that in their role as relationship managers, individuals should report directly to the CEO or another senior executive with a firmwide perspective, such as the head of investment banking or other major businesses in the firm. As a practical matter, this is in fact what does occur for senior bankers who are responsible for the firm's most important accounts, whatever their official place in the organization chart. Because relationship management is based on an agency role intended to represent the CEO's perspective, it is reinforced when the person in the role reports directly to the CEO or someone charged with taking a similar perspective. In discussing accounts with this person, the relationship manager benefits from the broad perspective of the senior executive. The relationship manager is also subject to the senior executive's influence for balancing the best interests of the firm with the best interests of the customer.

In addition to fostering a balanced perspective, such reporting relationships are a source of influence and authority over specialists. (Influence is also obtained through behavioral style. Lawrence and Lorsch described the person who is effective in an integrator role: "Effective integrators prefer to take significantly more initiative and leadership; they are aggressive, confident, persuasive, and verbally fluent. . . . Effective integrators seek status to a greater extent; they are ambitious, active, forceful, effective in communication, and have personal scope and breadth of interests. . . . Effective integrators have significantly more social poise; they are more clever, enthusiastic, imaginative, spontaneous, and talkative. . . . Effective integrators prefer more flexible ways of acting; they are adventurous, humorous, and assertive.")[9] This is an important way for a relationship manager to obtain sufficient control over the customer interface in order to integrate specialists' efforts. These specialists know that the person or persons with relationship management responsibility are in direct contact with a senior executive who will want to know whether or not they are acting in a way that balances the overall interest of the firm with the overall interest of the customer.

Reporting relationships, which emphasize the importance of relationship management, can be reinforced by measures of how effectively relationship managers are performing their responsibilities. Some of the same measures already described in the chapter on systems are useful for evaluating individuals who have relationship management responsibilities. These include, for each customer and for the customer base as a whole, fees earned, market shares of the firm and major competitors, and data from cross–evaluation surveys such as contributions to the market shares of others. Increasingly sophisticated management information systems can contribute both to managing relationships and to evaluating relationship managers. When product specialists also have relationship management responsibilities, they will appear in both categories in the cross–evaluation surveys. Through these surveys, along with conversations and observations, one can draw a general picture of the debits and credits within the network of ties.

The utility of the measures is enhanced when the senior executive to whom the relationship manager reports reviews them with each relationship manager, since this reinforces the agency nature of the role. One opportunity for doing so is near bonus time, when a performance review should be conducted. Although difficult, when a product specialist also has relationship management responsibilities, an effort should be made to evaluate separately both types of contributions. This is also a good opportunity for the senior executive to share his thinking about the direction of the firm in order to shape the relationship management function. Although there are ongoing conversations concerning deals, it is worthwhile to take the time to step back from the day-to-day frenzy in order to review the firm's standing with its customers.

The third implication is that senior managers, including the CEO and other top managers, have some responsibility for managing relationships with customers. This even includes those executives who are primarily concerned with the internal management of the firm. One reason for this is that customers expect to have access to the senior managers in a service organization, and in many cases established ties with them as they were going up the ranks, and it would be foolish to sever these. Direct contact with customers can also produce information about customer needs and perceptions useful to senior managers.

Senior managers can also be helpful to more junior bankers who have been assigned relationship management responsibility. This was important at Salomon Brothers, for example, because its strong ties with assistant treasurers and treasurers did not easily lead to contact with customer CEOs. Through the use of what one junior banker called "senior stardust," progress had been made in establishing higher-level relationships.

In helping with relationships, senior managers in the firm need to be careful not to take them over. One problem with this is that if the customer begins to expect contact with a senior manager, the manager will have insufficient time to attend to the internal needs of the firm. Another problem with customers' expectations is that they can actually make it harder for others in the firm to contribute in the capacity of relationship manager. This can inhibit the development of relationship management capabilities throughout the firm, which becomes a constraint on the size of the firm's customer base. Top management at Drexel was concerned that the firm had so few excellent relationship managers, and many of them had administrative responsibilities as well. This was one of the reasons for the creation of the Investment Banking Group.

The problem of senior executives spending too much time on customer relationships, to the detriment of their internal management responsibilities, is a very real one. The vast majority came into the investment banking business in order to do deals or trades, not to become managers. For most of them, working with customers is perceived to be more fun than administering their own firm. The challenge for them is to balance these external and internal management responsibilities by acting as what Lorsch and Mathias called "producing managers."[10] This is one of the many management challenges facing senior executives of firms competing in the investment banking industry.

FUTURE MANAGEMENT CHALLENGES

In this book we have presented a theory for understanding management in the investment banking industry. Our theory is grounded in an analysis of the network nature of the business, including its mediation function, economic characteristics, and production process. These three aspects of the business drive management practices, including the way strategy is formulated, the design of organizational structures, the management control systems used, the process for determining bonuses, and how relationships are managed. We developed our theory by observing existing practices, identifying patterns of similarity and difference, and showing how the practices logically follow from the network nature of the business.

Our theory was developed by studying practices in an industry that was at a peak of prosperity. We believe it is equally applicable to times of adversity unless adversity leads to fundamental changes in the function, economic characteristics, and production process of the business. Similarly, there is nothing intrinsic to increased size and complexity of firms that obviates our theory unless size and complexity change one or more of the fundamental aspects of the business. Nevertheless, times of adversity, as well as larger and more complex firms, make it more difficult to apply the theory, since managing is more difficult in these situations.

The theory should also be relevant to companies entering the investment banking business, either through acquisitions or directly. Large manufacturing companies, insurance companies, and diversified financial services companies that have acquired investment banks may mistake the management practices of investment banks as examples of "poor management." But companies acquiring investment banks should be careful about confusing good management in one business with good management in investment banking. Although some adjustment in management practices may be necessary after an acquisition, to insist on practices that are inappropriate to investment banking is to risk inhibiting the effectiveness of the acquired firm.

Other companies, especially commercial banks, are attempting to enter the business more directly through existing resources and hiring people from investment banks. So far, the Glass-Steagall Act has prevented commercial banks from acquiring investment banks, or vice versa, except for consumer banks. Commercial banks attempting to carve out a position for themselves in the investment banking industry will have to make dramatic changes in their management practices. Given the decline of the traditional corporate lending business of commercial banks, a strategic decision to enter investment banking is much easier to make than to implement.

All companies that have entered or seek to enter the business face a similar challenge. Despite the frequent comments made by investment bankers that doing deals is more fun than managing, they have developed an implicit theory of management for their industry. In contrast, commercial banks, insurance companies, diversified financial services firms, and manufacturing companies have developed a rhetoric that more explicitly values the management function. The specific practices to which the general term *management* refers, however, are not necessarily appropriate to investment banking. To the extent this is true these companies must make changes in their management practices.

Review of the Theory

The central concept for explaining how the function, economic characteristics, and production process of investment banking determine effective management practices is that of a *network*. To mediate the flow of assets between issuers and investors, investment banks create a network of external ties with customers and each other. External ties determine the pattern of internal ties within the firm that are necessary for doing deals and making markets in securities and other assets. Changes in the external ties necessarily require changes in the internal ties. This is facilitated by the fact that a large proportion of the professionals in the firm (excluding operations) participate directly in these ties.

In the past, investment banks participated in one-bank relationships with issuing customers and the range of products and services offered was relatively limited. The result was a fairly stable and well-ordered set of ties. Ties with customers were simple because of the limited number of products involved, and those with other investment banks were extensive because of the large syndicates formed to distribute securities. Consequently, the internal ties were comparatively few and the pattern fairly simple and stable.

A small number of people were involved with each customer and had little interaction with people involved with other customers. And because firms relied heavily on syndicates to distribute securities, internal ties linking the issuer side of the firm with the investor side were relatively simple.

During the past two decades the one-bank model has been replaced by most issuing customers, particularly sophisticated and heavy users of investment banking services, by a set of investment banks. With some of these investment banks the customer has a relationship and with others transactions are done on an opportunistic basis and are not embedded in relationships. Customers are also much more willing to engage in conversations with firms that they might do business with.

A profound consequence of the shift from single to multiple relationships, and to transactions that are not embedded in any kind of a relationship, is the perception by both customers and investment banks that the interface between them has become more transactional. This is an inevitable result of each party attempting to obtain the advantages of both single and multiple relationships. The resulting tensions are exacerbated by the loose linkage between services provided to customers and revenues earned from doing deals.

Two models for the interface have been developed by customers in their attempt to strike the right balance between a pure relationship orientation and a pure transactional orientation. In the dominant bank model, in which one investment bank clearly stands out as the single most important relationship and gets the majority of a firm's business, more emphasis is given to the advantages of a single relationship. In contrast, the core group model, in which there is a small group of roughly equal relationships, places more emphasis on the transactional advantages that come from multiple relationships. Both models have resulted in an increase in the number of ties between customers and investment banks.

This increase, accompanied by a growth in the number of products and services on which these ties are based, has increased the complexity of internal ties, which involve a number of relationship managers and product specialists. In addition, in conjunction with the decline in syndicate size, a number of external ties between firms emphasizing origination and firms emphasizing distribution have now been internalized by firms that have developed strengths in dealing with both sides of the market interface. Furthermore, the rate of change in the capital markets has increased the speed with which external ties change and thus the speed of the corresponding changes in the internal ties as well.

The external ties between investment banks and between them and their customers are an important determinant of the industry's structure. Firms vary in the extent to which their customer ties are with financially sophisticated companies that make extensive use of investment banking services or are with less sophisticated companies that are more modest users. Firms also vary in terms of the number of products on which these ties are based and the distribution of their business across these products. These two dimensions define four strategic groups. In competing within and across strategic groups, the image of firms is important. Thus firms seek to create and take advantage of positive reputations of themselves as well as negative reputations of their competitors.

The complexity of the business and the speed with which market opportunities come and go necessitates a strong grass-roots or bottom-driven approach to strategy formulation. The people who are dealing directly with issuers and investors are in the best position to create products and particular deals based on these products that facilitate the flow of assets between the two sides of the market interface. Implementing these strategies requires a self-designing organization that is a flat, fluid, and complex network of relationships. Flatness is required in order to process information in a timely fashion. Fluidity is required because of the constant change in internal ties created by constant change in external markets.

Complexity is required because of the mediation function, economic characteristics, and production process of investment banking. Matching issuers and investors requires a large number of ties between those who have contact with each side of the market interface. The loose linkage between services provided and revenues earned requires ties between the different people who service an account so that they can share information and help one another identify opportunities for deals. And because each deal requires a unique and changing mix of specialist resources, ties are created between the people who work together to get it done.

The greater the number of specialists who must work together, the greater is the complexity of the pattern of network ties. Especially in the largest firms, the investment banking business is now conducted by specialists (investment bankers, sales personnel, traders, and research analysts) who are further specialized according to function, product, or market. This specialization results in differences in attitudes and behavior (differentiation), which complicates the necessary coordination (integration) between specialists. A number of structural devices are used to create the necessary ties for ensuring that integration takes place, including multiple reporting relationships, shared management responsibilities, and units with integrating roles such as the capital markets desk.

As external ties change, these structural devices are used to create the corresponding change in internal ties. Much of this change is implemented by the people concerned, with little involvement or initial awareness by top management. Because of the large extent to which people throughout the firm directly determine its network structure, we consider investment banks to be self-designing organizations.

Despite the self-designing property of investment banks, their structures are shaped and reshaped within broad parameters established by top management. And however malleable, because these structures are designed within certain constraints, they limit the range of future strategies. Top management can overcome this shortcoming through an annealing process in which it alternates between heating up the organization through important changes in strategy, structure, and personnel and letting it cool down, during which time grass-roots strategies and self-designed structures dominate top management's influence.

Complementing the loose structures in a self-designing organization are tight management control systems designed and installed by top management. These systems direct the energies of people throughout the firm and are thereby an important way by which top management exercises control. Call reports and the tracking of deals done away emphasize the importance of external customer ties; the distribution of call reports also signals important ties internally and disseminates information along them. Customer evaluation and cross-evaluation surveys produce information on the external and internal network of ties, respectively. The internal surveys are an important integrating device when their results are reviewed with the people involved. Measures of revenues and profits are another integrating device when they are reported for high levels of aggregation.

Financial measures of results are also useful for evaluating performance and making investment decisions, but they are necessarily imperfect and are subject to manipulation. They also give an incomplete picture of a person's overall contribution to the firm, and create temptations for local optimization at the expense of what is best for the firm as a whole. Thus the bonus determination process used in investment banks attempts to subjectively evaluate a person's overall contribution to aggregate levels of current performance and the long-term health of the firm. Just as systems compensate for the inherent shortcomings of self-designing network structures, the bonus determination process compensates for shortcomings inherent in the systems. Individuals receive bonuses from a pool established at a fairly high level of aggregation, such as a division or even the firm as a whole, based upon their contribution to current revenues—both their own and others'—marketing and client development, and recruiting and training. Basing bonuses on collective outcomes is another powerful integrating device.

Data from a number of systems, as well as information generated directly from the network of relationships in the firm structure, are used in evaluating an individual's performance. The complex networks found in investment banks facilitate the process, transmitting information beyond that produced by the management control systems. The information, used as part of a careful and time-consuming bonus determination process, helps minimize charges that such a subjective process is unfair.

Structure, systems, and bonuses form a triad of organizational character-istics. Each plays an important role that includes compensating for flaws inherent in another. Taken as a group, the characteristics of the organization are complemented by the individual role of relationship manager. Persons in this role are needed, since the organizational characteristics alone cannot ensure that the right balance is struck between the resources of the firm and the return on these resources. Taking a firmwide perspective, relationship managers act as agents of the investment bank's CEO with respect to cus-tomers. In the agency role, they stand outside the existing structure to some extent, which enables them to integrate the firm's resources in ways that product specialization may inhibit.

For very important customers, a firm's most senior executives often have important relationship management responsibilities. Time spent managing customers is time not spent managing the firm and this can be detrimental to its effectiveness. But time spent managing customers is also an effective control on senior executives who would *over*manage the firm by interfering with grass-roots strategy formulation and the self-designing organization. The tension between external and internal management is acutely felt by many senior executives. The presence of some tension, however, should not be misinterpreted as requiring executives to choose between one or the other. Effective management of the customer interface necessarily requires effective management within the firm.

Relevance of the Theory

Most of our field data on the management practices used in investment banks were collected in 1986, with some follow-up data collection in 1987. The quantitative data on deals done used for analyzing the customer and investment bank interface and the industry structure were for the period 1984 to 1986. This period capped a five-year bull market starting in 1982, which was marked by rising stock prices, falling interest rates, substantial M&A activity, and important new products such as mortgage-backed securities.

A number of firms, especially the special bracket firms and Drexel Burn-ham Lambert, took advantage of this period of prosperity to grow substan-tially in revenues and personnel. At First Boston, for example, revenues grew more than fourfold between 1981 and 1986. In the same period, First Boston, Morgan Stanley, Salomon Brothers, and Goldman, Sachs more than doubled in size, from roughly two thousand employees each to more than five thousand. A disproportionate share of this increase came from staffing their London and Tokyo offices. Morgan Stanley, for example, started its London office in 1976 with fewer than fifty employees; by 1987, its staff had grown to nearly four hundred. Similarly, its Tokyo office employed fewer than thirty people in 1984 but three years later had close to four hundred.

In addition to rapid growth, the structure of investment banking firms became increasingly complex because of their higher degree of specialization. Increased size alone makes further specialization for a given set of products possible, since minimum scale economies can be obtained for a more refined division of labor. But increased specialization also resulted with the emergence of a number of new products, including mortgage-backed securities, swaps, takeover defense, and shelf-registered security offerings.

At the time of our study, senior executives were feeling the strain that comes with increased size, complexity, and geographic dispersion. The question must be asked if at some point further movement in these directions will invalidate our theory about management in the investment banking industry. Our answer is that the theory will remain relevant as long as increases in these variables do not cause fundamental changes in the function, economic characteristics, and production process of investment banking. Because these aspects of the business determine management practices, if the network nature of the business remains the same, then our theory about management should still be relevant.

This is not to say that no change is necessary.[1] In particular, greater complexity resulting from product and geographic diversification means that systems will become more important. Despite the belief in the industry about the interrelatedness of markets, by 1987 even the largest firms were finding themselves under pressure to make choices about which businesses to emphasize or whether to even be in them. The pressures came from both capital constraints, despite the rapid increase in capital in the largest firms, and management limitations.[2] Systems measures, particularly measures of product and geographical profitability, will play an increasingly important role in making these decisions. A further reason for improving these measures is so that beliefs about the interrelatedness of markets and customer buying behavior can be tested empirically. Producing useful measures will not be easy for the reasons we described in chapter 7 on the difficulties inherent in measuring product profitability. Nevertheless, this challenge cannot be avoided.

Meeting this challenge also has its risks. When the quality of performance measurement of specific departments, products, or even individuals improves, too much emphasis may be placed on systems measures, whether intentionally or unintentionally. This can lead to more centralized and overly cautious strategy formulation that misses market opportunities, to local optimization, which is not in the best interest of the firm as a whole, to an excessive emphasis on activities that are measured by systems (such as revenues and profits) at the expense of activities less easy to capture in a quantitative way (such as recruiting and training), and to an unwillingness to build ties throughout the firm outside one's department.

More generally, an increased emphasis on systems can disrupt the balance in the triad of a self-designing structure, management control systems, and the bonus determination process. To prevent this from occurring, more effort needs to be made to maintain the structural flexibility of the self-designing organization, as well as a bonus determination process based on a subjective assessment of an individual's contribution to collective outcomes. Unless this is done, more powerful systems may lead to a more rigid structure and to bonuses based more on individual or departmental financial measures. Similarly, more effort will be required to preserve the firm's capability for grass-roots strategy formulation and for relationship management that crosscuts the firm's organizational design.

Obviously, as firms become larger, more complex, and more geographically dispersed (which introduces problems of cultural and time zone differences), it becomes more difficult to manage using the practices we describe. For example, making a subjective assessment of an individual's contribution to collective outcomes is much more difficult. This increasing difficulty means that more people will have to spend more time developing and using particular techniques for achieving the organizational characteristics described here.

Although it is difficult if not impossible to anticipate what these techniques will be, what can be predicted is that the annealing process will become more important. In order to foster grass-roots strategy formulation and to preserve the firm's self-designing capabilities, top management cannot and should not intercede much in the day-to-day activities and decisions of people in the firm. At the same time, larger and more complex firms will invariably find themselves persisting in businesses that are no longer attractive, failing to create internal ties of the appropriate strength, and ignoring strategic opportunities that require a different organizational structure. These limitations can be addressed through more frequent heating-up phases to produce dramatic changes in strategy, structure, and personnel. The greater intensity of the annealing process will foster the development of management techniques for managing larger and more complex firms. It will also improve top management's knowledge about what is going on in the larger and more complex firms, since change generates information.

Systems are also more important when more emphasis is placed on controlling costs instead of simply maximizing revenues. During the data collection phase of our study, a number of the investment bankers we talked to described their business as "revenue driven" to emphasize that getting the necessary resources for taking the fullest advantage of business opportunities was more important than worrying about the costs of the resources.

This perception was reinforced by the belief that personnel costs, a large proportion of total costs, contained a large variable cost element in the form of bonuses, which were not paid out unless the revenues were earned.

The emphasis on increasing revenues rather than controlling costs is reflected in data on pretax profit margins and return on equity. Data from the Securities Industry Association for "large investment banks" show that pretax profit margins declined from a high of 17.4 percent in 1982 to 13.5 percent in 1986, and were down to 8.8 percent for the first half of 1987. Correspondingly, pretax return on equity declined from 54.8 percent in 1982 to 34.2 percent in 1986, and to 18.4 percent in the first half of 1987.[3] Similar trends were reported for national full-line firms and the industry as a whole.

Thus, while the record 508 point drop in the Dow Jones Industrial Average on Black Monday (October 19, 1987) signaled an end to the bull market and triggered concerns about the industry, firms were already experiencing tougher times. Growth in revenues was providing profits, but well before this historic event the industry was experiencing adverse conditions stemming from the high level of competition, falling bond prices in 1987, and a decline in the municipal market.[4]

In late 1987, a number of investment banks were taking advantage of a weaker market to trim some of the excess that had emerged during the prior boom period. Salomon Brothers eliminated eight hundred jobs when it exited the commercial paper and municipal businesses. Goldman, Sachs announced plans to trim up to four hundred people. L.F. Rothschild dismissed 875 people after reporting a loss of $44 million in its arbitrage department in October. Kidder, Peabody reduced its municipal department by one-third and later announced layoffs of a thousand people. Shearson Lehman Brothers was another firm cutting back in municipals along with staff reductions in London. It also announced plans to fire between five and six thousand people who were made redundant when Shearson Lehman Brothers acquired E.F. Hutton.[5] Just before the holidays Merrill Lynch reported retrenchment plans that could result in the dismissal of up to two thousand employees.[6]

Boom and bust cycles are not new to the industry and responding to cycles continues to be a difficult problem.[7] But since our data on management practices were gathered during the top of a boom cycle, we must ask how relevant the underlying management theory is to firms when the industry is experiencing less abundant times. Perhaps in times of adversity, changes may occur in the network nature of the business. For example, under pressure from customers and competitors, firms may charge fees that are directly tied to services provided, as consulting and law firms generally do. This will reduce the loose linkage between services and revenue and perhaps allow for a simpler network of internal ties. Similarly, under cost pressures, firms and the markets may shift to more standard financing deals that would allow some aspects of mass production. (Shelf registration may be a first step in this direction.) This would also allow simplification of the internal network of relationships. But unless adverse economic conditions lead to these or other fundamental changes in the function, economic characteristics, and production process of investment banking, there is no reason to believe that the basic management practices should be changed.

As with increased size and complexity, adverse economic conditions will make it more difficult to implement these practices. Such conditions also make systems for measuring revenues and profitability more important. When the firm is facing resource constraints, it has to be more careful about how it allocates its resources. Products and markets with unattractive returns and bleak prospects must be sacrificed for those with better current or future returns.

On the other hand, the risk of excessive reliance on systems in management is especially high in periods of modest or negative profitability. In its desire to tighten up the ship, top management may interfere with grassroots strategy formulation and the self-designing organization. Top management needs to make a special effort to preserve these characteristics within the limitations of the firm's resources by restraining itself from controlling too much.

This caution about getting too involved with strategy and structure should be complemented by getting even more involved in the bonus determination process. The difficulties of evaluating what an individual's total contribution is to the short- and long-term viability of the firm as a whole, and distributing bonuses that are both responsive to market prices and perceived as fair, are multiplied many times over when there are fewer bonus dollars to spread around. To the extent that top management wants to maintain an emphasis on the importance of total firm outcomes, it must not be perceived as awarding bonuses to people and departments strictly based on their own revenues and profits. If it wants all people in the firm to feel that everybody is in the same boat, a process that awards bonuses based on a subjective evaluation of a person's overall contribution must be used in good times and in bad. Failure to do so will have long-term negative consequences for the ability of the bonus determination process to act as an effective integrating device.

The difficulty in determining bonuses when there are fewer dollars to go around is especially acute when one's firm does poorly compared to the rest of the industry. In these circumstances, failing to reward top revenue producers their market value risks losing them to competitors. But in matching market prices, the perception that individual or departmental revenues are the only thing that counts is reinforced and there are even fewer dollars to reward those who have made other contributions to the firm. This can hurt morale for some time to come.

Reduced profitability for the industry as a whole actually creates opportunities for top management to revise the financial expectations of their employees. A number of senior executives expressed the concern that junior bankers did not realize that the period of prosperity was not the norm. Peter Buchanan, CEO of First Boston, observed, "This is a very unreal environment. Young people don't understand this, having never seen a bad year."

During our interviews we were also struck by the number of senior executives in the industry who expressed outrage at what they had to pay recruits and junior people, but who did so lest they lose business opportunities to competitors. When times are bad, however, employees quickly shift from worrying about how large their six-figure bonus is going to be to whether or not they will have a job next year. Concern for security is increased when layoffs suggest that other opportunities will only be found by leaving the industry. And most of these opportunities, many of which would require a move outside New York City, pay at about the same level that investment banking pays in hard times.[8]

Even if all firms in the industry face a bust period together and are successful in substantially revising downward the financial expectations of employees, the problem remains of how to get the necessary level of hard work and commitment required in a firm with grass-roots strategy formulation and a self-designing organization. During the course of our research we were impressed by the willingness of investment bankers to work incredible hours for a sustained period of time in order to get deals and get them done. Firms that rely upon the self-initiative of their people depend heavily upon them to pay more attention to what they should do rather than to what they are simply required to do.

The personal sacrifices required for this high level of commitment are easier to make when the financial rewards are handsome. Furthermore, it is more exhilarating to work hard at chasing deals when the probability of getting one is high. In a more competitive environment with fewer deals and deals with lower margins, top management needs to find ways to maintain high levels of commitment through other than financial rewards. Here too the annealing process is useful. Those who truly enjoy the business will appreciate the opportunities created to try new and different things. Those who came into the business purely for the money or to follow their friends will be selected out, increasing the average quality of the firm's human resources. G. Chris Andersen, a managing director at Drexel Burnham Lambert, described this process: "There's a people cycle. What happens is that you go through a period of ascendancy. Ultimately you get to the point where you have a critical mass of people who have never seen the bottom of the trough. They tip things over and when you go down the other side you schuck off a percentage of them and then start over again."

Thus down markets, however painful they may be, are an opportunity. They force managers to get rid of marginal personnel, which is always an unpleasant task, but is especially difficult to face when business is booming and everybody can be used. A number of executives we interviewed also pointed out that down markets create the biggest opportunities for some firms to significantly upgrade their competitive position. The quality of a firm's management is especially revealed by how well positioned the firm is to take advantage of the unpredictable but inevitable improvement in market conditions following a period of slow or declining business activity.

Applications of the Theory

The companies that have the greatest opportunity to improve their competitive capabilities by applying the management practices we describe are those that are new to the investment banking business. Most of these companies have developed management practices appropriate for businesses that are different from investment banking in terms of function, economic characteristics, and production process. New competitors can improve their competitive effectiveness in the investment banking business by adopting these management practices.

A number of large commercial banks, such as Bankers Trust, Chase Manhattan, Chemical Bank, Citicorp, Continental Illinois, First Chicago, Manufacturers Hanover Trust, Morgan Guaranty, and Security Pacific, have, to varying degrees, been building up their investment banking business within the constraints of the Glass-Steagall Act. A number of other large commercial banks, including some regional and so-called super-regional banks, are also increasing their emphasis on investment banking. If Glass-Steagall is repealed, many of these companies will increase their efforts even more. Their primary reason for doing so is the simple economic fact that their basic business of lending money to large corporations has been interrupted by the investment banks, who raise money for companies through the capital markets. Commercial banks need to find other ways to earn revenues while serving corporate and other large customers. The lucrative fees found in M&A and advisory work look particularly attractive.

The two major obstacles cited by commercial banks to success in the investment banking business—which are also cited by their investment bank competitors—are skilled people and culture. The typical corporate loan officer is perceived as lacking in the financial sophistication necessary in the investment banking business. Commercial banks are addressing this weakness through massive internal training programs and by recruiting from investment banks. Cutbacks in personnel and hiring by investment banks will create opportunities for commercial banks to build up their human resources.

Concerns about cultural differences cover a variety of issues; it has become a catchall phrase. One issue is the perception that loan officers are too risk averse. Commercial bankers are also perceived as being insufficiently aggressive and unwilling to call on the higher levels of the customer, such as the CFO and CEO. Banks are also addressing these concerns through training programs and changes in their credit management process. Nevertheless, there is clearly a legitimate reason for commercial bankers to be concerned about credit risk, as investment banks doing bridge loans are aware.

Although people and cultural issues are real, it is more useful to contrast the management practices of commercial banks and investment banks in the terms used here. Even though commercial banks are in the business of providing money to corporations, the function, economic characteristics, and production process in traditional commercial banking are very different from those of traditional investment banking. This has led to major differences in their process for formulating strategy, organizational structure, management control systems, process for determining bonuses, and relationship management. For commercial banks attempting to be successful in the investment banking business, we believe they will have to move significantly toward the practices used by investment banks, as a few commercial banks have begun to do.

The mediation function in investment banking requires a direct link between issuers and investors in that the security issued by a borrower, for example, must be designed to be of interest to potential investors. In traditional commercial banking, the bank performs an intermediation function that, in effect, breaks or at least greatly reduces the link between issuers and investors. Commercial bank lenders need not be well informed about the types of securities that the other side of the bank is selling to fund the institution and thus do not have contact with investors. But now that the larger banks have started selling a significant share of their loans into the market, those originating loans with issuers must form ties with the salespeople who are responsible for distributing them in order to be able to design securities (loans) that meet market needs. Before this change, the internal ties needed within commercial banks were much simpler than those in investment banks.

Internal networks have also been simpler because the economic characteristics of the traditional corporate banking business are different. Commercial banks have not had the same loose linkage between revenues received and services provided that exist in the investment banking business.

There is some looseness in pricing, as illustrated by disputes between banks and customers about whether the customer's deposit balances are adequate to compensate for noncredit services as well as meeting loan compensating balance requirements. But such issues are usually resolved in annual or other reviews of pricing arrangements, in sharp contrast to investment banking in which services provided in one year may or may not lead to a deal in another part of the firm in the future.

Finally, there are considerable differences in the production process. Whereas investment banks process unique deals drawing from resources throughout the firm, the commercial bank has a traditional product, corporate loans, which come in a small number of relatively standard varieties provided by a well-defined set of people. Because of the need to carefully manage credit risk, the process for "producing" loans is also quite standardized and includes an institutionalized credit management process.

Given these differences in the traditional function, economic characteristics, and production process, it is not surprising that commercial banks have management practices that differ considerably from those in investment banking (see table 10.1). A few commercial banks, particularly those that have made the most inroads into the investment banking business, have shifted toward new management practices, but it is not an easy transition.

Compared to investment banks, commercial banks have less product diversification and much longer product life cycles. As a result strategy can be largely formulated at the top and it changes relatively infrequently. Most commercial banks have a regular and relatively formal strategic planning process in which units of the bank are asked to develop strategies within guidelines established by senior management. Unlike investment banks, however, the head of a business unit, such as the southeast corporate group, has relatively little room to be innovative to take advantage of a shift in the market.

Allowing more grass-roots strategy formulation will probably only be possible with major changes in structure. Partly because of practices developed to manage credit risk, the organizational structure in commercial banks is a tall and rigid hierarchical network, unlike the flat and flexible networks of investment banks. Furthermore, these networks are designed by the most senior executives with little or no self-designing capabilities. (This suggests that as investment banks increase their bridge loan activity, their structures may become more similar to those of commercial banks. So far the number of bridge loans has been small enough that top management can be involved in each decision and it has not been necessary to institutionalize a credit management process.) A consequence of the tall and rigid hierarchy is that communication flows up and down rather than across departmental lines, making it more difficult for various product specialists and others serving corporate customers to work as a team.

TABLE 10.1. Management Practices in Investment Banks
and Commercial Banks

Management Practice	Investment Banks	Commercial Banks
Strategy Formulation	Grass-roots strategy formulation within broad guidelines set by top management.	Formal top-down process with little room for innovation by people at customer interface.
Organizational Structure	Self-designing organization that is a flat, flexible, and complex network.	Tall and relatively rigid hierarchical network with strong departmental boundaries.
Management Control Systems	Measure revenues and profits at aggregate levels. Call reports, customer surveys, and internal cross-evaluations. Risk control systems for underwriting and trading.	Measure profits at aggregate, unit, and customer levels. Call reports and customer evaluations. Risk control systems for credit, trading, global interest rate, and foreign exchange risk.
Bonus Determination Process	Subjective process by senior managers. Large share of compensation. Highly variable across people and independent of hierarchical position.	Little senior management time. Small share of compensation. Little variation across people and amount is tied to level in hierarchy.
Relationship Management	Senior people heavily involved. Role is highly variable, depending on customer, seniority of banker, firm strategy, etc. Person may or may not control customer interface, and may or may not have product responsibility.	Senior people have little involvement. Relationship manager almost always has product responsibility (corporate loans) and retains control of the customer interface.

Shifting from a rigid hierarchy to a self-designing organization that is flexible and flat will be difficult and will require changes in values as well. Unlike investment banks, commercial banks have long emphasized the importance of managerial careers. In some banks, relatively young vice presidents are placed in charge of a lending unit and they give up account responsibility at this time. At an investment bank, this person would be just beginning to take over responsibility for major accounts, not give it up. Just as investment banks must more explicitly recognize the importance of management, so must commercial banks recognize the importance of careers in which senior people primarily manage important customers rather than parts of the firm.

Control systems are the management practice in which commercial and investment banks have the greatest similarity. For both kinds of institutions, external ties with customers are important. Thus, both actively use call reports and customer evaluations, but commercial banks have traditionally not needed, and generally do not have, internal cross-evaluations to monitor internal ties. Both also have extensive risk management systems for trading and other asset management activities, although commercial banks naturally have tended to invest more in credit management systems. Because of their geographic spread, large commercial banks have also developed aggregate risk measures, such as a system to manage global foreign exchange risk. In general, commercial banks have more extensive measures of financial performance than do investment banks, including better measures of profitability for business units and products of the bank, down to the level of individual customers. (Loose linkage militates against strict profit measures.) To the extent this helps with resource allocation and similar decisions, investment banks might learn something from commercial banks, but performance measurement systems also tend to encourage units of the organization to pursue the performance of their own unit.

In investment banks a tendency to pursue one's own self-interest is addressed through the bonus determination process. Firms are willing to pay bonuses that are many multiples of a person's base salary, with the size of the multiple not particularly related to seniority or place in the firm's hierarchy. There is also a substantial variation in the size of bonuses in which individuals who make an outstanding contribution to the firm receive much higher bonuses than average performers. Commercial banks, in contrast, have traditionally paid only modest bonuses as a share of total compensation. Furthermore, the size of the bonus is largely related to a person's hierarchical position, with little difference between what is given to outstanding performers and mediocre ones. Thus the only way in a commercial bank to make substantially more money is to advance up the managerial hierarchy, which, as already noted, substantially removes the person from customer contact; compensation practices are actually a disincentive to managing external relationships.

Not surprisingly, compensation has turned out to be a major source of conflict in commercial banks, in terms of the absolute and relative amounts paid and for what it is paid. In matching market prices for their investment bankers, or perhaps exceeding them to build a staff, commercial bankers are stirring up strong feelings of unfairness. But trying to minimize the differences in total compensation risks losing good people to competitors who are not attempting to preserve internal equity. Although the total amount of money paid in bonuses must be kept in line with the performance of the bank, commercial banks have little choice but to implement a process for determining bonuses similar to that which is found in investment banks. This will require more senior management attention than has historically been the case. It will also require improved systems and different organizational structures in order to generate the necessary information for evaluating performance.

Just as companies used to be served by an investment banker generalist who provided all the services of the firm, so were they served by a loan officer who took care of all of their commercial banking needs. And as in investment banks, product proliferation in noncredit services and investment banking products has made it impossible for any one person to adequately serve a large and sophisticated customer of a commercial bank. Instead, product specialists are coordinated in various ways through one or more relationship managers. Thus commercial banks face the same problems of investment banks in relationship management.

Commercial banks, however, generally approach the problem more rigidly. In almost all commercial banks, the relationship manager is a loan officer who retains credit responsibility, and typically retains tight control over the contacts with the customer. Thus commercial banks typically use just one approach to the relationship management problem, that of a loan officer acting as a penetrator. This approach is fraught with all the problems discussed in chapter 9, such as a product specialist who has little interest or is ineffective in selling other products. The problem of relationship management is made worse when only one approach is inflexibly used.

A more severe problem, mentioned above, may be that commercial banks have typically assigned relationship management responsibility to a fairly young person who calls on the customer at a low level for a short period of time before being promoted up a largely managerial career path. If commercial banks are to be successful in getting access to customers who buy investment banking products, particularly the CFO and CEO for M&A and advisory work, they must assign relationship management responsibilities to more senior people and preserve continuity in their customer relationships. Again, this will require a change in values to make this activity as attractive as internal management responsibilities.

The magnitude of the challenge facing commercial banks that seek to transform at least part of an organization into a successful investment banking business cannot be underestimated. They must transform themselves from large, hierarchical, and slow-moving organizations into organizations that are flat and flexible with self-designing capabilities. In the process they will shift from being a conservative organization with high security but modest rewards for most employees into a leaner, more risk-prone, and quicker one where job security is less but the rewards for outstanding performance are higher.

This is not to say that commercial banks do not have advantages of their own. In addition to their large capital bases, managers in the money center banks have experience in managing large organizations of substantial cultural diversity because of the large number of branches spread throughout the world. It is only recently that the largest investment banks have reached a size similar to that of the wholesale portions of commercial banks (this convergence being accelerated by aggressive shrinking in most money center banks after the decline in their traditional business). And most investment banks are neophytes in operating in foreign locations, particularly on the institutional side of the house.

It takes time to learn how to operate within the customs and regulations of a foreign country, to build an infrastructure, to establish a strong enough reputation to attract quality people, and to develop a global risk management system. Commercial banks have a great deal more experience in this area than do the investment banks. (At the time of our study many of the latter were struggling mightily with just managing their London and Tokyo offices.) The comparative strength of commercial banks in foreign locations, along with their freedom in most instances from any equivalent of the Glass-Steagall Act, has led some to a strategy of developing their investment banking capabilities outside U.S borders. One consequence may be that they are better positioned to become effective should Glass-Steagall be repealed.

In addition to commercial banks, other companies are getting into the investment banking business but they are doing it primarily through acquiring investment banks. Ignoring the acquisitions of one investment bank by another (such as Shearson Lehman Brothers' acquisition of E.F. Hutton), this strategy is being used by insurance companies (Prudential acquired Bache Halsey Stuart Shields; Equitable acquired Donaldson, Lufkin & Jenrette; Travelers acquired Dillon, Read), diversified financial service companies (American Express acquired Shearson Hayden Stone and later Lehman Brothers Kuhn Loeb, and Primerica acquired Smith Barney, Harris Upham), commodity brokers (Phibro "acquired" Salomon Brothers), retail companies (Sears acquired Dean Witter Reynolds), and diversified manufacturing and service companies (General Electric acquired Kidder, Peabody).[9] The diversity of these acquirers in terms of their own management practices and the differences in their plans for the nature and extent of the integration between the investment bank and their other businesses make it more difficult to make general statements about applying our theory.

One point that can be made, however obvious, is that these acquirers should proceed with caution in making sudden and dramatic changes in their investment bank acquisitions. Research studies of acquisitions continue to show that many if not most fail to live up to their economic and strategic expectations because of implementation problems in melding two organizations together (and the often high price paid for the acquired company).[10] Although this evidence has yet to quell the enthusiasm of CEOs or investment bankers for this activity, its importance is much more immediate to an investment bank that is itself acquired.

The general perception within the American business community, which is shared by many in the investment banking industry, that investment banks are not well managed creates an obvious temptation for acquirers to implement "sound management practices."[11] Whatever these practices are, they should be analyzed in terms of whether or not they supplement the management practices we have identified in investment banks, those that are based on the function, economic characteristics, and production process of the business. We suspect that acquirers can be most helpful in developing systems for measuring revenues and profits, and should be most cautious about implementing changes in the other management practices. In particular, acquirers that explicitly value internal management of the firm should recognize the importance of external management of customers.

The Management Challenge

Our discussion of the relevance of our theory to investment banks under conditions of increased size, complexity, and economic adversity, and the application of the theory to companies seeking to get into the business, can be summarized in terms of a dilemma that represents a management challenge to executives in investment banking and in other industries as well. On the one hand, the investment banking industry is suffused with a rhetoric about how it comprises people who like to do deals rather than manage. Nevertheless, it is our conclusion that this industry of deal doers has developed a set of management practices that are in many ways appropriate to the business. On the other hand, a number of companies seeking to get into the business more explicitly value management, although not necessarily the specific management practices used in investment banks. For incumbents, new entrants, and aspiring entrants, the challenge is to create a rhetoric for the management appropriate to the investment banking business.

A number of senior executives we interviewed in the investment banking industry acknowledged the importance of management. For example, Peter Buchanan, CEO of First Boston, observed, "We're spending a lot of time thinking about management. Management is very important and is not given enough attention in this firm or any other firm." The chairman of First Boston, Alvin Shoemaker, even went so far as to say, "In the future the firm with the best management will perform the best."

Recognition of the importance of management was mixed with some ambivalence about doing it. Shoemaker noted, "We have prided ourselves on being producers first, the fun end of the business, and on being managers second." Tom Strauss, the president of Salomon Brothers, remarked, "I think management is essential but there is nobody I know who wouldn't rather be doing a deal. A lot of management issues are the sheer drudgery of running a business."

The lower status of managers in investment banking is reinforced when producers make more than managers. Max Chapman, who was made president of Kidder, Peabody, noted, "The rewards are for people who develop new sources of revenue." After a person has become wealthy, he or she is more likely to trade off income for the lower status of being a manager in an investment bank, but such a person may not have the qualifications. Bill Mayer, a member of the Executive Committee at First Boston, mused, "We have some managing directors who say they want to manage. This often happens after they have already made a lot of money. Sometimes they get bored and want to get beyond a producing role." Some firms had responded to this problem by seeing to it that managers were paid as well as or better than producers of comparable seniority. Strauss explained that since "there is a notion that senior managers are just hired hands," his firm had decided to "consciously reward people for being good managers."

As senior executives in investment banking come to recognize the need for improving the rhetoric and financial rewards for managing the firm, we can ask whether there are any lessons about management to be learned from investment bankers. At first glance this question might be absurd given the perception that the industry is not well managed. But, we have argued, convincingly we hope, that investment bankers have developed management practices that are appropriate to their business. Thus it logically follows that any business similar in function, economic characteristics, and production process should have similar management practices. Indeed, there is evidence that this is the case. The Japanese trading companies, or *sogo shosha,* are in a business similar to investment banking in terms of the three key aspects, and they have a number of similar management practices.[12]

More generally, investment banks compete in a complex and dynamic industry, in which the number of products and rate of product innovation and obsolescence is high, and the interactions with customers are particularly intense. To the extent that investment banks are facing conditions in a more extreme form than is the case for companies in other industries, investment bankers can only look to their own experience for identifying effective management practices. But their experience can be the basis of management insights for executives in other industries.

Thus, somewhat ironically, we conclude that in this supposedly poorly managed industry, there are a number of practices that potentially have more general applicability to firms in complex and dynamic industries and to firms with intensive interactions with their customers, which include but are not limited to other types of professional services firms. We think that executives in such industries should give careful consideration to using grass-roots strategy formulation; flat, flexible, and complex network structures that are self-designed within the organization; customer surveys and cross-evaluation systems; a bonus determination process, for potentially large amounts that vary substantially according to performance, that uses substantial subjective judgment in order to evaluate an individual's overall contribution to collective outcomes; and the assignment of relationship management responsibilities to individuals, many of whom are very senior, who act as agents of their CEO with respect to particular customers. Implementing these practices will require that senior executives shift attention from managing the firm to managing customer relationships. This is felicitous, since more focus on customers will better enable people lower down in the organization to formulate grass-roots strategies, which they can in turn implement within a self-designing organization.

In the study of management, practice precedes theory. Firms confronting new or forgotten problems develop management practices; these become the basis for a general theory that can be applied by other firms that face similar problems. As students of management, we examined the management practices used in investment banks in order to make explicit the theory underlying them. The theory can be used to further the development of these practices, as well as to identify other situations in which these practices might be relevant. Such application of our theory will, in turn, contribute to its further development.

DESCRIPTION OF DATABASE AND ANALYSIS

The quantitative analysis for this book is based upon a uniquely organized database of investment banking deals. For particular customers, the database allowed us to study the number and variety of investment banking services used and the firms used to lead manage and co-manage these transactions. Looking at the data from the perspective of investment banks, we were able to explore their product and customer profiles. Finally, for particular kinds of products, we were able to study the customers and investment banks that were active in these products.

The Database

The data for this study were purchased from the Securities Data Company (SDC) and were used with the company's permission. SDC collects data for four databases: new issues of corporate securities, tax-exempt security issues, mergers and acquisitions, and international security issues. (We purchased only part of the international database, publicly issued international bonds.) The data are deal-based and contain such information about the deal as the issuer, the type of deal, the price, the amount of the deal, the terms, and the securities firms involved as lead managers and co-managers. Large and important deals are well covered in the database. Thus the SDC data contain nearly all of the large deals in which the role of an investment bank is especially important. Because domestic public security issues have to be registered with the Securities and Exchange Commission (SEC), the data on deals of this type are complete. Private transactions are less completely reported. Based on our interviews, it is clear that many small M&A deals are not reported and therefore not included in the SDC database.

The SDC databases are frequently used by investment banks and other firms on a time-sharing basis to study how well they are doing in particular product areas, such as noninvestment-grade bonds or IPOs. The databases are also used by various trade publications to produce league table rankings for various product categories. Such analysis of the databases by investment banks and trade publications is organized by product, not client, and is performed for each of the databases rather than across the four databases.

For our purposes, however, it was important to track customers and investment banks across all four databases. Thus, we standardized key data items, such as customer and investment bank names, across the databases and formed one combined database. Merging the databases allowed us to link customers, products, and investment banks, and perform unique analyses. Since the combined database was quite large, we made decisions about the time period, products, customers, and investment banks we would study.

Although the SDC database included deals done from 1981 to 1986, we concentrated on the most recent three-year period, 1984 to 1986. We assumed the three-year period was long enough to minimize the influence of unusual features of any one year, yet short enough to present relatively steady investment bank and customer relationships through the data. Furthermore, this period had the advantage of being two years after the start of shelf registration, so that any transitional effects of the implementation of Rule 415 on the data were minimal.

Most of the analysis of the data reported here is based on the "number of deals" done rather than dollar volume or fees. Deals and dollar volume are highly (although not perfectly) correlated—those companies that did a large dollar volume of deals tended to do a large number of deals as well. Dollar volume was not used because the database did not include dollar-volume figures for some private transactions and for many M&A transactions. We did not use investment banking fees in the analysis because fees were unevenly reported and fees on underwriting are not particularly relevant by themselves. We had no data on after-market behavior, so we did not know how aggressively the issue was priced relative to the market.

The combined database contained a huge number of product categories, making analysis unwieldy. To facilitate our study of the database, we put each product into one of twelve categories. These are relatively standard product categories and each represents a market segment, such as investment-grade bonds and noninvestment-grade bonds (see table A.1).

Customers

In our analysis of customers, we focused on companies that did three or more deals over the three-year period. In generating this set of customers,

TABLE A.1. Deals by Product Category, 1984–1986

Product Category	Number of Deals
Noninvestment-Grade Bonds	620
Convertible Bonds	484
Investment-Grade Bonds	1,827
Mortgage-Related Securities	2,490
Privately Placed Securities	3,548
Common Stock	1,556
Initial Public Offerings	2,145
Preferred Stock	746
International Bonds	4,318
Tax-Exempt Bonds	14,955
Advice to M&A Targets	1,869
Advice to M&A Acquirers	1,612

we excluded entities formed for the sole purpose of issuing mortgage-backed securities. Although mortgage-backed and other mortgage-related securities are a new and important type of security, they were excluded in our analysis of customers. The number of these deals for a particular customer behaves very differently from other kinds of securities. For example, their deal count can be readily inflated as institutions buy mortgages and issue mortgage-backed securities to take advantage of arbitrage opportunities. Thus we did not include mortgage-related securities when we computed items such as number of deals per customer, but they were included in our analysis of investment banks and their product profiles, discussed below.

Our primary focus was on domestic companies, since it would have been unrealistic to focus on the full range of non-U.S. issuers and their investment banks. After excluding foreign companies and mortgage-related security issuers, we had a set of 1,167 customers, each of which had done three or more deals from 1984 to 1986.

We further divided customers into subsets of "most active" companies, including the "most active 100" and "most active 500" companies. Subsets were generated from the SDC database on the basis of deals done by company (see table A.2).

Investment Banks

In similar fashion to our analysis of customers, we focused on a particular set of investment banking firms in our analysis. In selecting the investment banks to study, we looked at the firms ranked in the top twenty-five invest-

TABLE A.2.   Characteristics of Most Active Customers, 1984–1986

Most Active Corporate Customers	Number of Companies	Number of Deals Done	Average Number of Deals	Avg. No. of Investment Banks Used as Lead Manager
Group I	106	13 or more	23.3	6.6
II	80	9 to 12	10.4	3.8
III	103	7 to 8	7.4	3.3
IV	81	6	6.0	2.5
V	137	5	5.0	2.4
VI	232	4	4.0	2.0
VII	428	3	3.0	1.7
Total	1,167			

NOTE: The "most active 500" customers group contain the 507 companies doing five or more deals that make up Groups I–V.

ment banks in each of several product categories from 1984 to 1986. We chose those firms that were well represented in the majority of the product categories. The resulting set of firms contained nineteen relatively large and diversified investment banks. Since nineteen is not a round number, we attempted to choose a twentieth but could not. All the candidates were firms strong in narrow product categories, purely regional firms, or varied in the strength of their performance through the three-year period.

For some purposes, we concentrated on the six special bracket firms: First Boston, Merrill Lynch, Morgan Stanley, Salomon Brothers, Shearson Lehman Brothers and Goldman, Sachs. In chapter 4, we used fourteen banks for our analysis, excluding five of the nineteen firms from our analysis because they were not the primary bank for many of the "most active 500" companies.

Ties between Customers and Investment Banks

Merging the four SDC databases enabled us to identify all investment banks that had done deals with a particular customer. The investment bank that did the most deals for a company was defined as the primary bank. The secondary bank was the investment bank that did the second most deals for a company. Investment banks tied in the count of deals were considered co-primary or co-secondary banks, depending on their position.

Knowing which investment banks worked with which customers and how many deals each firm did for a customer, we were able to study how companies managed their investment banking relationships. As discussed in chapter 4, we found two models that explain customer and investment bank relationships. The two models are the dominant bank model, in which a customer awards a substantial amount of its business to one investment bank, and the core group model, in which the customer allocates the bulk of its business among a small group of roughly equal investment banks. To identify the approach used, we defined a company as using the dominant bank model if its primary bank led at least 50 percent of its deals *and* if this investment bank led at least twice as many deals as the secondary bank. Companies not meeting this test were considered to be using the core group model (see table A.3). It is conceivable that some companies might use a purely transactional approach rather than one of the two models, but in a large, random sample of active companies we could find no evidence that this approach was used. We also found no evidence for a transactional approach in our interviews with twenty-one companies.

Ties among Investment Banks

Investment banks have numerous ties with each other (see table A.4). They compete for customers; they work together in syndicates; and they negotiate across the M&A table. Data on these ties are reported in the text. For example, investment banks competing at the customer interface are discussed in chapter 4. In chapter 5 we report lead manager and co-manager relationships in syndicates as well as the number of times firms worked on opposite sides in M&A advisory work. The number of ties between lead managing and co-managing investment banks are obviously much more extensive than those of the six special bracket firms discussed in chapter 5.

There is an interesting contrast between the patterns of syndicate ties and M&A ties. Some of the syndicate ties are much more frequent than would be expected given the number of lead-manager and co-manager positions of several of the firms. For example, Salomon Brothers and Merrill Lynch used each other as co-managers extensively because of their excellent distribution capabilities. Other combinations were used much less than would be expected statistically (see table A.5). When significance tests were performed for the entries in the M&A table, however, none of the entries was

TABLE A.3. Use of the Dominant Bank and Core Group Models, 1984–1986

Corporate Customers	% Using Dominant Bank Model	% Using Core Group Model
Group I: "100" Most Active	37.7	62.3
Groups II–V: Next "400"	63.4	36.6
"Most Active 500" Total	55.6	44.4

TABLE A.4. Lead Manager and Co-Manager Investment Banks, 1984–1986

Lead Managers	Co-Managers										
	Salomon Brothers	First Boston	Goldman, Sachs	Drexel	Shearson Lehman	Merrill Lynch	Paine-Webber	Morgan Stanley	Kidder, Peabody	Pru–Bache Securities	E.F. Hutton
Salomon Brothers	0	161	123	23	86	243	34	73	36	19	23
First Boston	118	0	159	15	100	111	20	122	35	19	6
Goldman, Sachs	98	64	0	11	46	57	10	49	30	4	5
Drexel	9	12	7	0	17	21	7	1	17	5	5
Shearson Lehman	78	99	75	8	0	59	17	28	15	24	25
Merrill Lynch	123	98	47	16	63	0	15	32	24	27	17
PaineWebber	28	18	6	8	30	19	0	2	10	8	11
Morgan Stanley	93	65	57	32	21	56	6	0	28	12	16
Kidder, Peabody	22	11	22	16	13	31	3	7	0	7	17
Pru–Bache Securities	2	7	2	2	5	3	1	0	3	0	4
E.F. Hutton	4	2	4	5	2	1	1	0	1	3	0
Smith Barney	9	2	3	3	8	4	7	4	4	1	9
Bear, Stearns	2	8	2	4	4	6	5	3	1	1	1
Dean Witter	3	9	6	3	8	7	3	0	6	5	12
Dillon, Read	3	9	4	0	3	2	0	1	2	0	2
Alex. Brown	3	2	2	4	3	3	1	2	5	0	2
DLJ	1	1	0	1	2	0	2	2	0	1	7
L.F. Rothschild	2	0	0	0	6	1	1	0	1	0	7
Lazard Frères	1	3	5	0	4	7	1	0	3	3	1
Other	11	8	1	9	13	13	14	3	0	0	5
Total	610	579	525	160	434	644	148	329	221	139	169

TABLE A.4. Lead Manager and Co–Manager Investment Banks, 1984–1986 (cont.)

Lead Managers	Co–Managers									No. of Times Bank Is the Lead Bank
	Smith Barney	Bear, Stearns	Dean Witter	Alex. Brown	Dillon, Read	DLJ	L.F. Rothschild	Lazard Frères	Other	
Salomon Brothers	20	17	15	7	4	4	7	18	121	1,522
First Boston	11	27	2	7	2	4	2	3	81	1,094
Goldman, Sachs	10	1	18	4	15	1	3	7	87	874
Drexel	12	23	10	0	5	8	2	2	83	862
Shearson Lehman	33	8	21	5	10	8	2	2	136	826
Merrill Lynch	11	20	13	2	14	9	5	7	143	792
PaineWebber	6	4	2	1	1	0	3	0	45	577
Morgan Stanley	15	18	8	4	7	9	9	3	90	551
Kidder, Peabody	19	2	4	3	1	7	2	0	82	509
Pru–Bache Securities	4	5	5	0	0	4	4	0	62	325
E.F. Hutton	6	5	11	1	1	2	1	2	39	279
Smith Barney	0	6	9	0	3	2	0	0	35	194
Bear, Stearns	1	0	1	1	1	1	1	1	33	175
Dean Witter	9	5	0	2	0	4	1	5	33	174
Dillon, Read	2	1	2	0	1	2	0	0	8	120
Alex. Brown	1	0	0	0	0	1	3	3	51	115
DLJ	0	0	0	0	1	0	0	0	33	101
L.F. Rothschild	2	2	4	0	3	2	0	0	27	96
Lazard Frères	0	1	0	1	0	1	1	0	8	46
Other	4	6	4	3	16	2	6	0	586	4,816
Total	166	151	129	41	85	71	52	53	1,783	14,716

TABLE A.5.   Significance of Frequency of Lead Manager and
               Co-Manager Relationships, 1984–1986

	Co-Managers					
Lead Managers	First Boston	Salomon Brothers	Goldman, Sachs	Merrill Lynch	Shearson Lehman	Morgan Stanley
First Boston	—	9	75*	4	28*	69*
Salomon Brothers	38*	—	18*	111*	−3	7
Goldman, Sachs	4	32*	—	−8	2	17*
Merrill Lynch	17*	34*	−22*	—	5	−11
Shearson Lehman	24*	−4	12	−21*	—	−12*
Morgan Stanley	4	26*	5	−10	−23*	—

NOTE: Entries in the table are "residuals"; that is, the difference between the number of times a firm was used as a co-manager and the number that would be expected given the frequency with which it served as a co-manager generally. An asterisk indicates a residual that is statistically significant at the .05 level.

significant (these tests are not shown). We expected this result because unlike lead manager and co-manager positions in which investment banks choose to work together, firms have little opportunity to choose which investment bank they work against in M&A advisory work.

Product Diversification of Investment Banks

Finally, in addition to studying the ties among investment banks, we studied the product profile and product diversification of the nineteen investment banks (see table A.6).

We used these data to design a diversification measure for each investment bank. We considered a fully diversified firm to have equal market share in the twelve product categories. A less diversified firm had relatively weak positions, or chose not to compete, in some product areas, and was comparatively strong in others. To capture this definition, the measure of diversification was calculated by taking the average market share for the three products in which a firm was the weakest, that is, a firm's three lowest market shares, and dividing this average by the firm's average market share for all twelve products. This diversification measure potentially ranges from zero (0), for firms that did no deals in at least three product categories, up to one (1), for firms that had equal market shares in all twelve product lines.

We used market shares rather than the number of deals for the diversification measure to reflect that the number of deals varies substantially across product markets. A given number of M&A transactions would represent a larger market share (and substantial revenue if the deals were large) than

TABLE A.6. Investment Bank Market Share by Product, 1984–1986

Bank	Inv.-Grade Bonds	Private Placmt. Bonds	Int'l. Bonds	Convert. Bonds	Noninv.-Grade Bonds	Mortgage-Related Securities	Tax-Exempt Bonds	Common Stock	IPOs	Pref. Stock	M&A Acq.	M&A Target	Total Market Share
Salomon Brothers	22.2	7.1	3.5	2.7	7.4	26.8	3.5	5.5	0.8	9.5	6.5	6.2	6.8
Merrill Lynch	16.2	1.9	2.7	9.5	5.0	5.0	7.6	6.5	4.0	5.1	6.5	5.3	6.2
First Boston	13.5	6.8	8.6	7.4	4.5	17.6	2.4	3.1	0.9	4.6	6.1	6.9	5.7
Goldman, Sachs	15.3	8.3	2.0	3.9	3.5	2.9	4.4	6.4	1.6	7.0	7.4	11.0	5.4
Shearson Lehman	7.2	5.9	1.2	5.2	4.8	9.2	3.0	6.4	1.8	8.2	5.5	7.5	4.3
Kidder, Peabody	3.6	3.9	0.5	4.1	1.8	4.2	3.5	6.4	1.8	4.0	4.4	7.1	3.5
Drexel	1.8	7.2	0.2	20.2	34.7	1.9	1.0	5.2	3.4	8.0	5.1	5.0	3.3
Morgan Stanley	9.7	2.2	4.3	3.5	6.6	3.3	1.6	4.4	1.4	7.6	7.4	5.3	3.3
PaineWebber	1.9	8.5	0.0	1.4	2.3	3.2	2.9	4.0	2.2	4.2	2.3	3.0	3.1
Pru–Bache Sec.	0.3	3.6	0.1	2.9	3.5	2.0	3.5	3.7	1.3	2.4	2.5	2.1	2.6
E.F. Hutton	0.9	4.5	0.0	2.1	1.3	0.6	3.4	2.1	0.9	2.3	1.0	1.3	2.3
Smith, Barney	2.4	1.6	0.2	2.1	2.3	0.2	3.7	2.1	1.3	0.8	1.7	1.8	2.3
Bear, Stearns	0.8	0.5	0.0	2.5	4.2	1.2	1.0	2.5	1.3	0.9	2.8	3.0	1.2
Dean Witter	0.4	1.2	0.0	1.4	0.6	1.8	1.3	1.9	1.2	1.7	0.6	0.7	1.1
Dillon, Read	1.4	2.0	0.0	1.0	0.3	0.0	0.7	0.7	0.2	0.3	2.1	2.4	0.8
Alex. Brown	0.1	0.0	0.0	1.0	0.0	0.0	0.4	2.8	1.8	3.4	1.4	2.9	0.7
DLJ	0.0	0.7	0.0	2.7	1.1	0.0	0.5	1.5	1.0	1.6	1.7	1.6	0.7
L.F. Rothschild	0.1	0.3	0.0	2.9	1.8	0.0	0.8	1.9	1.0	1.3	0.4	0.5	0.6
Lazard Frères	0.3	0.2	0.0	0.6	0.0	0.0	0.1	1.2	0.5	0.3	2.7	2.8	0.5
Total	97.9	66.5	23.5	77.3	85.8	80.2	45.3	68.4	28.3	73.2	68.2	76.7	54.2

would the same number of tax-exempt securities issues (which would probably also represent less revenue).

Like all measures that reduce many numbers to a single statistic, this
measure of diversification has its shortcomings. The most obvious is illustrated by comparing a firm that has zero market share in eight products
with one that has zero market share in three. Both firms would end up with
a diversification measure of zero. Thus it is an especially imperfect measure
for low levels of diversification. The measure does, however, work well for
the nineteen investment banks, since these firms were chosen on the basis
of their relatively high market share in the twelve products. An alternative
measure of diversification would explore an investment bank's concentration in its most successful products. This measure, however, penalizes firms
that are particularly successful in one or two products when in fact they
may be successful across all product lines.

GLOSSARY

Arbitrage: occurs when there is an opportunity to buy one security and sell another security and make a riskless profit. An arbitrage opportunity exists when two securities are mispriced relative to each other, so that it is possible to buy one and sell the other and make a risk-free profit. In the investment banking context, the term *arbitrage* is often used to refer to an activity when an acquisition is announced at a higher price than the current stock price of the target firm. The risk arbitrage department of an investment bank then decides whether to buy the stock to take advantage of the higher offer price.

Asset-Backed Securities: a security backed by a pool of assets, such as automobile loans. The cash flow from the pool of assets is used to make interest and principal payments on the securities.

Asset Valuations: usually refers to the valuation of assets in a merger and acquisition transaction. An investment bank is asked to estimate the value of the various parts of the firm that might be acquired.

Block Trading: trading of a large quantity of securities. The New York Stock Exchange considers a block trade to be equal to ten thousand or more shares.

Bond: see **Debt.**

Bought Deal: in securities underwriting, a firm commitment to purchase an entire issue outright from the issuing company. In recent years this term has been used to mean a firm commitment by one or a small number of investment banking firms.

Boutique: a small, specialized securities firm that deals with a limited clientele and offers a limited product line. In the context of this book *boutique* refers to a small, specialized firm that deals primarily with advisory services for issuers.

Bridge Loan: a short-term loan made by an investment bank to facilitate a transaction. It is made in anticipation of a security issue that would repay the loan.

Note: The definitions given here are intended to explain terms as used in this book, and do not necessarily cover all possible meanings of the terms.

Call Date: the date on which issuers have the right to call in or redeem outstanding bonds before their scheduled maturity.

Capital Markets Desk: a group of investment bankers who typically sit on the trading floor. They provide a direct link between issuing customers and the market.

Collaterized Mortgage Obligation (CMO): a security backed by mortgage bonds. The cash flows from the mortgage bonds are typically separated into different portions (e g., they can be separated into short-, intermediate, and long-term portions of the mortgages). Each class is paid a fixed rate of interest at regular intervals.

Co-Manager: works with a lead manager and often a group of other co-managers to manage a security underwriting.

Commercial Paper: a short-term debt with maturities ranging from 2 to 270 days, issued by corporations and other short-term borrowers.

Common Stock: a security representing ownership in a public corporation. Owners are entitled to vote on the selection of directors and other corporate matters. They typically receive dividends on their holdings, but corporations are not required to pay dividends. In the event that a corporation is liquidated, the claims of creditors and preferred stockholders take precedence over the claims of those who own common stock.

Convertible Bond: a bond that can be exchanged for a specified number of shares of common stock.

Credit Rating: typically refers to bond and commercial paper ratings assigned by Standard & Poor's, Moody's, or other credit-rating agencies.

Debt: a security that indicates a legal obligation of a borrower to repay principal and interest on specified dates. It is a general name for bonds, notes, mortgages, and other forms of credit obligations.

Distribution: the sale of a new security issue to investors.

Divestiture: the sale of a corporate asset such as a division.

Due Diligence: a process investment banks undertake to assure that information provided in a security offering is accurate.

Earnings per Share (EPS): the net income of a corporation divided by the number of shares outstanding.

Equity: represents ownership in a public corporation as evidenced by holding of common stock or preferred stock.

Eurobond: bond denominated in U.S. dollars or other currencies and sold to investors outside the country whose currency is used (e.g., a U.S. corporation could issue U.S. dollar-denominated securities to European investors).

Fixed-Income Security: a security that pays a fixed rate of return, such as a fixed rate of interest on a corporate bond.

Floating-Rate Debt: a security with interest payments that vary or "float" in response to prevailing interest rates, such as U.S. Treasuries.

Full-Service Firm: an investment bank that offers a wide range of financial services. The term is also used to refer to securities firms that have both extensive retail brokerage and investment banking services for large institutions.

Hedge: an investment strategy used to reduce risk. It typically involves the purchase or sale of a contract designed to offset the change in value of another security.

Hostile Takeover: an acquisition that takes place against the wishes of the management and board of directors of the target company.

Initial Public Offering (IPO): a corporation's first offering of common stock to the public.

Institutional Investor: an organization that holds and trades large volumes of securities such as pension funds, life insurance companies, and mutual funds.

International Bond: a bond issued outside the home country of the borrowing entity. International bonds can be subdivided into Eurobonds and foreign bonds. Foreign bonds are bonds sold primarily in the country of the currency of the issue.

Investment-Grade Bond: typically regarded as a bond with a credit rating of A or better.

Junk Bond: see **Noninvestment-Grade Bond.**

Lead Manager: works with a group of co-managers to form a syndicate to underwrite a security issue. A lead manager normally "runs the books" (manages the underwriting and determines distribution allocation) and is usually the investment bank that originated the deal.

League Table Rankings: published in various trade magazines, they rank security underwriters by the volume of securities underwritten.

Lease: a contract granting use of real estate, equipment, or other fixed assets for a specified period of time in exchange for a series of payments.

Leveraged Buyout (LBO): the purchase of a company, or part of a company, using borrowed funds. The target company's assets frequently serve as security for the loans taken out by the acquiring firm. These loans are then repaid out of the acquired company's cash flow.

Make a Market: trading a security in order to provide liquidity and market prices to investors.

Master Limited Partnership: a limited partnership comprises a general partner, who manages a project, and limited partners, who invest money but have limited liability. Frequently, limited partnerships are found in real estate and in oil and gas. A master limited partnership is a limited partnership that is publicly traded to give the investors liquidity.

Merchant Banking: in the context of U.S. investment banking, merchant banking refers to activities in which the firm commits its own capital to a transaction, as it does with bridge loans or when it makes equity investments in a company.

Mergers and Acquisitions (M&A): a general term that refers to various combinations of companies. A merger occurs when two or more companies combine; an acquisition occurs when one company takes over a controlling interest in another. M&A groups in investment banks work on these transactions, and they also advise on other kinds of related transactions, such as divestitures and repurchase of significant amounts of corporate stock.

Money-Market Paper: a short-term instrument such as commercial paper that is purchased by corporations and institutions that hold short-term liquid investment portfolios.

Money-Market Preferred Stock: a preferred stock instrument that has been structured to appeal to short-term investors such as investors that purchase regular money-market paper. The preferred stock is repriced every forty-nine days so that it trades like an instrument with a forty-nine-day maturity. From the point of view of the buyer, the advantage of preferred stock is that corporate holders of preferred and other stock only pay income tax on 15 percent of the dividend.

Mortgage-Backed Security: a security backed by a pool of mortgages. The cash flow from the pool of mortgages is used to make interest and principal payments on the security.

Noninvestment-Grade Bonds: technically, bonds with credit ratings of less than A. They are typically issued by companies without a long track record of sales and earnings or by companies that have experienced difficulty and have questionable credit strength. These securities are often used as a means to finance takeovers.

Origination: obtaining a mandate from an issuer to manage the underwriting and distribution of a new security issue.

Preferred Stock: a class of security that lies somewhere between bonds and common stock. Like interest on debt, dividends are paid on preferred stock at a specified rate, and holders of preferred stock take precedence over holders of common stock in the payment of dividends and liquidation of assets. Creditors, however, are ahead of preferred stock holders in the event of liquidation, and the company does not have a legal obligation to pay preferred stock dividends. Most preferred stock is cumulative, so that if its dividends are not paid for any reason, they accumulate and must be paid before dividends are paid to common stock holders.

Preliminary Prospectus: the first document released by an underwriter describing a new issue to prospective investors. It offers financial details about the issue but does not contain all of the information that will appear in the final prospectus. Portions of the cover page of the preliminary prospectus are printed in red ink, so it is popularly called a red herring.

Primary Market: the first time a security is sold to investors.

Private Placement: securities that are directly placed with an institutional investor, such as an insurance company, rather than sold through a public issue. Private placements do not have to be registered with the Securities and Exchange Commission, so these placements can occur more rapidly and with less information made available to the public.

Recapitalization: a change in a corporation's capital structure such as when the corporation exchanges bonds for outstanding stock. Some companies have been recapitalized in this fashion to make them less attractive targets for takeover.

Refinancing: when outstanding bonds are retired by using proceeds from the issuance of new securities. Refinancings are undertaken to reduce the interest rate or to otherwise improve the terms of the outstanding debt.

Restrictive Covenants: terms in a debt agreement that are designed to protect the creditor's interests. Covenants normally cover such matters as minimum amounts of working capital, maximum debt-equity ratios, and limits on dividend payments.

Retail Distribution: the capability of a securities firm to distribute securities to individual investors through retail brokers.

Secondary Trading: trading of securities which have already been issued in the primary marketplace. Thus, proceeds of secondary-market sales accrue to selling dealers and investors, not to the companies that originally issued the securities.

Securities and Exchange Commission (SEC): the federal agency created by the Securities Exchange Act of 1934 to administer that act and the Securities Act of 1933. The SEC is made up of five commissioners, appointed by the president. The statutes they administer are designed to promote full public disclosure and protect the investing public against malpractice in the securities markets. All issues of securities in the United States must be registered with the SEC.

Shelf Registration (Rule 415): a rule adopted by the SEC in 1982 that allows a corporation to preregister a public offering of securities. That is, they can preregister for up to two years prior to a public offering of securities. Once the security has been registered it is "on the shelf" and the company can go to market with the security as conditions become favorable.

Special Bracket Firm: an investment banking firm that leads the bulk of securities underwritten in the United States. The six special bracket firms are First Boston; Goldman, Sachs; Merrill Lynch; Morgan Stanley; Salomon Brothers; and Shearson Lehman Brothers.

Swap: has two meanings in the context of the securities markets. First, *swap* refers to the act of swapping from one type of security to another, such as an investor who swaps out of bonds into equities. Second, in a more recent use of the word, *swap* refers to debt obligations that are swapped between two borrowers (e.g., a borrower with floating-rate debt may swap its interest payment obligations with a borrower of fixed-rate debt; thus, the floating-rate debt issuer converts its debt into a fixed-rate obligation).

Syndicate: a group of investment banks that agree to purchase a new issue of securities from an issuer for resale to the investment public. These investment banks agree to underwrite the securities. That is, they guarantee to purchase the securities. This group of banking firms is normally part of the selling group that distributes the security to the ultimate investors.

Syndicate Desk: coordinates the underwriting function at an investment bank. It helps price the security, works with the other members of the syndicate, and determines the allocation between retail and institutional investors.

Tax-Exempt Bond: a bond whose interest is exempt from taxation by federal, state, or local authorities. It is frequently called a municipal bond even though it may have been issued by a state government or agency or by an entity that is not a municipality. General obligation bonds are backed by the full faith and credit of the issuing entity. These bonds may be underwritten by commercial banks as well as by investment banks. Revenue bonds are backed by the anticipated revenues of the issuing authority. Under present legislation, commercial banks may not underwrite revenue bonds.

Tender Offer: an offer to buy shares of a corporation for cash or securities, or both, often with the objective of taking control of a target company. The Securities and Exchange Commission requires a corporate investor accumulating 5 percent or more of a target company to disclose the investment.

Thrift Institution: the major forms of thrift institutions are savings and loans and savings banks. These and other organizations receive consumer savings deposits and invest most of their assets in residential mortgages.

Tombstone: an advertisement placed in newspapers and magazines by investment bankers to announce an offering of securities. It gives basic details about the issue and lists the underwriting group members in a manner that indicates the relative size of their participations.

Underwrite: securities firms underwrite a securities issue by assuming the risk of buying the issue and then reselling the securities to the public either directly or through dealers.

U.S. Treasuries: securities issued by the federal government to borrow money.

Wirehouse: a national or international brokerage firm that has a large retail network of branch offices.

NOTES

Chapter 2

1. This information and similar examples reported later in the chapter are based upon an analysis of deals included in the Securities Data Company database for 1984 through 1986. A three-year period was used to minimize the influence of unusual features of any one year. See the Appendix for more detailed discussion of the methodology for the quantitative analysis reported here.

2. For data on the number of equity portfolio managers, traders, and security analysts in investing institutions of various types and sizes see Greenwich Associates, *Institutional Equity Services 1986: Report to Participants* (Greenwich, CT: Greenwich Associates, 1986).

3. Another example of how external network ties influence the management of a firm is a study of two publishing companies by Walter W. Powell, *Getting into Print: The Decision-Making Process in Scholarly Publishing* (Chicago: University of Chicago Press, 1985).

4. For a review essay on how the concept of a network can be applied to organizations and some of the analytical techniques for doing so, see Noel M. Tichy, *Handbook of Organizational Design, Vol. 2, Remodeling Organizations and Their Environments,* eds. Paul C. Nystrom and William H. Starbuck (New York: Oxford University Press, 1981), pp. 225–249.

5. See Phyllis Feinberg, "Should Investment Bankers Be Paid by the Hour?," *Institutional Investor* (May 1979), pp. 110-122, for a discussion of some experimental efforts to charge for services rendered that are not tied to deals and the advantages and disadvantages of this practice.

6. In discussing the "uncomfortable properties" of information, Arrow noted that "there is a fundamental paradox in the determination of demand for information; its value for the purchaser is not known until he has the information, but then he has in effect acquired it without cost." Kenneth J. Arrow, *Essays in the Theory of Risk-Bearing* (Chicago: Markham, 1971), p. 152.

7. For a discussion of M&A fees see Peter Field, "The Attack on the M&A Barons," *Euromoney* (May 1985), pp. 89–96, and Peter Petre, "Merger Fees That Bend the Mind," *Fortune* (January 20, 1986), pp. 18–23.

8. "Salomon Securities Unit Won't Hire Pending Study," *The Wall Street Journal* (August 20, 1987), p. 39.

9. For one of the earliest theoretical treatments of how job-shop technologies require management practices different from other technologies, such as mass assembly and continuous process, see Joan Woodward, *Industrial Organization: Theory and Practice* (Oxford: Oxford University Press, 1965). See also James D. Thompson, *Organizations in Action* (New York: McGraw-Hill, 1967).

10. Brooke Kroeger, "Feeling Poor on $600,000 a Year," *New York Times* (April 26, 1987), pp. F-1, F-8. Discussions about the compensation of investment bankers are usually accompanied by questions about whether they are worth it, and about the contribution investment banking makes to the general welfare of society. On this point see Adam Smith, "But What Do Investment Bankers *Do?*," *Esquire* (November 1986), pp. 97–98, and Benjamin J. Stein, "Not Worthy of the Name? Investment Banking Isn't What It Used to Be," *Barron's* (July 13, 1987), pp. 6–7, 26, 28, 30, 32.

11. The classic treatment of management in the construction industry is Arthur L. Stinchcombe, "Bureaucratic and Craft Administration of Production: A Comparative Study," *Administrative Science Quarterly* 4 (September 1959), pp. 168–187. For a critique of this article and an alternative interpretation see Robert G. Eccles, "Bureaucratic versus Craft Administration: The Relationship of Market Structure to the Construction Firm," *Administrative Science Quarterly* 26 (September 1981), pp. 449–469. See also Robert G. Eccles, "The Quasifirm in the Construction Industry," *Journal of Economic Behavior and Organization* 2 (1981), pp. 335–357.

12. Paul R. Lawrence and Jay W. Lorsch, *Organization and Environment: Managing Differentiation and Integration* (Homewood, IL: Richard D. Irwin, 1967). This book is one of the earliest works in a management perspective labeled "contingency theory," which holds that management practices that will be most effective depend upon circumstances as determined by such variables as technology and environmental heterogeneity and dynamism. Other important works in this tradition include Arthur L. Stinchcombe, "Bureaucratic and Craft Administration," pp. 168–187; Tom Burns and G. M. Stalker, *The Management of Innovation* (London: Tavistock, 1961); Alfred D. Chandler, Jr., *Strategy and Structure: Chapters in the History of the American Industrial Enterprise* (Cambridge, MA: MIT Press, 1962); Woodward, *Industrial Organization;* Thompson, *Organizations in Action;* Charles Perrow, "A Framework for Comparative Organizational Analysis," *American Sociological Review* 32, 2 (April 1967), pp. 194–208; and Raymond E. Miles and Charles C. Snow, *Organizational Strategy, Structure, and Process* (New York: McGraw-Hill, 1978).

Chapter 3

1. This is confirmed by data from Greenwich Associates, *Investment Banking 1986: Report to Executives,* Greenwich, CT: (Greenwich Associates, 1986), which reports an average of 3.7 investment banks used by the 1,490 companies surveyed.

2. See John Thackray, "The Rise of Do-It-Yourself Corporate Finance," *Institutional Investor* (June 1982), pp. 194–209. Ipsen discussed a similar increase in the sophistication of internal M&A departments. Erik Ipsen, "The Growth of In-House M&A Departments," *Institutional Investor* (August 1984), pp. 202–208.

3. Michelle L. Collins and Michael F. Goss, *The Impact of Relationships on the Investment Banking Industry: Exhibit and Tables,* Field Study on the Management of Financial Service Organizations, sponsored by Donaldson, Lufkin & Jenrette, Harvard Business School, May 5, 1986, Table 1, p. 7.

4. Greenwich Associates, *Investment Banking 1986,* p. 24.

5. Sender stated that "even sophisticated treasurers complain they are inundated with financing techniques that often turn out to be obscure, expensive and inappropriate." Henny Sender, "The Client Comes Second," *Institutional Investor* (March 1987), p. 90.

6. Collins and Goss, *The Impact of Relationships,* p. 6.

7. For discussions on how principal activities can lead to client distrust and conflicts of interest, see Sender, "The Client Comes Second," pp. 84–87, 90, 95, 98; Benjamin J. Stein, "Not Worthy of the Name? Investment Banking Isn't What It Used to Be," *Barron's* (July 13, 1987), pp. 6–7, 26, 28, 30, 32; Stratford P. Sherman, "C.E.O.s Take on Their Investment Bankers," *Fortune* (April 27, 1987), pp. 57–64.

8. "First Boston Bounced from Citicorp Deal," *Investment Dealers' Digest* (September 14, 1987), p. 12; and Peter Truell, "First Boston Removed from Offering, Denies Charge of Conflict by Citicorp," *The Wall Street Journal* (September 14, 1987), p. 3.

9. Neil Osborn, "The Creativity Game," *Institutional Investor* (January 1983), p. 65.

10. For discussions of the role of these "quants," which include a number of former finance professors, mathematicians, and physicists see Michael Rogers, "Professors Who Work on Wall Street," *Fortune* (November 25, 1987), p. 83; Barbara Donnelly, "The Academic Invasion of Wall Street," *Institutional Investor* (December 1984), pp. 73–78; Barbara Donnelly, "Wall Street's Quants Come into Their Own," *Institutional Investor* (November 1984), pp. 181–188; and Joe Kolman, "Revenge of the Nerds," *Institutional Investor* (September 1987), pp. 84–94.

11. For a discussion of the development of the preferred stock product see Peter Grant, "What Hath Gallatin Wrought? The Preferred Stock Wars," *Investment Dealers' Digest* (May 11, 1987), pp. 18–25.

12. For a discussion of the role of these new product development groups see Osborn, "The Creativity Game," pp. 65–72; Michael Blumstein, "Creating New Financial Products," *New York Times* (August 8, 1982), p. F-6; and Gregory Miller, "The Knockoff Artists," *Institutional Investor* (May 1986), pp. 81–84.

13. The concept of a lead user was developed by von Hippel. See Eric von Hippel, "Lead Users: A Source of Novel Product Concepts," *Management Science* 32, 7 (July 1986), pp. 791–805, and Eric von Hippel, *The Sources of Innovation* (New York: Oxford University Press, forthcoming).

14. For a discussion of Sallie Mae's role as a lead user see Jill Dutt, "Wall Street's First Call: Why Sallie Mae Gets a Peek at the Hottest New Ideas," *Investment Dealers' Digest* (October 27, 1986), pp. 20–24.

15. Grant, "What Hath Gallatin Wrought?," p. 22. For a discussion of how new product groups work at copying the new products of others as well as developing new products of their own see Miller, "The Knockoff Artists," pp. 81–84, and Osborn, "The Creativity Game," pp. 65–72.

16. Greenwich Associates, *Investment Banking 1986*, p. 21.

17. For a discussion that product innovation has gone too far see David Shirreff, "Down with Innovation!," *Euromoney* (August 1986), pp. 23–31, and Andrew Marton, "How Much Is Too Much?," *Institutional Investor* (August 1984), pp. 238–250.

18. Of course, there is no consensus that the rate of innovation will continue to be as high as it has been the past twenty years. Miller has suggested that although further opportunities for innovation will continue to exist, since many are based on regulations and taxes, the rate of innovation may slow down in the future. Merton H. Miller, "Financial Innovation: The Last Twenty Years and the Next," *Journal of Financial and Quantitative Analysis* 21, 4 (December 1986), pp. 459–471.

19. Schumpeter made a similar argument about the inherent limitations of technological progress, which he saw as one cause for the ultimate end of capitalism. Joseph A. Schumpeter, *Capitalism, Socialism, and Democracy*, 3d ed. (New York: Harper & Row, 1950).

20. Michael M. Thomas, "The Elusive Partnership: Corporate America's Problem with Wall Street," *Corporate Finance* (November 1986), p. 48. Sender notes the

opinion of some that "Wall Street has now entered a third era: the era of adversarial banking, where the banker and his client begin negotiations in an atmosphere of distrust and hostility." Sender, "The Client Comes Second," pp. 85–86. But he concludes that "so for all the antipathy, Wall Street and its clients still need each other." Ibid., p. 98. Sherman posits a relationship that combines both adversarial and collaborative elements: "The relationship of the [Fortune] 500 to Wall Street's financiers is a peculiar mix of heart-felt antagonism and profound dependence." Sherman, "C.E.O.s Take on Their Investment Bankers," p. 57.

21. This concern about an inappropriately priced security is one reason why some companies avoid a competitive bidding procedure in selecting an investment bank for an underwriting. See Miriam Rozen, "Treasurers Starting to Shun Competitive Bidding," *Investment Dealers' Digest* (November 17, 1986), p. 12.

22. Shelby White, "More Pay, More Work," *Corporate Finance* (March 1987), pp. 49–51. For other data on investment bankers' compensation see "Coining It on Wall Street," *Institutional Investor* (July 1986), pp. 73–88, and David Carey, Lisa Kaplan, Stephen Kindel, Tani Maher, Deborah Mittel, Margaret Price, and Stephen Taub, "Wall Street's Superstars," *Financial World* (July 14, 1987), pp. 34–115. The *Financial World* top 100 ranged from a high of $125 million to a low of $3 million.

23. Tracy Kidder, *The Soul of a New Machine* (Boston: Atlantic-Little, Brown, 1981).

24. According to Sherman, "A more immediate worry for executives of [Fortune] 500 companies is the question of whether to trust their investment bankers." Sherman, "C.E.O.s Take on Their Investment Bankers," p. 60.

25. Granovetter noted the importance of personal or social relationships "for the production of trust in economic life." Mark Granovetter, "Economic Action and Social Structure: The Problem of Embeddedness," *American Journal of Sociology* 91, 3 (November 1985), p. 491. Causality goes the other way as well, since trust generated from economic exchanges forms the basis for personal relations.

26. Argyris argues that this tendency inhibits both individual and organizational learning in a way that will identify and correct the underlying causes of a problem. As applied to the customer and investment bank relationship, his ideas suggest that as long as the underlying issues are not discussed, they will not go away if the conditions causing them do not change, and may in fact grow worse. See Chris Argyris and Donald A. Schön, *Organizational Learning: A Theory of Action Perspective* (Reading, MA: Addison-Wesley, 1978).

Chapter 4

1. McGoldrick has also suggested the existence of a core group of three to six firms. She interprets this as a renewed emphasis on the importance of relationships by companies that became very transactional following Rule 415, shelf registration. Included in her argument is evidence from the Collins and Goss survey: Michelle L. Collins and Michael F. Goss, *The Impact of Relationships on the Investment Banking Industry: Exhibit and Tables,* Field Study on the Management of Financial Service Organizations, sponsored by Donaldson, Lufkin & Jenrette, Harvard Business School, May 5, 1986. Beth McGoldrick, "Who Said Relationships Are Dead?," *Institutional Investor* (May 1986), pp. 181–184.

2. The dominant bank model and the core group model bear some similarities, although they are not identical, to two models of industrial customer buying behavior discussed by Jackson. Barbara Bund Jackson, *Winning and Keeping Industrial Cus-*

tomers: The Dynamics of Customer Relationships (Lexington, MA: Lexington Books, 1985).

3. Baker refers to this as *shadow competition,* which he defines as "pricing as if one is in a real bidding contest against other firms." Wayne E. Baker, "The Organization-Market Interface: Corporations' Relations with Investment Banks," Harvard Business School Working Paper No. 87–043 (second draft), April 16, 1987, p. 55.

4. Data supplied by Greenwich Associates in a special report for the authors.

5. Greenwich Associates, *Investment Banking 1986: Report to Executives* (Greenwich, CT: Greenwich Associates, 1986), p. 15.

6. Ibid., p. 17.

7. The best fit of the data was a statistical equation using logs of the number of deals and investment banks. The resulting equation was

Number of Investment Banks $= .856$(Number of Deals)$^{.691}$

This equation explained 45.5 percent of the variance.

8. Thackray reports that "according to one recent survey, no less than 40 percent of the CEOs of the largest American corporations came up via the finance ranks." (Unfortunately, he does not identify the survey.) John Thackray, "The Rise of Do-It-Yourself Corporate Finance," *Institutional Investor* (June 1982), p. 194. In a carefully done sixty-year longitudinal study, Fligstein has shown that the percentage of presidents of the hundred largest American corporations with a financial background has risen from 7.6 percent in 1919 to 27.5 percent in 1979. He attributes this to the increased importance of diversification, especially through mergers and acquisitions, in corporate strategy. Neil Fligstein, "The Intraorganizational Power Struggle: Rise of Finance Personnel to Top Leadership in Large Corporations, 1919–1979," *American Sociological Review* 52 (February 1987), pp. 44–58.

Chapter 5

1. For a perspective on the status hierarchy reflected in syndicate structures see Samuel L. Hayes, III, "Investment Banking: Power Structure in Flux," *Harvard Business Review* (March–April 1971), pp. 136–152, and Samuel L. Hayes, III, "The Transformation of Investment Banking," *Harvard Business Review* (January–February 1979), pp. 153–170.

2. Kenneth N. Gilpin, "Split in 'Tombstone' Ranks," *New York Times* (October 5, 1987), p. D-1.

3. Ibid., and "Prior Restraint," *Investment Dealers' Digest* (September 28, 1987), p. 12.

4. Michael E. Porter, *Competitive Strategy: Techniques for Analyzing Industries and Competitors* (New York: Free Press, 1980), pp. 129–155.

5. Joseph Auerbach and Samuel L. Hayes, III, *Investment Banking and Diligence: What Price Deregulation?* (Boston: Harvard Business School Press, 1986), p. 141. For the opposite view, see Alexandra Clough, "Shelf Filing Hits Regionals Hard, SEC Admits," *Investment Dealers' Digest* (February 2, 1987), p. 16.

6. The network of lead manager and co-manager relationships is much more extensive than that among the special bracket firms. In the Appendix, lead manager and co-manager combinations for nineteen leading investment banks are given.

7. Carol Davenport, "DLJ Loses 11-Person Group to Smith Barney Harris Upham," *Investment Dealers' Digest* (October 20, 1986), p. 8, and Ida Picker, "Hut-

ton MBS Team Quits En Masse for LFRUT," *Investment Dealers' Digest* (September 16, 1986), p. 6.

8. Evan Simonoff, "Salomon's Muni Bankers Market Themselves as a Group," *Investment Dealers' Digest* (October 19, 1987), p. 22, and Evan Simonoff and Mark Fadiman, "Salomon Muni Team Move May Cause Friction at Dean Witter," *Investment Dealers' Digest* (October 26, 1987), p. 11. Dean Witter actually took out an ad in this publication to announce the hiring of twenty-three municipal bankers. *Investment Dealers' Digest* (November 9, 1987), p. 17.

9. "Lost Luggage," *Investment Dealers' Digest* (November 9, 1987), p. 11.

10. "If at First You Don't Succeed . . . " *Investment Dealers' Digest* (May 4, 1987), p. 12.

11. Porter, *Competitive Strategy,* p. 129. Porter makes the important point "that for purposes of defining strategic groups, the strategic dimensions must include the firm's relationship to its parent." Porter, *Competitive Strategy,* p. 130. The recent acquisitions of a number of investment banks make this point especially germane. It is too soon to assess, however, what the consequences will be in terms of the role the investment bank's strategy will play in the strategy of the parent company as a whole.

12. Other examples of industry-focused firms are discussed in Eric Laursen, "On the Waterfront (West): The Investment Banking Bosses of San Francisco," *Investment Dealers' Digest* (March 30, 1987), pp. 25–30, and other examples of regional firms are discussed in Phyllis Feinberg, "The Deal Hunters: How Regional Firms Survive Now That the Big Game Is Gone," *Investment Dealers' Digest* (February 16, 1987), pp. 22–26.

13. In his discussion of "horizontal strategy" Porter explores many of the issues involved in managing interdependent businesses. Michael E. Porter, *Competitive Advantage: Creating and Sustaining Superior Performance* (New York: Free Press, 1985), pp. 364–442. Diversified investment banks can be described as managing a large number of complicated horizontal strategies.

14. For a discussion of the growing importance of capital in serving large customers, especially for firms attempting a global strategy, see Beth McGoldrick, "How Much Capital Is Enough?," *Institutional Investor* (November 1986), pp. 183–187.

15. Samuel L. Hayes, III, A. Michael Spence, and David Van Praag Marks, *Competition in the Investment Banking Industry* (Cambridge, MA: Harvard University Press, 1983), pp. 63–77. They used customers to define four strategic groups of investment banks based upon the probability that members of each group would have a common set of corporate clients.

16. Ibid., pp. 70–73.

17. For some discussions of investment banks putting their own capital at risk see Fred R. Bleakley, "Wall St.'s Merchant Bankers," *New York Times* (November 19, 1984), pp. D-1, D-5; Beth McGoldrick, "Wall Street Puts Its Own Money on the Line," *Institutional Investor* (June 1984), pp. 61–75; James Sterngold, "Deep-Pocketed Deal Makers," *New York Times* (April 14, 1987), pp. D-1, D-8; Peter Lee, "View from Bridge Makes Bankers' Heads Spin," *Euromoney* (May 1987), pp. 64–73; and Ida Picker, "The Big Bet: The Dilemma of Bridge Financing," *Investment Dealers' Digest* (June 1, 1987), pp. 16–20.

18. See Lynn Brenner and Beth McGoldrick, "Investment Banking's New Boutiques," *Institutional Investor* (May 1983), pp. 179–189, and John Thackray, "The Catchy Rhythm of the One-Man Bank," *Euromoney* (May 1986), pp. 27–46.

19. The concept of strategic differentiation should not be confused with Lawrence and Lorsch's organizational concept of differentiation. Nevertheless, since strategic differentiation does lead to differences in attitudes and behaviors of people in differ-

ent firms, there are actually some advantages in using the same word to describe these related strategic and organizational phenomena.

20. Paul J. DiMaggio and Walter W. Powell, "The Iron Cage Revisited: Institutional Isomorphism and Collective Rationality in Organizational Fields," *American Sociological Review* 48 (April 1983), p. 151.

21. "Project 89" was how the firm referred to its objective of becoming one of the top five, or at least very highly ranked, investment banking firms by 1989. See Glenn A. Kessler, "George Ball's 'Project '89': Pru-Bache's Plan for Investment Banking," *Investment Dealers' Digest* (October 13, 1987), pp. 24–32.

22. For a description of the industry's consensus on Goldman, Sachs see Beth McGoldrick, "Inside the Goldman, Sachs Culture," *Institutional Investor* (January 1984), pp. 53–67.

23. Ken Auletta provides some glimpses into the culture of Lehman Brothers Kuhn Loeb in the period just before its acquisition by Shearson/American Express in his book: Ken Auletta, *Greed and Glory on Wall Street: The Fall of the House of Lehman* (New York: Random House, 1986).

24. Beth McGoldrick, "Salomon's Power Culture," *Institutional Investor* (March 1986), pp. 67–76.

25. Ida Picker, "Malicious Whispers: Wall Street Declares War on Drexel," *Investment Dealers' Digest* (March 16, 1987), p. 28.

26. Drexel was reported to have been one of the most profitable firms on Wall Street in 1986 with net profits estimated at $600 to $700 million. Marci Baker, "Drexel's Record Year Eases Scandal's Pain," *Pension & Investment Age* (January 12, 1987), pp. 1, 36.

27. Picker, "Malicious Whispers," p. 28. This article also noted the disparity between Drexel's treatment in the press and that of its competitors: "When Kidder and Goldman officials were nabbed, the general reaction was: 'What a shame. They're such nice people. And those are such fine, respectable firms.'" One story in the *New York Times,* for example, emphasized that Robert Freeman, the Goldman partner (indicted for insider trading), is "a great family man who manages a Little League team." Ibid., p. 24. An article in *Business Week* reported that based on an "extensive inquiry" conducted by this magazine, "whatever action the government brings against Drexel will probably be a good deal less monumental and far-reaching" than the rumors that this was the biggest scandal involving the securities industry since the 1920s." Chris Welles, "The Case against Drexel: Will the Government Come up Short?," *Business Week* (August 10, 1987), p. 56.

28. Stratford P. Sherman, "Drexel Sweats the Wall Street Probe," *Fortune* (March 16, 1987), p. 41.

29. For a historical perspective on the investment banking industry, and the rises and declines in the fortunes of some of its members, see Vincent P. Carosso, *Investment Banking in America: A History* (Cambridge, MA: Harvard University Press, 1970); Hayes, "Investment Banking," pp. 136–152; and Hayes, "The Transformation of Investment Banking," pp. 153–170.

Chapter 6

1. Kenneth Andrews, *The Concept of Corporate Strategy,* 3d ed. (Homewood, IL: Richard D. Irwin, 1987), p. 13.

2. Michael Porter's popular book *Competitive Strategy* (New York: Free Press, 1980) largely focuses on formulating business strategies.

3. The grass-roots strategy formulation process is similar to what Burgelman called "autonomous strategic behavior," which he described as "conceptually equivalent to entrepreneurial activity—generating *new* combinations of productive resources—in the firm. It provides the basis for radical innovation from the perspective of the firm." Robert A. Burgelman, "Corporate Entrepreneurship and Strategic Management: Insights from a Process Study," *Management Science* 29, 12 (December 1983), p. 1350. See also Robert A. Burgelman, "Designs for Corporate Entrepreneurship in Established Firms," *California Management Review* 26, 3 (Spring 1984), pp. 154–166. Grass-roots strategy formulation is also similar to what Mintzberg described as the "adaptive mode" of strategy making. Henry Mintzberg, "Strategy-Making in Three Modes," *California Management Review* 16, 2 (Winter 1973), pp. 44–53, and Henry Mintzberg, "Patterns in Strategy Formation," *Management Science* 24, 9 (May 1978), pp. 934–948. Most recently, Mintzberg himself has used the term *grass-roots strategy formulation* to describe a strategy-making process similar to what is found in investment banks. See Henry Mintzberg and Alexandra McHugh, "Strategy Formulation in an Adhocracy," *Administrative Science Quarterly* 30 (June 1985), pp. 160–197, and Henry Mintzberg, "Crafting Strategy," *Harvard Business Review* (July–August 1987), pp. 66–75.

4. "Underwriting Leadership: The First Six Months," *Institutional Investor* (October 1976), p. 97.

5. In an interesting and curious article, Hedberg, Nystrom, and Starbuck suggested the concept of a self-designing organization by describing its characteristics but without specifying how to create it. Bo L. T. Hedberg, Paul Nystrom, and William H. Starbuck, "Camping on Seesaws: Prescriptions for a Self-Designing Organization," *Administrative Science Quarterly* 21 (March 1976), pp. 41–65.

6. Paul R. Lawrence and Jay W. Lorsch, *Organization and Environment: Managing Differentiation and Integration* (Homewood, IL: Richard D. Irwin, 1967), p. 11.

7. Ibid.

8. For a general discussion of the relationship between organizational size and the division of labor see Peter M. Blau, "A Formal Theory of Differentiation in Organizations," *American Sociological Review* 35, 2 (April 1970), pp. 201–218.

9. Julie Rohrer, "Revenge of the Bond Trader," *Institutional Investor* (April 1986), pp. 89–94, discusses the increased importance of the fixed-income trading function. Pamela H. Roderick, "Sales vs. Trading vs. Research," *Investment Dealers' Digest* (November 18, 1985), pp. 17–19, presents evidence of this in terms of higher compensation. "The Traders Take Charge," *Business Week* (February 20, 1984), pp. 58–64, analyzes why the trading function has become more important and reviews some prominent investment banking executives with trading backgrounds.

10. For an excellent historical account of how large functional structures were transformed into product-based multidivisional structures see Alfred D. Chandler, Jr., *Strategy and Structure* (Cambridge, MA: MIT Press, 1962). For a more general discussion of organizational design and the relationship between strategy and structure see Henry Mintzberg, *The Structuring of Organizations: A Synthesis of Research* (Englewood Cliffs, NJ: Prentice-Hall, 1979).

11. Bartlett and Ghoshal discuss the need and techniques for achieving integration in a multinational enterprise, techniques that balance product, functional, and geographical dimensions. Enterprises that are successful at doing so are termed *transnational organizations*. Christopher A. Bartlett and Sumantra Ghoshal, "Managing across Borders: New Strategic Requirements," *Sloan Management Review* (Summer 1987), pp. 7–17, and Christopher A. Bartlett and Sumantra Ghoshal, "Managing

across Borders: New Organizational Responses," *Sloan Management Review* (Fall 1987), pp. 43–53.

12. Mark S. Granovetter, "The Strength of Weak Ties," *American Journal of Sociology* 78, 6 (May 1973), pp. 1361–1381. See also Judith R. Blau, "When Weak Ties Are Structured," preliminary report of work in progress, Department of Sociology, State University of New York at Albany, January 18, 1979 (cited with author's permission), and Judith R. Blau, "Paradoxical Consequences of Excess in Structural Complexity: A Study of a State Children's Psychiatric Hospital," *Sociology of Health and Illness* 2, 3 (1980), pp. 277–292.

13. Geanne Perlman, "Road Warrior: How First Boston's Driven Away with the Asset-Backed Securities Market," *Investment Dealers' Digest* (December 22, 1987), p. 33.

14. Lawrence and Lorsch, *Organization and Environment*, p. 13.

15. Tom Burns and G. M. Stalker, *The Management of Innovation* (London: Tavistock, 1961).

16. Ibid., p. 121.

17. Judith R. Blau, "When Weak Ties Are Structured," and Yoshino and Lifson also show the importance of debits and credits between individuals for resolving conflict. The Japanese trading companies studied by Yoshino and Lifson, or *sogo shosha,* which mediate the flow of assets between sellers and buyers, perform a number of services without direct compensation, and execute trades that are generally unique, also bear some strong similarities in organizational structure to investment banks. M. Y. Yoshino and Thomas B. Lifson, *The Invisible Link: Japan's Sogo Shosha and the Organization of Trade* (Cambridge, MA: MIT Press, 1986).

18. The organizational structures of investment banks bear a number of similarities to the structural form that Mintzberg calls an adhocracy. See Henry Mintzberg, *The Structuring of Organizations.*

19. Jay W. Lorsch and Peter F. Mathias, "When Professionals Have to Manage," *Harvard Business Review* (July–August 1987), pp. 78–83.

20. For a general discussion of these human resource flows see Michael Beer, Bert Spector, Paul R. Lawrence, D. Quinn Mills, and Richard E. Walton, *Managing Human Assets* (New York: Free Press, 1984).

21. For a description of recruiting techniques used by investment banks see Beth Selby, "Recruiting Rites at the Harvard B-School," *Institutional Investor* (March 1986), pp. 78–84.

22. Rosabeth Moss Kanter, "When a Thousand Flowers Bloom: Structural, Collective, and Social Conditions for Innovation in Organizations," in *Research in Organizational Behavior,* Vol. 10, eds. Barry Staw and Larry Cummings (Greenwich, CT: JAI Press, 1988), pp. 169–211. See also Rosabeth Moss Kanter, *The Change Masters* (New York: Simon and Schuster, 1983).

23. Fran Hawthorne, "1 + 1 = 1," *Institutional Investor* (October 1986), pp. 297–301.

24. Ibid. Reference for Salomon Brothers is Jill Dutt, "Salomon Merges Health Care Financing Groups," *Investment Dealers' Digest* (October 13, 1986), p. 23.

25. Jill Dutt, "Constructing the New Municipal Bond," *Investment Dealers' Digest* (September 29, 1986), pp. 27–35.

26. Miriam Bensman, "Smith Barney Creates Short-Term Securities Unit," *Investment Dealers' Digest* (October 5, 1987), p. 9.

27. Robert G. Eccles and Jeffrey L. Bradach, "Structure as Problem Solving," Harvard Business School, Draft paper, September 23, 1987.

28. For discussions of how structure influences strategy see Joseph L. Bower, *Managing the Resource Allocation Process: A Study of Corporate Planning and Investment*

(Boston: Division of Research, Harvard Business School, 1970); Raymond E. Miles and Charles C. Snow, *Organizational Strategy, Structure, and Process* (New York: McGraw-Hill 1978); Henry Mintzberg, "Patterns in Strategy Formation"; Robert A. Burgelman, "A Model of the Interaction of Strategic Behavior, Corporate Context, and the Concept of Strategy," *Academy of Management Review* 8, 1 (January 1983), pp. 61–70; Bartlett and Ghoshal, "Managing across Borders: New Strategic Requirements"; and Bartlett and Ghoshal, "Managing across Borders: New Organizational Responses."

29. Eric M. Leifer and Harrison C. White, "Wheeling and Annealing: Federal and Multidivisional Control," in *The Social Fabric*, ed. James F. Short, Jr. (Newbury Park, CA: Sage Publications, 1986), p. 238. In some circumstances disorder actually increases for a cooler temperature before decreasing again. For a discussion of this phenomenon see James S. Walker and Chester A. Vause, "Reappearing Phases," *Scientific American* 256, 5 (May 1987), pp. 98–105.

30. Ibid., p. 238.

31. Mintzberg referred to this as the "entrepreneurial mode" of strategy formation "where a powerful leader takes bold, risky decisions toward a vision of the organization's future." Mintzberg, "Patterns in Strategy Formation," p. 934. See also Mintzberg, "Strategy-Making in Three Modes."

32. Steve Swartz, "Salomon Charge Is Estimated at $70 Million," *The Wall Street Journal* (October 13, 1987), pp. 3, 26; Anthony Bianco, "Can Salomon Grow by Shrinking?" *Business Week* (October 26, 1987), pp. 30–31; "Street Says Cutting CP May Hurt Other Desks at Salomon," *Investment Dealers' Digest* (October 19, 1987), p. 58; Robert J. Cole, "Salomon to Dismiss 12% of Staff and End Its Municipal Bond Role," *New York Times* (October 13, 1987), pp. A-1, D-9.

33. Ann Monroe, "Salomon Aide Lewis Ranieri Leaves Firm," *The Wall Street Journal* (July 15, 1987), p. 4.

34. Edith Penrose identified the same phenomenon in her seminal work *The Theory of the Growth of the Firm,* where she argued that firms expand in order to take the fullest advantage of managerial capacity. Edith Penrose, *The Theory of the Growth of the Firm* (White Plains, NY: M. E. Sharpe, 1959).

Chapter 7

1. For example, Merchant discussed how to make control systems tighter or looser. Kenneth A. Merchant, *Control in Business Organizations* (Boston: Pitman, 1985), pp. 57–70.

2. For a discussion of the theoretical and practical issues involved in defining a business see Derek F. Abell, *Defining the Business: The Starting Point of Strategic Planning* (Englewood Cliffs, NJ: Prentice-Hall, 1980).

3. For a discussion of the futility of ever finding the scientifically correct transfer price, and of how transfer prices must be determined in light of strategy and the administrative process, see Robert G. Eccles, *The Transfer Pricing Problem: A Theory for Practice* (Lexington, MA: Lexington Books, 1985). For a general discussion of some of the problems involved in transfer pricing and cost allocation see Richard F. Vancil, *Decentralization: Managerial Ambiguity by Design* (Homewood, IL: Dow Jones-Irwin, 1978).

4. Kaplan noted that "the allocation of joint costs gets the accountant involved in some of the more arbitrary and difficult-to-defend decisions associated with the profession." Robert S. Kaplan, *Advanced Management Accounting* (Englewood Cliffs,

NJ: Prentice-Hall, 1982), p. 390. In a classic case study, Dalton detailed the arbitrariness and political nature of cost allocation procedures in one company. Melville Dalton, *Men Who Manage* (New York: Wiley, 1959).

5. These firms collect data on all publicly reported deals. The data are used to generate the league table rankings given in various publications such as *Institutional Investor* (Securities Data Company) and *Investment Dealers' Digest* (IDD Information Services). In addition, through time-sharing services sold by these vendors, firms can calculate market shares for segments defined in a number of ways in order to calculate the performance of units of the firm.

6. Investment banks that participate in the McLagan Partners survey furnish data on the amount of business done for six hundred major institutional investors. Participating firms (which do not include Goldman, Sachs, Salomon Brothers, and Merrill Lynch) receive a report telling them their market share and the market shares of unidentified others of specific rank. These market shares are reported by product and by market segment.

7. One of the classic studies of this problem is Peter M. Blau, *The Dynamics of Bureaucracy* (Chicago: University of Chicago Press, 1955). See also Chris Argyris, *The Impact of Budgets on People* (Ithaca, NY: School of Business and Public Administration, Cornell University, 1952). For a more general discussion see Merchant, *Control in Business Organizations*.

Chapter 8

1. For further discussion of the importance of internal equity or fairness and how differences in pay result in differences in status see Robert H. Frank, *Choosing the Right Pond: Human Behavior and the Quest for Status* (New York: Oxford University Press, 1985). For a discussion of how imperfections in systems can lead to concerns about fairness see Robert G. Eccles, *The Transfer Pricing Problem: A Theory for Practice* (Lexington, MA: Lexington Books, 1985).

2. See Steve Swartz, "Merrill Lynch Posts $250 Million of Mortgage-Issue Trading Losses," *The Wall Street Journal* (April 30, 1987), pp. 2, 8; Steve Swartz, "Merrill Lynch Trader Blamed in Big Loss Had Been under Supervision, Aides Say," *The Wall Street Journal* (May 1, 1987), p. 6; Steve Swartz, "Merrill Ousts Aides Involved in Trading Loss," *The Wall Street Journal* (May 20, 1987), pp. 3, 27; and James Sterngold, "Anatomy of a Staggering Loss: Merrill Chose Risky Course," *New York Times* (May 11, 1987), pp. D-1, D-10.

3. See Benson P. Shapiro, *Sales Program Management: Formulation and Implementation* (New York: McGraw-Hill, 1977), pp. 299–311, for a discussion of and further references on sales force compensation practices.

4. As this book goes to press, Merrill Lynch was reported to be shifting from a commission to a salary-plus-bonus approach with sales and trading sharing a common bonus pool. Steve Swartz, "Merrill Lynch Plans Layoffs, Cutbacks to Save up to $370 Million on '88 Costs," *The Wall Street Journal* (December 15, 1987), p. 2.

5. For a discussion of the increased importance of fixed-income research see Barbara Donnelly, "The Rush for Fixed-Income Research," *Institutional Investor* (May 1985), pp. 165–170. Although this section is primarily about equity research, the evaluation and compensation practices and potential conflicts of interest are similar for fixed-income research.

6. For a discussion of how potential conflicts of interest create tensions for the research analyst see N. R. Kleinfield, "The Many Faces of the Wall Street Analyst,"

New York Times (October 27, 1985), pp. F-1, F-8; Nancy Welles, "Can Analysts Find True Happiness Doing Deals?," *Institutional Investor* (November 1983), pp. 201–207; Joe Kolman, "The Saga of a Merger-Hot Sector," *Institutional Investor* (April 1987), pp. 159–166.

7. See Derek F. Abell and John S. Hammond, *Strategic Market Planning: Problems and Analytical Approaches* (Englewood Cliffs, NJ: Prentice-Hall, 1979), for a discussion of portfolio planning.

Chapter 9

1. Michelle L. Collins and Michael F. Goss, *The Impact of Relationships on the Investment Banking Industry: Exhibit and Tables,* Field Study on the Management of Financial Service Organizations, sponsored by Donaldson, Lufkin & Jenrette, Harvard Business School, May 5, 1986, p. 2.

2. Harrison C. White, "Delegation by Agency," paper presented at the American Sociological Association Annual Meeting, Chicago, Illinois, August 19, 1987, pp. 4–5.

3. Ibid., p. 6.

4. Ibid., p. 5.

5. Ibid., p. 10.

6. Ibid., p. 10. See also Eric M. Leifer and Harrison C. White, "Wheeling and Annealing: Federal and Multidivisional Control," in *The Social Fabric,* ed. James F. Short, Jr. (Newbury Park, CA: Sage Publications, 1986), pp. 223–242; Robert R. Alford, *Health Care Politics: Ideological and Interest Group Barriers to Reform* (Chicago: University of Chicago Press, 1975); and John F. Padgett, "Hierarchy and Ecological Control in Federal Budgetary Decision-Making," *American Journal of Sociology* 87, 1 (July 1981), pp. 75–129.

7. White, "Delegation by Agency," p. 11.

8. For a discussion of this see M. Y. Yoshino and Thomas B. Lifson, *The Invisible Link: Japan's Sogo Shosha and the Organization of Trade* (Cambridge, MA: MIT Press, 1986).

9. Paul R. Lawrence and Jay W. Lorsch, "New Management Job: The Integrator," *Harvard Business Review* (November–December 1967), p. 150.

10. Jay W. Lorsch and Peter F. Mathias, "When Professionals Have to Manage," *Harvard Business Review* (July–August 1987), pp. 78–83.

Chapter 10

1. For discussions (albeit in the rhetoric of the investment banking industry not being well managed) of the dilemmas pushing investment banks to respond to increased size and complexity without eliminating those characteristics that have made them successful see Henny Sender, "Too Big for Their Own Good?," *Institutional Investor* (February 1987), pp. 63–66; "Managing Greed and Risk on Wall Street," *The Economist* (July 5, 1987), pp. 69–72; and Steve Swartz, "Wall Street's Growth Is Seriously Outpacing Management Systems," *The Wall Street Journal* (July 27, 1987), pp. 1, 12.

2. See Beth McGoldrick, "How Much Capital Is Enough?," *Institutional Investor* (November 1986), pp. 183–187.

3. Securities Industry Association, *Security Industry Trends* 13, 6 (October 30, 1987), pp. 10–11. The large investment bank category includes Bear, Stearns; Dillon, Read; First Boston; Goldman, Sachs; Kidder, Peabody; Lazard Frères; Morgan Stanley; L.F. Rothschild; Salomon Brothers; and Wertheim.

4. For discussions of the causes and consequences of increased economic adversity in the investment banking industry see Robert E. Norton, "Upheaval Ahead on Wall Street," *Fortune* (September 14, 1987), pp. 68–69, 72, 76–77, and Anthony Bianco with Christopher Farrell, "The Big Chill on Wall Street: Pink Slips, Slashed Bonus—And a New Set of Mergers," *Business Week* (December 7, 1987), pp. 54–56.

5. "Boom Ends for Financial Services Firms: Job Outlook Is Bleak Following Market Crash," *The Wall Street Journal* (December 11, 1987), p. 6.

6. Steve Swartz, "Merrill Lynch Plans Layoffs, Cutbacks to Save up to $370 Million on '88 Costs," *The Wall Street Journal* (December 15, 1987), p. 2.

7. For a cynical view of Wall Street's ability to cope with this inherent characteristic of the market, which is the lifeblood of investment banking firms, see Chris Welles, "Will the Street Ever Learn That Good Times End?," *Business Week* (December 7, 1987), p. 57.

8. For an early perspective on the consequences of decreased profitability in the investment banking industry, especially for younger employees, see Bill Powell and Carolyn Friday, "A Jolt for Wall St.'s Whiz Kids," *Newsweek* (October 26, 1987), pp. 55–56, 58.

9. Although Phibro Corporation, the world's biggest independent commodities trader, acquired Salomon Brothers in October 1981 for $554 million, within three years John Gutfreund of Salomon Brothers was named CEO of the holding company and Phibro's co-chairman, David Tendler, and president, Hal Beretz, resigned, thereby handing control of the holding company over to Gutfreund. Peagam described this as "a stunning coup for Gutfreund, although associates insist he never plotted to achieve it." See Norman Peagam, "How Salomon Turned the Tables on Phibro," *Euromoney* (November 1984), pp. 70–81.

10. For a careful study of the effects of acquisitions on the shareholder value of acquirers see Michael C. Jensen and Richard S. Ruback, "The Market for Corporate Control: The Scientific Evidence," *Journal of Financial Economics* 11 (1983), pp. 5–50. For a review of the literature on this subject see J. Fred Weston and Kwang S. Chung, "Do Mergers Make Money? A Research Summary," *Mergers & Acquisitions* (Fall 1983), pp. 40–48.

11. For a discussion of the experiences of Dean Witter (acquired by Sears) and Donaldson, Lufkin & Jenrette (acquired by Equitable Life Assurance Society), see Miriam Rozen, "Bearing Gifts: Wall Street's Best, and Worst, Corporate Parents," *Investment Dealers' Digest* (April 20, 1987), pp. 18–24. For a discussion of how General Electric managed the early stages of its acquisition of Kidder, Peabody, see Beth Selby, "GE Moves in on Kidder," *Institutional Investor* (August 1987), pp. 77–87.

12. M. Y. Yoshino and Thomas B. Lifson, *The Invisible Link: Japan's Sogo Shosha and the Organization of Trade* (Cambridge, MA: MIT Press, 1986).

BIBLIOGRAPHY

Abell, Derek F. *Defining the Business: The Starting Point of Strategic Planning.* Englewood Cliffs, NJ: Prentice-Hall, 1980.

Abell, Derek F., and John S. Hammond. *Strategic Market Planning: Problems and Analytical Approaches.* Englewood Cliffs, NJ: Prentice-Hall, 1979.

Alford, Robert R. *Health Care Politics: Ideological and Interest Group Barriers to Reform.* Chicago: University of Chicago Press, 1975.

Andrews, Kenneth R. *The Concept of Corporate Strategy.* 3d ed. Homewood, IL: Richard D. Irwin, 1987.

Argyris, Chris. *The Impact of Budgets on People.* Ithaca, NY: School of Business and Public Administration, Cornell University, 1952.

Argyris, Chris, and Donald A. Schön. *Organizational Learning: A Theory of Action Perspective.* Reading, MA: Addison-Wesley, 1978.

Arrow, Kenneth J. *Essays in the Theory of Risk-Bearing.* Chicago: Markham, 1971.

Auerbach, Joseph, and Samuel L. Hayes, III. *Investment Banking and Diligence: What Price Deregulation?* Boston: Harvard Business School Press, 1986.

Auletta, Ken. *Greed and Glory on Wall Street: The Fall of the House of Lehman.* New York: Random House, 1986.

Baker, Marci. "Drexel's Record Year Eases Scandal's Pain." *Pension & Investment Age* (January 12, 1987), pp. 1, 36.

Baker, Wayne E. "The Organization-Market Interface: Corporations' Relations with Investment Banks." Harvard Business School Working Paper No. 87-043 (second draft), April 16, 1987.

Bartlett, Christopher A., and Sumantra Ghoshal. "Managing across Borders: New Strategic Requirements." *Sloan Management Review* (Summer 1987), pp. 7-17.

————. "Managing across Borders: New Organizational Responses." *Sloan Management Review* (Fall 1987), pp. 43-53.

Beer, Michael, Bert Spector, Paul R. Lawrence, D. Quinn Mills, and Richard E. Walton. *Managing Human Assets.* New York: Free Press, 1984.

Bensman, Miriam. "Smith Barney Creates Short-Term Securities Unit." *Investment Dealers' Digest* (October 5, 1987), p. 9.

Bianco, Anthony. "Can Salomon Grow by Shrinking?" *Business Week* (October 26, 1987), pp. 30-31.

Bianco, Anthony, and Christopher Farrell. "The Big Chill on Wall Street: Pink

Slips, Slashed Bonus—And a New Set of Mergers." *Business Week* (December 7, 1987), pp. 54–56.

Blau, Judith R. "When Weak Ties Are Structured." Preliminary report of work in progress, Department of Sociology, State University of New York at Albany, January 18, 1979.

———. "Paradoxical Consequences of Excess in Structural Complexity: A Study of a State Children's Psychiatric Hospital." *Sociology of Health and Illness,* Vol. 2, No. 3 (1980), pp. 277–292.

Blau, Peter M. *The Dynamics of Bureaucracy.* Chicago: University of Chicago Press, 1955.

———. "A Formal Theory of Differentiation in Organizations." *American Sociological Review,* Vol. 35, No. 2 (April 1970), pp. 201–218.

Bleakley, Fred R. "Wall St.'s Merchant Bankers." *New York Times* (November 19, 1984), pp. D-1, D-5.

Blumstein, Michael. "Creating New Financial Products." *New York Times* (August 8, 1982), p. F-6.

Bower, Joseph L. *Managing the Resource Allocation Process: A Study of Corporate Planning and Investment.* Boston: Division of Research, Harvard Business School, 1970.

Brenner, Lynn, and Beth McGoldrick. "Investment Banking's New Boutiques." *Institutional Investor* (May 1983), pp. 179–189.

Burgelman, Robert A. "A Model of the Interaction of Strategic Behavior, Corporate Context, and the Concept of Strategy." *Academy of Management Review,* Vol. 8, No. 1 (January 1983), pp. 61–70.

———. "Corporate Entrepreneurship and Strategic Management: Insights from a Process Study." *Management Science,* Vol. 29, No. 12 (December 1983), pp. 1349–1364.

———. "Designs for Corporate Entrepreneurship in Established Firms." *California Management Review,* Vol. 26, No. 3 (Spring 1984), pp. 154–166.

Burns, Tom, and G. M. Stalker. *The Management of Innovation.* London: Tavistock, 1961.

Carey, David, Lisa Kaplan, Stephen Kindel, Tani Maher, Deborah Mittel, Margaret Price, and Stephen Taub. "Wall Street's Superstars." *Financial World* (July 14, 1987), pp. 34–115.

Carosso, Vincent P. *Investment Banking in America: A History.* Cambridge, MA: Harvard University Press, 1970.

Chandler, Alfred D., Jr. *Strategy and Structure: Chapters in the History of the American Industrial Enterprise.* Cambridge, MA: MIT Press, 1962.

Clough, Alexandra. "Shelf Filing Hits Regionals Hard, SEC Admits." *Investment Dealers' Digest* (February 2, 1987), p. 16.

Cole, Robert J. "Salomon to Dismiss 12% of Staff and End Its Municipal Bond Role." *New York Times* (October 13, 1987), pp. A-1 and D-9.

Collins, Michelle L., and Michael F. Goss. *The Impact of Relationships on the Investment Banking Industry: Exhibit and Tables.* Field Study on the Management of Financial Service Organizations, sponsored by Donaldson, Lufkin & Jenrette, Harvard Business School, May 5, 1986.

Dalton, Melvin. *Men Who Manage*. New York: Wiley, 1959.

Davenport, Carol. "DLJ Loses 11-Person Group to Smith Barney Harris Upham." *Investment Dealers' Digest* (October 20, 1986), p. 8.

DiMaggio, Paul J., and Walter W. Powell. "The Iron Cage Revisited: Institutional Isomorphism and Collective Rationality in Organizational Fields." *American Sociological Review*, Vol. 48 (April 1983), pp. 147–160.

Donnelly, Barbara. "Wall Street's Quants Come into Their Own." *Institutional Investor* (November 1984), pp. 181–188.

———. "The Academic Invasion of Wall Street." *Institutional Investor* (December 1984), pp. 73–78.

———. "The Rush for Fixed-Income Research." *Institutional Investor* (May 1985), pp. 165–170.

Dutt, Jill. "Constructing the New Municipal Bond." *Investment Dealers' Digest* (September 29, 1986), pp. 27–35.

———. "Salomon Merges Health Care Financing Groups." *Investment Dealers' Digest* (October 13, 1986), p. 23.

———. "Wall Street's First Call: Why Sallie Mae Gets a Peek at the Hottest New Ideas." *Investment Dealers' Digest* (October 27, 1986), pp. 20–24.

Eccles, Robert G. *The Transfer Pricing Problem: A Theory for Practice*. Lexington, MA: Lexington Books, 1985.

———. "Bureaucratic versus Craft Administration: The Relationship of Market Structure to the Construction Firm." *Administrative Science Quarterly*, Vol. 26 (September 1981), pp. 449–469.

———. "The Quasifirm in the Construction Industry." *Journal of Economic Behavior and Organization*, Vol. 2 (1981), pp. 335–357.

Eccles, Robert G., and Jeffrey L. Bradach. "Structure as Problem Solving." Harvard Business School, Draft paper, September 23, 1987.

Feinberg, Phyllis. "Should Investment Bankers Be Paid by the Hour?" *Institutional Investor* (May 1979), pp. 110–122.

———. "The Deal Hunters: How Regional Firms Survive Now That the Big Game Is Gone." *Investment Dealers' Digest* (February 16, 1987), pp. 22–26.

Field, Peter. "The Attack on the M&A Barons." *Euromoney* (May 1985), pp. 89–96.

Fligstein, Neil. "The Intraorganizational Power Struggle: Rise of Finance Personnel to Top Leadership in Large Corporations, 1919–1979." *American Sociological Review*, Vol. 52 (February 1987), pp. 44–58.

Frank, Robert H. *Choosing the Right Pond: Human Behavior and the Quest for Status*. New York: Oxford University Press, 1985.

Gilpin, Kenneth N. "Split in 'Tombstone' Ranks." *New York Times* (October 5, 1987), p. D-1.

Granovetter, Mark S. "The Strength of Weak Ties." *American Journal of Sociology*, Vol. 78, No. 6 (May 1973), pp. 1361–1381.

————. "Economic Action and Social Structure: The Problem of Embeddedness." *American Journal of Sociology,* Vol. 91, No. 3 (November 1985), pp. 481–510.

Grant, Peter. "What Hath Gallatin Wrought? The Preferred Stock Wars." *Investment Dealers' Digest* (May 11, 1987), pp. 18–25.

Greenwich Associates. *Institutional Equity Services 1986: Report to Participants.* Greenwich, CT: Greenwich Associates, 1986.

————. *Investment Banking 1986: Report to Executives.* Greenwich, CT: Greenwich Associates, 1986.

Hawthorne, Fran. "1 + 1 = 1." *Institutional Investor* (October 1986), pp. 297–301.

Hayes, Samuel L., III. "Investment Banking: Power Structure in Flux." *Harvard Business Review* (March–April 1971), pp. 136–152.

————. "The Transformation of Investment Banking." *Harvard Business Review* (January–February 1979), pp. 153–170.

Hayes, Samuel L., III, A. Michael Spence, and David Van Praag Marks. *Competition in the Investment Banking Industry.* Cambridge, MA: Harvard University Press, 1983.

Hedberg, Bo L. T., Paul Nystrom, and William H. Starbuck. "Camping on Seesaws: Prescriptions for a Self-Designing Organization." *Administrative Science Quarterly,* Vol. 21 (March 1976), pp. 41–65.

Ipsen, Erik. "The Growth of In-House M&A Departments." *Institutional Investor* (August 1984), pp. 202–208.

Jackson, Barbara Bund. *Winning and Keeping Industrial Customers: The Dynamics of Customer Relationships.* Lexington, MA: Lexington Books, 1985.

Jensen, Michael C., and Richard S. Ruback. "The Market for Corporate Control: The Scientific Evidence." *Journal of Financial Economics,* Vol. 11 (1983), pp. 5–50.

Kanter, Rosabeth Moss. *The Change Masters.* New York: Simon and Schuster, 1983.

————. "When a Thousand Flowers Bloom: Structural, Collective, and Social Conditions for Innovation in Organizations." In *Research in Organizational Behavior,* Vol. 10, eds. Barry Staw and Larry Cummings. Greenwich, CT: JAI Press, 1988, pp. 169–211.

Kaplan, Robert S. *Advanced Management Accounting.* Englewood Cliffs, NJ: Prentice-Hall, 1982.

Kessler, Glenn A. "George Ball's 'Project '89': Pru-Bache's Plan for Investment Banking." *Investment Dealers' Digest* (October 13, 1987), pp. 24–32.

Kidder, Tracy. *The Soul of a New Machine.* Boston: Atlantic-Little, Brown, 1981.

Kleinfield, N. R. "The Many Faces of the Wall Street Analyst." *New York Times* (October 27, 1985), pp. F-1, F-8.

Kolman, Joe. "The Making of a Merger-Hot Sector." *Institutional Investor* (April 1987), pp. 159–166.

————. "Revenge of the Nerds." *Institutional Investor* (September 1987), pp. 84–94.

Kroeger, Brooke. "Feeling Poor on $600,000 a Year." *New York Times* (April 26, 1987), pp. F-1, F-8.

Laursen, Eric. "On the Waterfront (West): The Investment Banking Bosses of San Francisco." *Investment Dealers' Digest* (March 30, 1987), pp. 25–30.

Lawrence, Paul R., and Jay W. Lorsch. *Organization and Environment: Managing Differentiation and Integration.* Homewood, IL: Richard D. Irwin, 1967.

———. "New Management Job: The Integrator." *Harvard Business Review* (November–December 1967), pp. 142–150.

Lee, Peter. "View from Bridge Makes Bankers' Heads Spin." *Euromoney* (May 1987), pp. 64–73.

Leifer, Eric M., and Harrison C. White. "Wheeling and Annealing: Federal and Multidivisional Control." In *The Social Fabric,* ed. James F. Short, Jr. Newbury Park, CA: Sage Publications, 1986, pp. 223–242.

Lorsch, Jay W., and Peter F. Mathias. "When Professionals Have to Manage." *Harvard Business Review* (July–August 1987), pp. 78–83.

McGoldrick, Beth. "Inside the Goldman, Sachs Culture." *Institutional Investor* (January 1984), pp. 53–67.

———. "Wall Street Puts Its Own Money on the Line." *Institutional Investor* (June 1984), pp. 61–75.

———. "Salomon's Power Culture." *Institutional Investor* (March 1986), pp. 67–76.

———. "Who Said Relationships Are Dead?" *Institutional Investor* (May 1986), pp. 181–184.

———. "How Much Capital Is Enough?" *Institutional Investor* (November 1986), pp. 183–187.

Marton, Andrew. "How Much Is Too Much?" *Institutional Investor* (August 1984), pp. 238–250.

Merchant, Kenneth A. *Control in Business Organizations.* Boston: Pitman, 1985.

Miles, Raymond E., and Charles C. Snow. *Organizational Strategy, Structure, and Process.* New York: McGraw-Hill, 1978.

Miller, Gregory. "The Knockoff Artists." *Institutional Investor* (May 1986), pp. 81–84.

Miller, Merton H. "Financial Innovation: The Last Twenty Years and the Next." *Journal of Financial and Quantitative Analysis,* Vol. 21, No. 4 (December 1986), pp. 459–471.

Mintzberg, Henry. *The Structuring of Organizations: A Synthesis of Research.* Englewood Cliffs, NJ: Prentice-Hall, 1979.

———. "Strategy-Making in Three Modes." *California Management Review,* Vol. 16, No. 2 (Winter 1973), pp. 44–53.

———. "Patterns in Strategy Formation." *Management Science,* Vol. 24, No. 9 (May 1978), pp. 934–948.

———. "Crafting Strategy." *Harvard Business Review* (July–August 1987), pp. 66–75.

Mintzberg, Henry, and Alexandra McHugh. "Strategy Formulation in an Adhocracy." *Administrative Science Quarterly,* Vol. 30 (June 1985), pp. 160–197.

Monroe, Ann. "Salomon Aide Lewis Ranieri Leaves Firm." *The Wall Street Journal* (July 15, 1987), p. 4.

Norton, Robert E. "Upheaval Ahead on Wall Street." *Fortune* (September 14, 1987), pp. 68–69, 72, 76–77.

Osborn, Neil. "The Creativity Game." *Institutional Investor* (January 1983), pp. 65–72.

Padgett, John F. "Hierarchy and Ecological Control in Federal Budgetary Decision-Making." *American Journal of Sociology*, Vol. 87, No. 1 (July 1981), pp. 75–129.

Peagam, Norman. "How Salomon Turned the Tables on Phibro." *Euromoney* (November 1984), pp. 70–81.

Penrose, Edith. *The Theory of the Growth of the Firm*. White Plains, NY: M. E. Sharpe, 1959.

Perlman, Geanne. "Road Warrior: How First Boston's Driven Away with the Asset-Backed Securities Market." *Investment Dealers' Digest* (December 22, 1987), pp. 30–34.

Perrow, Charles. "A Framework for Comparative Organizational Analysis." *American Sociological Review*, Vol. 32, No. 2 (April 1967), pp. 194–208.

Petre, Peter. "Merger Fees That Bend the Mind." *Fortune* (January 20, 1986), pp. 18–23.

Picker, Ida. "Hutton MBS Team Quits En Masse for LFRUT." *Investment Dealers' Digest* (September 16, 1986), p. 6.

———. "Malicious Whispers: Wall Street Declares War on Drexel." *Investment Dealers' Digest* (March 16, 1987), pp. 26–32.

———. "The Big Bet: The Dilemma of Bridge Financing." *Investment Dealers' Digest* (June 1, 1987), pp. 16–20.

Porter, Michael E. *Competitive Strategy: Techniques for Analyzing Industries and Competitors*. New York: Free Press, 1980.

———. *Competitive Advantage: Creating and Sustaining Superior Performance*. New York: Free Press, 1985.

Powell, Bill, and Carolyn Friday. "A Jolt for Wall St.'s Whiz Kids." *Newsweek* (October 26, 1987), pp. 55–56, 58.

Powell, Walter W. *Getting into Print: The Decision-Making Process in Scholarly Publishing*. Chicago: University of Chicago Press, 1985.

Roderick, Pamela H. "Sales vs. Trading vs. Research." *Investment Dealers' Digest* (November 18, 1985), pp. 17–19.

Rogers, Michael. "Professors Who Work on Wall Street." *Fortune* (November 25, 1987), p. 83.

Rohrer, Julie. "Revenge of the Bond Trader." *Institutional Investor* (April 1986), pp. 89–94.

Rozen, Miriam. "Treasurers Starting to Shun Competitive Bidding." *Investment Dealers' Digest* (November 17, 1986), p. 12.

———. "Bearing Gifts: Wall Street's Best, and Worst, Corporate Parents." *Investment Dealers' Digest* (April 20, 1987), pp. 18–24.

Schumpeter, Joseph A. *Capitalism, Socialism, and Democracy.* 3d ed. New York: Harper & Row, 1950.

Securities Industry Association. *Security Industry Trends.* Vol. 13, No. 6 (October 30, 1987), pp. 10–11.

Selby, Beth. "Recruiting Rites at the Harvard B-School." *Institutional Investor* (March 1986), pp. 78–84.

———. "GE Moves in on Kidder." *Institutional Investor* (August 1987), pp. 77–87.

Sender, Henny. "Too Big for their Own Good?" *Institutional Investor* (February 1987), pp. 63–66.

———. "The Client Comes Second." *Institutional Investor* (March 1987), pp. 84–98.

Shapiro, Benson P. *Sales Program Management: Formulation and Implementation.* New York: McGraw-Hill, 1977.

Sherman, Stratford P. "Drexel Sweats the Wall Street Probe." *Fortune* (March 16, 1987), pp. 38–42.

———. "C.E.O.'s Take on Their Investment Bankers." *Fortune* (April 27, 1987), pp. 54–64.

Shirreff, David. "Down with Innovation!" *Euromoney* (August 1986), pp. 23–31.

Simonoff, Evan. "Salomon's Muni Bankers Market Themselves as a Group." *Investment Dealers' Digest* (October 19, 1987), p. 22.

Simonoff, Evan, and Mark Fadiman. "Salomon Muni Team Move May Cause Friction at Dean Witter." *Investment Dealers' Digest* (October 26, 1987), p. 11.

Smith, Adam. "But What Do Investment Bankers *Do*?" *Esquire* (November 1986), pp. 97–98.

Stein, Benjamin J. "Not Worthy of the Name? Investment Banking Isn't What It Used to Be." *Barron's* (July 13, 1987), pp. 6, 7, 26, 28, 30, 32.

Sterngold, James. "Deep-Pocketed Deal Makers." *New York Times* (April 14, 1987), pp. D-1, D-8.

———. "Anatomy of a Staggering Loss: Merrill Chose Risky Course." *New York Times* (May 11, 1987), pp. D-1, D-10.

Stinchcombe, Arthur L. "Bureaucratic and Craft Administration of Production: A Comparative Study." *Administrative Science Quarterly,* Vol. 4 (September 1959), pp. 168–187.

Swartz, Steve. "Merrill Lynch Posts $250 Million of Mortgage-Issue Trading Losses." *The Wall Street Journal* (April 30, 1987), pp. 2, 8.

———. "Merrill Lynch Trader Blamed in Big Loss Had Been under Supervision, Aides Say." *The Wall Street Journal* (May 1, 1987), p. 6.

———. "Merrill Ousts Aides Involved in Trading Loss." *The Wall Street Journal* (May 20, 1987), pp. 3, 27.

———. "Wall Street's Growth Is Seriously Outpacing Management Systems." *The Wall Street Journal* (July 27, 1987), pp. 1, 12.

———. "Salomon Charge Is Estimated at $70 Million." *The Wall Street Journal* (October 13, 1987), pp. 3, 26.

———. "Merrill Lynch Plans Layoffs, Cutbacks to Save up to $370 Million on '88 Costs." *The Wall Street Journal* (December 15, 1987), p. 2.

Thackray, John. "The Rise of Do-It-Yourself Corporate Finance." *Institutional Investor* (June 1982), pp. 194–209.

———. "The Catchy Rhythm of the One-Man Bank." *Euromoney* (May 1986), pp. 27–46.

Thomas, Michael M. "The Elusive Partnership: Corporate America's Problem with Wall Street." *Corporate Finance* (November 1986), pp. 46–50.

Thompson, James D. *Organizations in Action.* New York: McGraw-Hill, 1967.

Tichy, Noel M. *Handbook of Organizational Design.* Vol. 2, *Remodeling Organizations and Their Environments.* eds. Paul C. Nystrom and William H. Starbuck. New York: Oxford University Press, 1981.

Truell, Peter. "First Boston Removed from Offering, Denies Charge of Conflict by Citicorp." *The Wall Street Journal* (September 14, 1987), p. 3.

Vancil, Richard F. *Decentralization: Managerial Ambiguity by Design.* Homewood, IL: Dow Jones-Irwin, 1978.

von Hippel, Eric. *The Sources of Innovation.* New York: Oxford University Press, forthcoming.

———. "Lead Users: A Source of Novel Product Concepts." *Management Science,* Vol. 32, No. 7 (July 1986), pp. 791–805.

Walker, James S., and Chester A. Vause. "Reappearing Phases." *Scientific American,* Vol. 256, No. 5 (May 1987), pp. 98–105.

Welles, Chris. "The Case against Drexel: Will the Government Come up Short?" *Business Week* (August 10, 1987), pp. 56–60.

———. "Will the Street Ever Learn That Good Times End?" *Business Week* (December 7, 1987), p. 57.

Welles, Nancy. "Can Analysts Find True Happiness Doing Deals?" *Institutional Investor* (November 1983), pp. 201–207.

Weston, J. Fred, and Kwang S. Chung. "Do Mergers Make Money? A Research Summary." *Mergers & Acquisitions* (Fall 1983), pp. 40–48.

White, Harrison C. "Delegation by Agency." Paper presented at the American Sociological Association Annual Meeting, Chicago, IL, August 19, 1987.

White, Shelby. "More Pay, More Work." *Corporate Finance* (March 1987), pp. 49–51.

Woodward, Joan. *Industrial Organization: Theory and Practice.* Oxford: Oxford University Press, 1965.

Yoshino, M. Y., and Lifson, Thomas B. *The Invisible Link: Japan's Sogo Shosha and the Organization of Trade.* Cambridge, MA: MIT Press, 1986.

INDEX